Good News

For All People

Studies in the Gospel of Luke

~ LUMINAIRE STUDIES ~

Good News

For All People

Studies in the Gospel of Luke

Tim Geddert

WINNIPEG, MB CANADA

HILLSBORO, KS USA

Kindred Productions is the publishing arm of the Mennonite Brethren Churches. Kindred publishes, promotes and markets print and mixed media resources that help shape our Christian faith and discipleship from the Mennonite Brethren perspective.

Good News For All People

Published simultaneously by Kindred Productions, Winnipeg, Manitoba R3M 3Z6 and Kindred Productions, Goessel, Kansas 67053

Cover Design: Brandon Letkeman

Book layout: Brandon Letkeman

Printed in United States of America by Lightning Source

(Insert CIP info)

International Standard Book Number: 978-1-894791-48-9

Visit our website: kindredproductions.com

Table of Contents

Introduction to Luke's Gospel

I am reluctant to write a long introduction in which I tell all the things I think will emerge from this study of Luke. I would love instead simply to move into the text and examine it together. However, there are some introductory matters that are best dealt with right up front.

Who is the author of Luke?

Starting in the second half of the second century, early church traditions consistently attribute this Gospel to "Paul's dear friend, Luke, the doctor" (see Colossians 4:14). He was one of Paul's fellow-workers and companions in ministry (see Philemon 1:24; 2 Timothy 4:11). We cannot be certain that this Luke really was the author because we do not know on what basis second century leaders made that claim and the author never identifies himself in either Luke or Acts, at least not directly. But we can be detectives and try to verify those claims indirectly.

There are hints in Acts that the author was a companion of Paul. This is a plausible interpretation of something fascinating that happens in Acts 16. After writing a whole Gospel and more than half of Acts in the third person (he, she, they), the author suddenly switches pronouns. He has been reporting what "*they*" (all sorts of people, and in the immediate context, Paul and Silas) have been doing, when suddenly he changes to "*we*": "*We* got ready at once to leave for Macedonia" (Acts 16:10). It appears the author joined Paul and his missionary team in Troas, just before they crossed the Aegean Sea and planted a church in Philippi. And then it looks as though the author stayed in Philippi when the others left (see Acts 16:40), rejoined them later in Troas (see Acts 20:5) and then traveled with Paul to Rome (see Acts 27:1).

Was that person really Luke the doctor? If early church claims are based on reliable traditions, we should probably go with that. If they did not have reliable traditions, perhaps they were doing their own detective work, observing the "we sections" in Acts, eliminating all of Paul's missionary companions that are actually named in Acts and concluding Luke is the one left over. If that is what happened, then their guess is as good as ours!

In the end, it is not terribly important to be sure who wrote Luke and Acts. The author tells us that he was not an eyewitness, but that he had reliable sources that were. And he chooses to write anonymously. So we will simply choose to call the author Luke, along with the rest of the church that has for all these centuries done so. Whoever he (or she, for all we know) was, this author contributed more to our New Testament (not more books, but certainly more words) than anyone else, even Paul!

When was Luke written?

Some people reason like this:

- Luke wrote two volumes: The Gospel of Luke and The Book of Acts.

- Luke presumably wrote his Gospel before writing Acts.
- The Book of Acts ends with Paul still alive in Rome.
- Paul was martyred in Rome sometime between AD 64 and 68.
- Therefore Acts was written no later than that.
- Most probably, Acts was written in about AD 63 (the time of the last events recorded in Acts).
- Therefore, the Gospel of Luke was written before that date.

I think that the first four claims hold up well. It is, however, not at all obvious that The Book of Acts tells the story of the early church *right up to the time of the author's writing.* It could easily be that Luke ended the narrative of Acts with reference to the situation around AD 63, even though he was writing much later. Perhaps he even intended one day to write a third volume. We will never know.

At any rate, other considerations lead me to propose a later date for Luke. Scholars widely accept that Luke had access to – in fact heavily used – the Gospel of Mark in writing his own Gospel. My own personal study leads me to conclude that Mark was written shortly before AD 70 during the time of the Jewish war with Rome (AD 66-70). It appears as though Luke's version of that war is a post-war rewording of the way Mark's Gospel refers to it (compare Luke 21:20 and Mark 13:14). That would imply Luke wrote his Gospel after AD 70.

I think a time frame anywhere from 70 to 85 is plausible. But in all this uncertainty, here is the good news: it does not matter! The narrative Luke tells is based on eyewitness accounts and reliably preserved traditions (see Luke 1:1-4). Moreover, it was inspired by the Holy Spirit. We can be sure that it provided Theophilus with what he needed "that he might know the certainty of the things he had been taught" (see Luke 1:4). And we can be sure that it provides us with that as well.

Why was Luke written?

On the one hand, the answer to this question is simple: to tell the reader everything that he included in his narrative of Jesus! If we answer the question that way, then our best strategy is simply to start reading the Gospel and see what it contains.

However, it would be helpful to summarize a few of the unique characteristics and important themes of Luke, so that, as we read and study the Gospel, we can take special note of them.

I suggest seven points:

- **To make the case that the stories people were telling about Jesus were based on solid historical evidence.** Early Christians would have heard many stories about Jesus – his origins, his life, his teaching, his death and resurrection. But without apostles and other reliable eyewitnesses always ready at hand, it may have been hard to know which stories were based on fact. So Luke did the research (see Luke 1:1-4). And by writing it all down, he provided certainty for the reader.
- **To help people understand the meaning and implications of what they knew about Jesus.** Even if separating fact from fiction was not always the most pressing need (see previous point), there was and is always a need to probe more deeply into what the advent of Jesus *means.* What does it mean for our salvation? What does it mean for the nature and mission of the church? What does it mean for discipleship and obedience? As we dig deeply, we discover more and more clearly how to live as a result.
- **To make the story of Jesus come alive!** Luke is an amazing storyteller. His narratives are gripping, profound, lively, life-changing. Encountering the gospel does not always need to bring us more proofs and more lessons. Sometimes it simply needs to impress us all over again with its beauty and its transformative power. Luke, the master storyteller, provides that.

- **To highlight certain aspects of the gospel that were particularly dear to Luke's heart.** I would list at least the following:
  - History is unfolding according to God's plan;
  - The salvation Jesus brings is first for Israel and then for the whole world;
  - Jesus paid special attention to "low-status" people (women, children, the poor, the unclean, outsiders, Gentiles); so should we;
  - Jesus lived to demonstrate and promote a countercultural way of living, one that is out of step with the world's value systems, because it is in step with God's will and God's reign.
- **To instruct the church on faithful Christian living.** In his Gospel, Luke emphasizes prayer, songs of praise, generous giving, obedience to the true intent of the law, welcoming the outsider, sharing the good news, depending on the Holy Spirit, etc. All these emphases suggest he is encouraging Christians to learn from Jesus and from others who encountered him during his earthly life, so that they themselves can live the Christian life with integrity and with joy.
- **To assure Christians that their hope is in Jesus and therefore their allegiance must be to Jesus.** The Roman Empire and especially its emperors made huge claims for themselves: they bring good news, they are to be worshipped and feared, their armies assure peace on earth and they deserve titles like "Savior," "Lord" and "Son of God." Luke emphasizes that followers of Jesus are not seduced by such claims. They refuse idolatrous worship of the emperor and the pagan gods. They pledge allegiance to Jesus alone. And therefore they know that the real good news is in the counterclaim, made by heaven's armies to lowly shepherds: "Today a Savior has been born to you; he is the Messiah, the Lord.... Glory to God in the highest, and on earth peace" (Luke 2:11, 14).

- **To introduce Jesus to the readers.** Whatever else this Gospel does, it introduces Jesus. Luke, like the other evangelists, presents Jesus as the Savior and the hope of the world. Luke's Gospel emphasizes specific titles, specific roles, specific outcomes, but his message joins the chorus of the whole New Testament in proclaiming Jesus.

Luke, the Old Testament and the other three Gospels

As you read this commentary, you will undoubtedly notice I rarely interpret Luke in the light of the other three Gospels, but I regularly interpret it in the light of the Old Testament. It may seem inconsistent or strange, but consider this. The Old Testament (especially in its Greek translation) was the shared background knowledge of all early Christians. Indeed, they acknowledged it as their authoritative Scriptures. They interpreted *everything* in the light of these Scriptures. Luke could count on this and so Luke includes quotations from, and especially allusions to, many texts from the Old Testament.

The other three Gospels, on the other hand, were not considered authoritative Scripture in the early church at the time Luke was writing. Indeed, Luke's readers would have been quite unaware of these other Gospels. Even Luke, the author, probably knew only Mark's Gospel. Matthew's Gospel was almost certainly written independently of Luke, and possibly later. John's Gospel was almost certainly written later. If Luke expected his first readers to understand his narrative without reference to other Gospels, we should follow the author's cues, interpreting Luke's narrative without other Gospels' input. Otherwise we will find ourselves interpreting, not Luke, but our own harmony of the Gospels.

We can certainly use the other three Gospels to help us understand the first century world, its culture, its habits, its language, and that will help us interpret Luke. We should also use the other three Gospels if our goal is to get as full a picture as possible of all that Jesus said and did. But if the goal is to examine the unique portrait Luke gives us of Jesus, then we see that more clearly if we do *not* constantly examine what the other three Gospels say.

This commentary is not about "everything Jesus said and did." This commentary examines Luke's narrative, Luke's portrait, Luke's presentation. For that, we need to look closely at Luke and at everything he could assume his readers would know and take into account: that includes the Old Testament; it does not include the other Gospels.

How to use this book

This book is divided into thirteen sections, so that Luke can conveniently be studied in a thirteen-week (three month) series of Bible studies or lessons. However, a detailed study of each section requires more time than is possible in a single Bible study. For this reason, I have highlighted one theme that seems especially prominent in each of the sections and labeled that section accordingly.

Since each section studies, on average, almost two of Luke's chapters, it may sometimes be advisable for Bible study groups to study just one passage within each section, one that clearly develops the main theme of the section. Alternatively, a Bible study group could take more than three months to work through the book of Luke, or (better still) could invest many hours each week in studying the Scriptures. That could even replace personal, private Bible reading and study for a period of time. Let me say more about that.

We often imagine that Scripture was designed for personal, private Bible reading. But the first "readers" of Luke's Gospel encountered it, not actually as readers, but as listeners. The majority of Gentile readers (and those would probably have made up well over half of the original readers) did not know how to read. And in any case virtually no church members in the first century would ever own personal copies of any of the books now in our New Testament. Churches (we should imagine house fellowships of perhaps 30-40 people) would read and study books like Luke's Gospel *in their gatherings*, guided by apostles or other church teachers, drawing heavily on Jews within their fellowships who knew the Old Testament Scriptures so well, and could therefore interpret all the events initiated through Jesus' life, death and resurrection in the light of the Hebrew Scriptures. Reading and studying Luke in the first century, indeed in the first fifteen centuries of church history, was primarily *group* reading and studying.

When we gather in Bible study groups, led by those well trained in the Scriptures, we encounter Scripture most like the original readers of these texts did. We, of course, have the special opportunity to own copies of Scripture and the ability to ready them privately, making it quite possible to study books like Luke entirely on our own. But let's make that a supplement to, never a replacement for, studying the Bible in the community of God's people.

This commentary does not reproduce the entire text in Luke, though short passages are sometimes quoted within the text. Readers are encouraged to have a modern translation with them as they work through the commentary. My comments are related most closely to the New International Version (2011), but I recommend consulting other modern translations as well.

In The Form and Flow of the Text, I overview the section of Luke under consideration and provide an outline. Often this overview also builds bridges to preceding or following sections, so the reader can follow the progression of Luke's narrative.

In The Text Explained, I examine individual units. Reading the text of Luke in a modern translation before reading the comments is important. Occasionally a text will introduce a theme so important in Luke's Gospel, or perhaps so important for contemporary readers, that I draw attention briefly to that theme, even when it looks beyond the short passage under consideration.

In Implications of the Text for Today, I address a small set of issues that were prominent in the section of Luke we just examined. These issues may be theological – in which case, we should ask what the rest of the Scriptures say about these matters. Or they may be very practical – in which case, we should consider what present-day implications follow from what Luke has addressed.

Finally, I include some Personal Reflection Questions. If you are using this book to study Luke's Gospel on your own, take some time to reflect, or even to write down, how you would respond to these questions. If you are studying Luke with others, use these questions to facilitate group conversation.

I wish you much joy in studying Luke. It has brought me much joy preparing this book to help you do that.

The Birth and Childhood of Jesus

The Text: Luke 1:1 - 2:52 NIV

The Flow and Form of the Text

The first two chapters of Luke provide us with much material that is unknown from the other Gospels. A detailed account of the circumstances surrounding the birth of John the Baptist's is interspersed with considerable detail about the circumstances surrounding the birth of Jesus. The two narratives intersect at the point when the two expectant mothers, Elizabeth and Mary, meet to celebrate, prophesy and sing about the goodness of God.

Throughout these two chapters, we see divine interventions taking place through such diverse means as angelic visitations, two miraculous pregnancies, a baby kicking in the womb and an emperor's decree. And God's Spirit is at work filling people, inspiring prophetic words, doing miracles.

These chapters feature prophecies and songs (often these two flow together) by Elizabeth, Mary, Zechariah, an angel choir, Simeon and Anna. And through all these means, Luke introduces us to two important characters. The first is the great prophet John who will prepare for the ministry of Jesus. The second, of course, is Jesus, introduced already here as Messiah and Son of God, Savior and Lord. And there are clear hints that he is not only someone God has *sent*; he is in his very person the *presence of God* among us. But he will not fulfill his role as deliverer in ways that everyone will welcome and accept. Some will reject him, not so much because they misunderstand, but because they do understand he is doing something different than what they wanted their Messiah to do. He will deliver them from sin and death, but not from the might of Rome – not yet, at any rate. Yet ultimately he will establish a peace this world has never known.

We will examine these two chapters following the NIV's section divisions, though sometimes with modified titles.

Outline:
Introduction to Luke's Gospel (1:1-4)
Announcing the Coming of John (1:5-25)
Announcing the Coming of Jesus (1:26-38)
Two Expectant Mothers Praise God Together (1:39-45)
The Song of Mary (1:46-56)
John the Baptist is Born (1:57-66)
The Song of Zechariah (1:67-80)
Jesus is Born (2:1-7)
Shepherds Experience the Good News (2:8-20)
Ceremonies of Circumcision and Consecration (2:21-24)
The Prophecies of Simeon and Anna (2:25-40)
The Boy Jesus at the Temple (2:41-52)

The Text Explained

Introduction to Luke's Gospel (1:1-4)

> *Many have undertaken to draw up an account of the things that have been fulfilled among us, just as they were handed down to us by those who from the first were eyewitnesses and servants of the word. With this in mind, since I myself have carefully inves-*

tigated everything from the beginning, I too decided to write an orderly account for you, most excellent Theophilus, so that you may know the certainty of the things you have been taught. (1:1-4)

Christians confess that Luke's Gospel, along with every other book of the Bible, is more than just the product of a human writer – it is the inspired Word of God. Yet Luke very clearly reveals what he has written is indeed (also) a fully human book, taking its place alongside other ancient literature. He tells us his goal in writing, the carefulness of his research and the reliability of his sources. He even addresses his writing to someone named "Theophilus," a person whose identity remains a mystery to us.

When Luke decided to write his own Gospel, it was not because he saw deficiencies in what his predecessors had written. In fact, he based his work on theirs. He refers to them as "eyewitnesses" (original apostles and others who were with Jesus) and "servants of the word" (a term that might imply they were authorized by the apostles to pass on the reliable traditions they had learned and probably memorized).

We cannot be sure which sources Luke used, but he may well have used Mark's Gospel and some additional shorter collections of Jesus's sayings and perhaps some of his deeds, whether these were written accounts or oral traditions. So why did Luke want to add something new to what was already available? I suggest three reasons, based on what Luke says in the prologue:

- He wanted to turn individual pieces of tradition and short collections into a *narrative*. That is probably what he means by "an orderly account." The gospel story can be told in many ways. Some forms resemble documentaries of what happened. Some are more like evangelistic preaching. Luke's choice was to write *a narrative* – a narrative with characters (including "good guys" and "bad guys"), a plot, a narrator, etc. It is of course a true story – but it is a story!

- He wanted his reader to gain assurance in the faith through reading and studying Luke's story. We are not quite sure what "Theophilus" was missing. Did he know the meaning of the Jesus story, but needed to fill in historical details? Or did he know a lot of historical details but needed to learn what it all meant and how it applied to his life? Perhaps he needed help with both history and theology. Certainly we do! So Luke wrote to help him "know the certainty of the things he had been taught."
- He wanted readers everywhere to understand the origins of what they were experiencing in their day. Luke addressed his work to Theophilus, but he obviously wanted far more people to read it. It was written for the church, initially the church in which Luke himself participated, as well as surrounding congregations. Ultimately, however, it would be for the whole church of Jesus Christ, for all time, as Luke's writing was recognized as Scripture and included in the New Testament canon. By the time Luke wrote, perhaps four or five decades after Jesus died and rose again, there would have been hundreds or thousands of early Christians wanting to learn more about how the whole Christian movement got started. Luke researched carefully and wrote it all down for them in a narrative that is now part of God's inspired Word.

That is Luke's prologue. Interestingly, he does not even hint at what his narrative will be about. It is about "the things that have been fulfilled among us." Of course we know this will be the story of Jesus, but when Luke gets started, he starts elsewhere. The Old Testament does not prophesy only about the coming Messiah; it also contains words of prophecy about the one who would prepare the way for the Lord. And those prophecies were fulfilled in John the Baptist. An old couple about to become the parents of this John are the first two characters to appear in Luke's narrative.

Announcing the Coming of John (1:5-25)

Zechariah and Elizabeth are far too old to have children. They are a priestly couple, living blamelessly before God; and yet they are childless. In their world that would seem strange, for childlessness was often interpreted as God's punishment for something they were doing wrong. In her culture, Elizabeth would bear the shame of this; many would assume she was the one living under God's curse (see 1:25).

Yet early Christians reading Luke's Gospel, if they knew their Scriptures (the Old Testament), would read of Elizabeth's barrenness and already anticipate that God is about to intervene. We remember the mother of the great Old Testament prophet, Samuel, whose shame and grief were also removed by the birth of her son (see 1 Samuel 1). And we remember an old couple before them, Abraham and Sarah, who experienced the miracle of a child in their old age.

Luke gives a detailed narrative of how that miracle happened for Zechariah and Elizabeth. The announcement that they would have a son came to Zechariah while he was experiencing a once-in-a-lifetime opportunity to perform the evening sacrifice on behalf of the nation of Israel. Suddenly, while Zechariah is out of sight behind the temple curtain, the angel Gabriel appears – the first of multiple angelic visits in these first two chapters of Luke.

> *The angel said to him: "Do not be afraid, Zechariah; your prayer has been heard. Your wife Elizabeth will bear you a son, and you are to call him John." (1:13)*

Reading 1:13 might give the impression that Zechariah was behind the temple curtain praying for a son. After all, the angel says, "Your prayer has been heard. Your wife Elizabeth will bear a son." But that is not how we should read this verse. I suspect Zechariah and Elizabeth had stopped praying *for a son* decades before. But even if not, it would have been completely inappropriate for him to use the context of the evening sacrifice to pray for his own personal concerns. He was there to pray for the *redemption of Israel!* And that is the prayer that Gabriel announces will now come to fulfillment.

God was about to initiate a chain of events leading to the redemption of Israel! It would involve the coming of the great prophet who would prepare for the ministry of the greater Coming One, the Messiah, whose life and teaching, and ultimately whose death and resurrection, would redeem not only Israel, but the whole world. Of course, the angel Gabriel did not reveal all this to Zechariah right at first. Yet as one who knew the Scriptures, Zechariah would have known that if the redeemer of Israel was now coming, then the redemption of the world would follow! Yes, "your prayer (for Israel's redemption) has been heard." But then the angel continues: "And your wife Elizabeth will bear you a son." God's redemption work would begin through the birth of a son to Zechariah and Elizabeth.

And so, amazingly, the prayer this couple had prayed a thousand times would also be answered, as part of the means by which God would now answer Israel's prayer, offered to God by the presiding priest, Zechariah, in the evening sacrifice. I wonder how often the deepest longings and prayers of our own hearts are fulfilled precisely when we are concerned with the wider purposes of God for our neighbors, our nation and our world. We are reminded of Jesus's promise that when we seek first God's kingdom, all our own needs will be met as well.

The angel Gabriel explains to Zechariah what the miracle child will become: a joy to his parents and to many others; a servant of God fully dedicated to his ministry; a spirit-filled prophet; a reformer; a forerunner of God's promised redeemer. And how does Zechariah respond? He doubts that it will be so! "How can I be sure of this?" (1:18). It is clear from the angel's response that Zechariah's question expresses his unbelief. And so the angel provides the proof that it will be so, but it is more like a punishment than mere evidence. Zechariah will now be unable to speak (and apparently to hear as well – see 1:62), until God fulfills the promise that Zechariah had not trusted God to keep.

When Zechariah re-emerges into the public part of the temple, people know something extraordinary has happened, though because of Zechariah's inability to speak, they get few details.

Zechariah's response to all this had been inadequate. Elizabeth's response is presented as exemplary. She rejoices in the goodness of God (1:25). Her words, "In these days he has shown his favor and taken away my disgrace among the people," are probably filled with far more meaning than she herself realizes. She is thinking of the shame of a lifetime of childlessness. But Luke, the writer, knows that "these days" speak of a whole new era of redemption in which God will remove the shame of Israel's unfaithfulness, remove the guilt of Israel's sin and indeed restore Israel as a people who will bring God's message of redemption to the whole world. At this point in the narrative, Luke drops no hint that many in Israel will reject this good news. Those hints will come soon enough.

Announcing the Coming of Jesus (1:26-38)

Luke is a master storyteller. His narrative intricately weaves together the stories of John and Jesus: first the announcement of John's impending conception, then Jesus's. Later the news of John's arrival, followed by Jesus's. Words of prophecy and songs of praise are connected to all four of these events.

Six months after the angel Gabriel speaks to Zechariah, that same angel appears again, this time to Mary. Both times it is to announce an impending pregnancy. But notice all the differences. The first announcement was to an old man; this one is to a young girl. The parents of John had lived a lifetime childless; Mary is not yet married. The first announcement came in the Jerusalem temple; this one comes in a no-account Galilean village. The first spoke of a great prophet; this one announces the arrival of "The Son of the Most High." The first child will grow up to prepare Israel for God's salvation; this one will one day reign on David's throne – forever!

Gabriel's greeting has been the subject of much analysis and dispute. Catholics often say, "Hail, Mary, full of grace." The same words are usually translated by Protestants as "Greetings! You are highly favored." Catholics sometimes imply that God fills Mary with grace, so she is able to dispense it. Protestants often downplay the significance of Mary, worrying that she will be worshipped and deified. Luke's point of view is between the extremes. Mary plays significant roles in this Gospel: She is the mother of the Messiah, indeed of "God" (for that is how Luke will present Jesus); she is a model of faith; she is a model of obedience. In the end, her greatness will not be linked to her role as Jesus's mother as much as to her faithful, obedient response to Word of God (see 11:27-28).

Mary's response, "How will this be?" sounds somewhat like Zechariah's earlier response, "How can I be sure of this?" But there is a world of difference between *doubt* that God will fulfill a promise and eagerness *to learn how* God will do so! Unlike Zechariah, Mary is affirmed for believing God's message to her (see 1:45).

The Christian doctrine of the virgin birth is very important. But we should not imagine that it was the only way God could have entered our world as a sinless human person. God is not that limited! It is important because Scripture affirms it; and it is important because God chose this way of bearing witness to the uniqueness of Mary's child.

The angel tells Mary about Elizabeth's miracle pregnancy (1:36) and speaks that wonderful assurance, "No word from God will ever fail" (1:37). Mary's response says it all! "I am the Lord's servant. May your word to me be fulfilled" (1:38). We are invited to respond exactly like that, no matter what word God speaks to us, no matter how we are called to serve the Lord.

Two Expectant Mothers Praise God Together (1:39-45)

This part of Luke's Gospel intertwines two storylines, one about John's birth, the other about Jesus's. Mary's visit at Elizabeth's house brings the two together. Imagine the conversations they had, both miraculously with child, both promised sons who would play unprecedented roles in salvation history. Luke's short narrative highlights joy and blessing, the filling of God's Spirit, a sign from God prophetically interpreted and an amazing claim made about Mary and her baby. Mary is called "the mother of my Lord." Luke obviously refers to "God" when he uses "Lord" in 1:45; but just as obviously that same word, when used by Elizabeth in 1:43, refers to "Jesus." Luke, like the other evangelists, will present Jesus with many significant titles – Messiah (Christ), Son of the Most High (Son of God), Savior, Lord, etc. But most astonishing of all is the claim, sometimes only cautiously suggested between the lines: This baby is God!

The Song of Mary (1:46-56)

At this point, Mary bursts forth in song. Or maybe we should imagine she carefully composed this song on the long three-day trip to visit her Aunt Elizabeth, and decided this was the time to sing it!

> *"My soul glorifies the Lord*
> *and my spirit rejoices in God my Savior,*
> *for he has been mindful*
> *of the humble state of his servant.*
> *From now on all generations will call me blessed,*
> *for the Mighty One has done great things for me—*
> *holy is his name." (1:46-49)*

Mary's song, often called The Magnificat (after the first word in its Latin translation) seems to be modeled on Hannah's song of praise in the Old Testament (see 1 Samuel 2:1-10). Mary's version of the song highlights her joy. Yet it quickly moves beyond joy about God's special intervention in her life to what God would now do for the whole world. She, a humble servant girl, has experienced God's great blessedness. And that foreshadows what God is beginning to do for all people, everywhere, for all time.

The proud oppressor will be cut down; the humble will be lifted up, the hungry fed. God is keeping the ancient promises! Many in Israel were awaiting the day when Israel, now oppressed, would defeat and humiliate the enemy, at this point, the Romans. But Mary's song is not so much about turning the tables *upside down*, creating a new set of oppressors who pay back their enemies for all they have suffered. Rather, bringing down the mighty and raising those they have kept down means stopping the oppression, creating a community of equals where each cares for the other, where worldly power differences no longer count. Luke's second volume, the Acts of the Apostles, will tell the story of how that came about. Roman jailors, military officials, Jewish freedom fighters, foreign slave girls, fishermen, tax collectors – rich and poor, slave and free – become a family of equals, with only Jesus as Lord! That is the kind of restoration that Mary's song points toward, though it would take decades for all that to become reality.

John the Baptist is Born (1:56-66)

Naming children was always an important event for ancient Jews. The name Gabriel said to give the child, John (see 1:13), means "God has shown favor." It is an appropriate name for what God has now initiated. This really is the time of God's favor! It also speaks of newness. Neighbors and relatives want Zechariah's son to bear his name and carry on his legacy. The parents recognize that the legacy of their own family is now secondary. God will create a new family that transcends small circles of families and friends – that even transcends ethnic and national identities.

As soon as he names the child, Zechariah can speak again. Appropriately, his first words are praise to God. Luke's text creates the impression that bystanders know something unusual is happening: even the healing of Zechariah's muteness bears witness to that! They are filled with expectation, though they understand very little about what this all means (see 1:66). This will be the norm all the way through Jesus's ministry, and sometimes beyond that. People will be astonished by what they see and hear, but they will understand very little. Eventually the resurrected Jesus (see 24:27), the Holy Spirit poured out on the church (Acts 2) and (not to be overlooked) Gospels like Luke will interpret all these new things God is doing.

The Song of Zechariah (1:67-80)

Elizabeth's Spirit-filling and prophesying in 1:41-45 are now matched by her husband's Spirit-filling and prophesying (1:67). It is not his own son God has raised up as a "horn of salvation" (1:69); that line refers to Jesus. But his own son will prepare the way for the greater one to come, the one who will fulfill the ancient promises. Central to Zechariah's prophecy is the focus on deliverance from enemies (see 1:71, 74). For most in Israel, it would have seemed obvious that this must mean the Roman oppressors.

Yet Luke knows better. He knows that Jesus comes to establish God's reign *even while Rome continues to wield earthly power.* And precisely for this reason, many would reject Jesus. They did not want a Messiah who called them to love their enemies! Luke knows Jesus comes to defeat the real enemies of Israel and of all humanity – the powers of sin and death, and behind these, the principalities and powers that oppose God. By defeating these at the cross and through the resurrection, Jesus would inaugurate the reign of God, right in the middle of a world still controlled, from a worldly point of view, by Israel's enemies and their falsely named "Peace of Rome" (*Pax Romana*).

Zechariah's song, which Luke calls a word of prophecy, continues with specific foretelling about the role the newborn child would fulfill. John will be a prophet of God. He will prepare for the Lord's coming (now clearly referring to Jesus). The ministry of John, and of course the even greater ministry of Jesus to follow, will bring knowledge of salvation, forgiveness of sin, and finally, a path toward true peace, not the kind that Rome promised through its sword, but the kind God would make possible through the death and resurrection of Jesus.

And the child grew and became strong in spirit; and he lived in the wilderness until he appeared publicly to Israel. (1:80)

The final verse of this chapter sends the reader forward, right to the beginning of John's ministry. But before he tells that story, Luke devotes a whole chapter to the birth and the growth of Jesus, until these two servants of God meet at the Jordan River in Luke 3.

Jesus is Born (2:1-7)

In those days Caesar Augustus issued a decree that a census should be taken of the entire Roman world. (This was the first census that took place while Quirinius was governor of Syria.) And everyone went to their own town to register.

So Joseph also went up from the town of Nazareth in Galilee to Judea, to Bethlehem the town of David, because he belonged to the house and line of David. He went there to register with Mary, who was pledged to be married to him and was expecting a child. While they were there, the time came for the baby to be born, and she gave birth to her firstborn, a son. She wrapped him in cloths and placed him in a manger, because there was no guest room available for them. (2:1-7)

Luke has already indicated that Herod is king of Judea (see 1:5); now he names Augustus, the Roman emperor (2:1). In the next chapter, covering events 30 years later, he lists numerous other governing (3:1) and religious (3:2) officials. This not only assures us that Luke knows the facts of history. It means, first and foremost, that the gospel is now present on the "world stage." The gospel is not just about doctrines and divinity. God acts within human history, challenging real political and economic systems, bringing heaven's rule to bear on human culture and society. Jesus is born in troubled times, in a place where political authorities wield oppressive power. And he comes to set up God's kingdom!

That does not mean he comes to do only "spiritual things," leaving the world to run itself on its own terms. It means, rather, that he sets in motion a movement that would ultimately turn the world upside down, or perhaps better, right side up! That movement would take root among the Jews of Judea and Galilee, but would, within a few short generations, spread across the Roman Empire and beyond. And all along the way, it would challenge the ways of the world – never by taking up military and political power against worldly ways, always by teaching and modeling an alternative, even if it provokes violent responses, even if those embodying that gospel and living for that kingdom lose their lives in the process.

Luke's "Christmas story" in many ways hints that the movement of God now beginning would subvert the world's ways and, in the end, through non-violent means, bring them down!

Scripture foretold the coming king would be born in Bethlehem. Luke's narrative shows how God uses even the oppressive decrees of pagan rulers to move actors around and set the stage for the fulfillment of divine prophecies. And when the stage is set, the King of all the Earth is born, not in a palace, but in the most humble of circumstances, and laid in a manger. The first humans to bow down will not be rulers and kings, but humble shepherds.

The subversive nature of God's kingdom is already on display. Soon the movement will attract fishermen, tax collectors, prostitutes, the poor, crippled, blind and lame – ordinary and not so ordinary people who will bear witness to, and embody, a new sort of kingdom. Against such a kingdom, all the world's powerful rulers will be powerless to defend, whatever weapons they choose – swords and crosses, guillotines and bonfires, intimidation and imprisonment. God's kingdom will one day bring down the mighty from their thrones, just as Mary's song celebrates.

What Inn?

And now we must briefly challenge a common misconception. Jesus's parents almost certainly did not first check out an "inn" in Bethlehem; and the birth itself almost certainly did not take place in a "barn" – nor for that matter in a cave, as a minority have sometimes claimed.

Bible interpreter Kenneth Bailey first proposed, and many others have since confirmed, that the word usually translated "inn" in Luke 2:7 (*kataluma*) actually means "guest room." Commentaries on Luke have followed suit, and now translators are revising English versions of the Bible. See, for example, the NIV translation quoted above: "there was no *guest room* available for them."

Numerous factors have led Bible interpreters to re-imagine what Luke actually meant in his brief "Christmas story," including:

- First century Jewish peasants did not have separate buildings for animals; rather, on cold nights they brought animals into the house.
- Mangers were therefore inside ordinary houses.
- Animals would sleep in a lower level of a family's one-room split-level house; the family slept on a raised level. And the manger was likely built along the edge of the family's living area.
- Bethlehem was not along a trade route and therefore almost certainly would not even have had an inn.
- Even if it had an inn, Joseph, a native son of the village, and Mary, who has relatives in the hill country nearby, would certainly not have checked out an inn; they would have gone to stay with relatives and friends.
- A guest room (*kataluma*) would normally have been built on the roof. Luke refers to a large one in 22:11, 12.

Taking all this into account, what does Luke's narrative actually say? Not that an inn was full, so the couple had to go to a cold dark barn. Rather, that the family who took them in put them right in the living area because their guest room was already occupied by other guests. We will explore some of the implications of this reading later!

Shepherds Experience the Good News (2:8-20)

The story of the shepherds is familiar. But we do not always take into account how subversive it would have sounded to early Christians and their pagan neighbors in the Roman Empire of Luke's day. God's angel announces "good news" (*euangelion*). It is a word Roman emperors used to announce the birth of their children, or their own inauguration into power. The angel called the newborn babe a "Savior" (*sōter*), a title that appeared on Roman coins to designate emperors. And the baby is not only a Messiah (Jews would have recognized that term), but is also called Lord (*kurios*) – the early Christian confession "Jesus is Lord" was an intentional challenge to the primary confession of Rome's fastest growing and most powerful religion: "Caesar is Lord."

And when an *army* of angels joins the first messenger – yes, indeed, the word Luke uses refers to an army, and thus directly draws attention to the military might of Rome – it announces that, in this Jesus, the world will find peace. Could there be a more direct challenge to Rome's claim that their great gift to the world was the "*Pax Romana*" – a reign of terror that they called "Peace"?

Far more of Luke (and for that matter, Acts) stands as a frontal challenge to the claims of Roman power, as if the Christian church were saying to the greatest empire the world had ever known: "You think you are so mighty with all your pompous claims, economic clout and military prowess? Just wait until the little band of Jesus-followers carries out its campaign of love and self-sacrifice. Your pretentious claims will come crashing down at the foot of the cross you so proudly raised. As if you could stop the world's true king from taking his throne!

The rest of the "Christmas story" presents us with models of faithfulness. The shepherds model faith-filled hearing and obedient doing (2:15), then they model effective evangelism, bearing witness to what they had experienced (2:17, 18), and finally, they return to their ordinary work as changed people, filled with praise because they have seen what God is doing, heard it explained and experienced it firsthand. And in the middle of Luke's tribute to the shepherds is the notice, which he will repeat later (2:51), that mother Mary pondered all these things in her heart. That, too, belongs to our Christmas celebrations and to our daily lives as followers of this Jesus.

Ceremonies of Circumcision and Consecration (2:21-24)

The account of Jesus's circumcision reminds us that he came as a Jew into a Jewish context, and that, at least initially, his mission was to the Jews. The gospel will of course ultimately be for the whole world. Yet, in Luke's account of Jesus's ministry, Jesus rarely comes into direct contact with any Gentiles. His death and resurrection will be for all people and for all God's creation; his preaching and earthly ministry, however, will be first and foremost to prepare Israel for its mission: to bring the gospel to all nations. The book of Acts will show how the Jews who responded to Jesus's call did precisely that!

Luke portrays Mary and Joseph as faithful Israelites, carrying out the Law of Moses. Luke tells us their sacrifices were to "consecrate Jesus." Normally a firstborn child would also be "redeemed": parents offered sacrifices to God in place of the firstborn child (who belonged to God; see 2:23), so that the child could belong again to the earthly parents. Nothing is said about "redeeming" in Luke's text, implying that Jesus, even though he will grow up in Mary and Joseph's home and family, really belongs in God's house and God's family. Twelve years later, Jesus will chide his parents for not understanding that he must be in his (true!) Father's house (see 2:49).

The Prophecies of Simeon and Anna (2:25-38)

Luke 2:25-27 contains the fifth, sixth and seventh direct references to the Holy Spirit in this Gospel. God's Spirit is clearly on the move, filling people, moving them around, revealing words of prophecy, performing miracles. Simeon, by listening to and responding to God's Spirit, experiences something that apparently was on his "bucket list" (see 2:26, 29, 30). He was permitted to see God's Messiah, the baby Jesus, before he died. Indeed, his prophetic word speaks of God's salvation, now arrived in Jesus, as being not only for the glory of Israel, but on display for all the world to see.

His prophecy then takes an ominous turn. Not all in Israel will welcome the coming Messiah. The "falling and rising" of many means that some will accept Jesus as God's final deliverer and some will reject him, like a metaphorical "sword" dividing Israel in two. And a sword of another sort will also pierce Mary, alluding to what she will suffer when she loses her son to the cruelty of Rome's jealous power. Readers of Luke's Gospel have now heard prophecies of greatness and weakness, acceptance and rejection, peace and a sword. But through it all rings a message of hope and joy: through this child, God will bring about the world's redemption.

Luke so often balances stories about men with stories about women. Just as both Elizabeth and Zechariah spoke prophetic words, so also Simeon and Anna do. This time Luke does not quote the prophetic words, but assures us that Anna, a faithful Israelite, boldly witnesses to the new things God is doing.

> *When Joseph and Mary had done everything required by the Law of the Lord, they returned to Galilee to their own town of Nazareth. And the child grew and became strong; he was filled with wisdom, and the grace of God was on him. (2:39-40)*

The so-called "Christmas story" in Luke ends with a brief summary of how Jesus's life continues. Mary and Joseph move back to Galilee as obedient Jews and raise this miracle child in their family. Verse 40 is the first of two clear statements that Jesus grew and matured, in many ways just like any other boy (note the similarity to what is said of John in 1:80!). Yet always there are hints that Jesus is so much more than just an ordinary child.

The Boy Jesus at the Temple (2:41-52)

Luke 2 ends with the only account of anything Jesus did between his experiences as an infant and the beginning of his ministry 30 years later. It could be read as a story about a precocious boy, or about an adolescent causing his parents unnecessary concern. It could also be read as if the parents were careless and clueless. But Luke emphasizes other things. This is an account of a young man who knows and understands Israel's Scriptures at the deepest level, something even the Bible experts of the day can recognize. And it is about the boy Jesus's realization that his "real Father" is God in heaven and that therefore he belongs in God's house (at that time, still the temple).

What readers of Luke will learn as they keep reading through this Gospel and its sequel, the Book of Acts, is that even this temple is destined to be replaced by Jesus himself and his community of followers. Yes, God has chosen to dwell in this building made of stone, but for those with eyes to see, Jesus will from now on be the real place where heaven and earth meet, where followers offer true worship, where the Scriptures are understood and fulfilled.

> *His mother treasured all these things in her heart. And Jesus grew in wisdom and stature, and in favor with God and man. (2:51-52)*

The last two verses of this chapter re-emphasize two things Luke has already told us: Mary pondered all these things in her heart (see also 2:19). The child Jesus continues to grow up, physically, socially and spiritually (see also 1:40).

When I heard the Bible stories as a child, I somehow imagined the baby Jesus was already all-knowing and all-powerful, like the God of heaven – as if even the baby in the manger could have explained how to fix a computer or build a hybrid car. Luke tells the story differently. Jesus was a typical Jewish boy, except that he was already becoming aware of his unique mission and his unique destiny, not so much because of supernatural knowledge within him, but because he was filled with God's Spirit, because he listened to his Father's voice and because he diligently studied the Scriptures.

In Jesus, God truly became one of us, and so Jesus can also be a model for us in learning our own true nature and our calling.

Implications of the Text for Today

The Gospels and the Scriptures

We must remember that there was no New Testament when Jesus lived on earth, nor, for that matter, when Luke was writing his Gospel. For the characters in Luke's story and for the readers of Luke's Gospel, "the Bible" – the "Holy Scriptures" – contained the books we know now as the "Old Testament" or the "Hebrew Scriptures." For this reason, it was natural for people around Jesus and those reading Luke's Gospel to interpret everything they experienced and read in the light of these Scriptures. Moreover, the Jews of Jesus's day and the Jews in the Christian churches who read the Gospels would have known their Bible far better than most of us know ours. It was, after all, the only textbook they would have used in all their years of schooling. From it, they learned to read, they learned history, politics, religion and ethics – everything they needed to know to be God's people!

Yet each of the four Gospels builds on the Hebrew Scriptures in its own unique way. Mark, for example, rarely quotes it, but often makes subtle allusions to texts that shed a clearer light on what is happening. Matthew, by contrast, frequently quotes it, lining up events of biblical prophecy with their fulfillment in the time of Jesus. Luke is somewhere in between. He makes clearer references to the Old Testament than Mark, but fewer than Matthew.

Luke's strongest emphases are that faithful Jews awaiting their Messiah were people of faith who knew God would keep the ancient promises and they expressed their faith by a devout lifestyle in accordance with the Law of Moses. We see multiple examples in these first two chapters. Zechariah and Elizabeth are said to be "righteous in the sight of God, observing all the Lord's commands and decrees blamelessly" (1:6). Mary and Joseph are portrayed as fulfilling their obligations in relation to the Law of Moses, circumcising, performing purification rites, consecrating their firstborn, always "in keeping with what is said in the Law" (see 2:21-24). Simeon was "righteous and devout. He was waiting for the consolation of Israel" (2:25) and Anna "never left the temple but worshiped night and day, fasting and praying" (2:37).

For Luke, the ones who experience God's surprising interventions are often those who are faithful and obedient as they trust and wait – sometimes a whole lifetime. Yet, later in the Gospel, we will also encounter another scenario: people who were absolutely unfaithful (tax collectors, prostitutes and sinners) and were not at all waiting for God's interventions will encounter Jesus and find in him their hope and salvation.

What does that mean for us? Nobody is beyond the reach of the gospel! Yet, if we want to experience all that God has in store for us, we are called to be like those models of faith and obedience we encounter in Luke's first two chapters. And often the key to that faithful obedience is knowing the Scriptures as they did, believing the promises found there, living according to God's directions revealed there. The good news God has in store for us will always be a fulfillment of what God has previously revealed in the Word!

God is in Control

Luke's Gospel makes very clear that God is a God who intervenes in history, moving actors around the stage, communicating with them, sending divine messengers, doing miracles. But we should not read this as though God has every event in world history pre-planned, nor as though God micromanages all the affairs of our daily lives, nor as though God exerts so much influence on people that they all eventually do whatever God decrees. That is an extreme version of God's sovereignty that some Christians find comforting, or consider biblical. But worked out to its logical implications, it falls apart and in the end portrays a very different version of God from the one we encounter in Scripture.

Yes, God knows that some will reject the message of salvation, but

God does not "make them do it." Yes, God uses oppressive decrees from worldly authorities to accomplish divine purposes, but God does not always protect people from the horrible consequences of evil human acts. Yes, God provided miracle babies for Elizabeth and Mary, but often couples remain childless despite their prayers, and some expectant mothers experience miscarriages and stillbirths. God is a sovereign God who will bring about the fulfillment of all God's good purposes, one day! Until that day comes, God punctuates human existence with occasional surprising interventions, but is constantly with us and working among us in those times when evil still happens, whether caused by humans, by a still unredeemed natural world, or by God's supernatural enemy. And so, just as Simeon and Anna waited for God's salvation to appear, we wait still!

Which Prayer Was Answered?

Gabriel's message to Zechariah was "Your prayers have been heard!" As we suggested above, the prayer God heard was the prayer of God's people Israel, uttered through their consecrated priest, for God to intervene and bring salvation. Now God would do it! And precisely as God would now answer this prayer, God would also answer Zechariah's and Elizabeth's lifelong prayer for a son. Zechariah sought first the kingdom of God; God saw to it that the private prayer of a lonely and shamed couple was also answered.

Clearly there are times to pray our "private prayers" – to pray for daily bread, for health, for safety when we drive, even for a parking spot. But if all our prayers are about our "lesser needs," we take our eyes off of God's mighty deeds in bringing salvation to the world. Perhaps the Lord's Prayer, which we will encounter in Luke 11, can be a model. We concern ourselves first with the honor of God's name and the coming of God's reign (11:2), and then trust God also to give us our daily bread (11:3). Both Zechariah and Mary experienced God's goodness to them as a result and as an implication of God's greater concern for the salvation of the whole world. Let that be our highest concern as well.

The "Christology" of Luke

We use the word "christology" to speak of Jesus's identity, titles and roles. The word is not quite appropriate, since it comes from the word "Christ," and Jesus's identity is not centered around any one specific title, not even the title "Christ," as important as it is. There are many ways of saying who Jesus is and what he does.

Each Gospel has its own unique christology; that is, each centers on Jesus, but not always in identical ways. Matthew's Gospel, for example, opens with indications that Jesus is the Son of Abraham (a true Israelite), Son of David (the one who will reign forever) and Messiah (the one who brings an end to Israel's long exile). Those are the titles embedded in Matthew's opening 17 verses. Later we learn that Jesus is Immanuel (God with us; 1:23) and God's own Son (3:17).

Mark's Gospel introduces Jesus explicitly as "Christ" and "Son of God" right from the start (see 1:1). Almost immediately, Mark drops hints – but only hints – that this is also the Lord God (*Yhwh; I Am*) embodied in the human Jesus (Mark 1:2-3). All in all, much more secrecy surrounds the identity of Jesus in Mark's Gospel than in Matthew's.

John's Gospel first introduces Jesus as "the Word" who is identified as "God" (1:1) and then makes the astonishing claim that this Word "became flesh"; that is, he took on human nature and a physical body (1:14). In John, Jesus frequently refers to himself with the divine name (*I Am*) and at the same time as "the one God sent."

Luke, the focus of our study, will reveal the identity of Jesus gradually. There is no christology in the first verses as there is in the other three Gospels. In fact, there is no explicit mention of Jesus or his coming until 1:31, though there are hints already in 1:17. Yet before the first two chapters are over, the reader learns that Jesus will be "Son of the Most High God" (1:32, 35), that he will rule on David's throne forever (1:33), that he is Lord (1:43, 76; 2:11), Horn of Salvation (1:69), Savior (2:11) and Christ (2:11,

26). And the very first time we hear Jesus speak, he refers to God as his own Father (2:49). We will see many of these titles recurring and their meaning clarified. Perhaps most impressive is the way in which Luke will use two titles carefully reserved for God in the Old Testament and conspicuously applied to Caesar in the first century world, and apply them directly to Jesus: "Lord" and "Savior."

Celebrating Jesus's Birth

Some who learn that Jesus was probably not born in a cold, dark barn fear that they will need to start all over again finding appropriate Christmas decorations. But maybe the opposite is true! Maybe we can finally with good conscience set up our Christmas decorations as we usually do without the uncomfortable feeling that we have violated what really happened.

I have seen numerous manger scenes that have the heavenly star shining down on the manger scene, even though we are told in Scripture that the star shone down on the *house* where the couple was when the wise men came to honor him (Matthew 2:9-11). We've usually imagined the holy couple must have moved from the stable to somebody's house between the shepherds' visit and the wise men's visit. So not only do we put the star in the wrong place (over the stable), but we put the wise men there along with it, and have them kneeling beside the shepherds. We set it up all wrong, don't we? Not necessarily.

If a manger would normally be in a house and if Mary and Joseph were staying there all along (even though the guestroom on the roof was occupied by other visitors), perhaps the shepherds Luke reports and the wise men Matthew reports really did all visit baby Jesus on the "first Christmas night" and perhaps the heavenly star really did shine down on them all! We cannot be sure, but it really is possible – just the way we usually set up our Christmas displays.

What really changes when we read the story as I propose is that it does not illustrate the hard-heartedness of people who make no room for Mary and Joseph and thus cause Jesus to be born in a cold, dark barn. Rather, it illustrates a warm-hearted reception by a family whose house was already full of other guests. Maybe that can be our motivation to do the same when we celebrate Jesus's birth. Yes, the house may be full of guests, but Jesus is invited right into the middle of the celebration.

Personal Reflection Questions

- When have you had Zechariah's experience of being surprised that God not only blessed your service, but was, in the process, answering prayers you had long given up expecting God to answer?
- Which view of God's divine sovereignty do you consider most biblical and most helpful for your own spiritual journey: the view of God that sees God in control of everything, or almost everything (so that even the negative things we experience are attributed to God's plan); or the view that God only occasionally intervenes miraculously to bend circumstances and/or people's will to God's purposes? What would it mean for God to be our companion and fellow-sufferer when we experience evil things in this life?
- How does Luke's narrative of the events preceding and surrounding Jesus's birth motivate you to celebrate Christmas in meaningful ways? To live faithfully all through the year?

Preparations for Jesus's Ministry

The Text: Luke 3:1 - 4:13 NIV

The Flow and Form of the Text

Everything in this passage prepares for the ministry of Jesus. This involves two primary components:

- John's ministry prepares Israel for the arrival and ministry of God's Messiah;
- God prepares Jesus for his own role as the world's Savior.

Luke has already introduced John as a prophet who will "go on before the Lord to prepare the way for him" (1:76). Now Luke tells us about John's prophecy and baptism ministries. Using the words of ancient prophets, Luke characterizes John as a "voice" and as a "preparer." His role is to get Israel ready for the coming of the Messiah, the one who will deliver them from oppression and restore them for their God-given ministry of bringing God's salvation to the rest of the world. As we will see, this preparation for ministry involves his hearers' renewed commitment to God, a restored covenant relationship based on faith and obedience, not racial, ethnic or national identity. And it will require a transformation of life in anticipation of the kind of kingdom Jesus will inaugurate.

God prepares Jesus himself for his ministry in multiple ways. At his baptism, a voice from heaven proclaims his identity and alludes to key aspects of his life's work. The descending dove symbolizes the Spirit who empowers Jesus for what lies ahead. Jesus, the Son of God, is thereby linked in the most intimate way with both his heavenly Father and the Holy Spirit. This is not yet the Trinity as the church later tries to define it, but it is the data which the later church will take into account in its reflections on the nature of God.

In this section, Luke makes it clear Jesus is not only linked to God the Father and the Holy Spirit; Jesus is also a fully human person. His baptism identifies him in the closest possible way with covenant Israel, of whom he is a member, whom he came to deliver and restore, whom he explicitly joins anew through baptism. And then the genealogy Luke provides links Jesus to all of humanity, to those Jesus came to save and return to their rightful place as caretakers of and rulers over the rest of creation.

Then, as if Jesus were a new Adam, ready to be the head of a whole new humanity, he faces (as did our first parents) Satan's temptations. The devil tempts Jesus to act in ways that would disqualify him from his divinely given role. Jesus resists all temptations – temptations to pursue self-interest, to compromise with evil and to take shortcuts in living out his mission. And so Jesus is ready for his ministry, ready as the Son of God and ready as the sinless human. To accomplish all he came to do, he had to be both. What a theologically rich section of Luke's Gospel!

Outline:

John Fulfills Prophecy (3:1-6)
John Baptizes, Preaches Judgment and Calls for Justice (3:7-20)
The Baptism of Jesus (3:21-22)

Jesus's Human Lineage (3:23-38)
Jesus is Tested in the Wilderness (4:1-13)

The Text Explained

Introduction

As indicated above, this lesson is all about preparation. John, the preparer, baptizes and preaches. Various groups within Israel hear the call to repent, be baptized and live transformed lives. And in multiple ways, Jesus undergoes preparation for his public ministry.

But we should not overlook another set of preparations: Luke is preparing the reader as well! Luke is telling the reader all the ancient promises are now being fulfilled. Luke says this explicitly when he quotes Isaiah's prophecy (3:4-6) and declares John as the fulfillment. But it happens in numerous more subtle ways as well:

- The heavenly voice alludes to three different Old Testament texts that suggest central aspects of Jesus's ministry;
- The genealogy Luke provides is designed to link Jesus with Adam, into whose lineage he was born and whose divinely given role he will now re-establish;
- The temptation narrative reveals the importance of knowing Scripture well; how else will we be able to resist the temptations that threaten our own ministry callings?
- And the temptation narrative also makes clear that it is not enough to "find a verse somewhere." Faithful biblical interpretation includes discerning which texts apply to which persons in which situations.

If we learn these lessons, we will be well equipped to understand Jesus's ministry and well equipped to join Jesus in his work as we learn from him.

John Fulfills Prophecy (3:1-6)

The word of God came to John son of Zechariah in the wilderness. He went into all the country around the Jordan, preaching a baptism of repentance for the forgiveness of sins. As it is written in the book of the words of Isaiah the prophet:
"A voice of one calling in the wilderness,
'Prepare the way for the Lord,
make straight paths for him.'" (3:2b-4)

Even before Luke interprets John's ministry, he locates John both in "world history" and in "salvation history." The first two verses remind us of 2:1, 2. When Jesus was born, Caesar Augustus was Rome's emperor. Thirty years have passed. Rome's emperor is now Tiberius Caesar. Luke also names other rulers: Pontius Pilate (the governor who will condemn Jesus to death); several other Herods (the New Testament refers to six of them); Caiaphas and Annas (powerful religious leaders in Jerusalem).

By naming all these, Luke is saying a series of important things:

- Luke's narrative is not some "interesting story that teaches good lessons." Luke's account is a report of what really happened to concrete people in specific times and places. And it is a narrative about God's divine invasion into a world that was being ruled (at least from an earthly perspective) by powerful political, military and religious rulers.
- God's kingdom will not be a secret inner spirituality. It will be God powerfully breaking into the real world of politics and social systems, of economics and religion, turning the world upside down, or perhaps better: right side up.
- Jesus and the gospel he brings challenge the rulers of this world to recognize that, for all their worldly power, they must and one day will submit to God's reign through Jesus – a far more powerful reign, established not with swords and spears, not with religious laws and ceremonies, but with love and self-sacrifice, a cross and the miracle of resurrection.

When the world thinks it has things under control, God speaks a divine word and turns the world upside down. The divine word is spoken first by John, and then, more powerfully still, by Jesus. John's ministry is "in the wilderness" and "around the Jordan." Both of these phrases are loaded with significance. In the ancient past, Israel spent decades "in the wilderness" experiencing hardship and testing as they waited and longed for the day they would enter the Promised Land. Now John, and after him Jesus, will lead Israel into the new Promised Land of God's arriving kingdom. Israel has experienced hardship, testing, waiting. Now will be the time of fulfillment.

John's baptism is "around the Jordan." The Jordan River, of course, was the last obstacle Israel had to cross before entering the Promised Land (see Joshua 3). Last time, God miraculously piled up the waters so Israel could cross on dry ground. This time, those ready to enter the new "Promised Land" are plunged beneath the waters of Jordan to cleanse their hearts and lives and emerge ready to welcome God's deliverer.

John's was not the first voice crying in the wilderness, not the first "fulfiller" of Isaiah's prophecy. But he will be the greatest fulfiller, the one who fills the prophecy all the way full. After him "the Lord" arrives.

More than any other New Testament writer, Luke firmly locates John at the end of the old era, and Jesus at the beginning of the new era. Their births and their childhoods were intertwined, but their ministries are kept separate. John's ministry completes the time of the "Law and the Prophets." Jesus's ministry inaugurates the kingdom of God (see 7:28 and 16:16-17).

One more point: we should not underestimate how radical it was for John to be baptizing Jews. Jews had their own cleansing ceremonies, but baptism itself was reserved for non-Jews who wanted to convert to biblical faith. By baptizing Jews John was saying: It is not enough to be born into a Jewish family; it is not enough to have attended synagogue school, to worship regularly, to bring sacrificial animals to the temple; it is not enough to identify with ethnic or national Israel. What matters is the condition of the heart. Even "Jews" need to become "true Jews" if they want to live under God's loving rule.

John Preaches Judgement and Calls for Justice (3:7-20)

Produce fruit in keeping with repentance! (3:8)

For centuries, Israel had been longing for "The Day of the Lord" to arrive. They were sure they understood what that would mean. It would mean, on the one hand, judgment on all who had oppressed Israel through the centuries, and on the other hand, salvation and sovereignty for Israel. John's message sounds like it preserves the focus on judgment, but look closely: It is not judgment on foreign rulers, it is judgment on unfaithful Israelites.

Later Peter will write these words: "It is time for judgment to begin with God's household." (1 Peter 4:17) That seems to have been John's message. In order to prepare for God's salvation, hearts needed to turn back to God. Repent! (i.e. change your minds and hearts) Be baptized! (i.e. become a "true Jew" through the transformation of the heart, not by claiming Abraham as an ancestor). Produce fruit! (i.e. live consistent with your renewed status as God's covenant people!)

The specific instructions are merely "rules"; they are designed to teach attitudes. Sharing a second shirt means to give up selfish hoarding and care for others. Collecting no more (taxes) than required means living with integrity. Avoiding extortion and being content with one's pay means serving faithfully for the benefit of others.

John is calling for life transformation. Without that, religious rituals do not count for much. The radical renewal John called for and the widespread success of his ministry has an unintended result: some begin to speculate that John is the promised Messiah. But John vigorously denies this. He is only the preparer. He knows the one to come is greater still. He knows his own baptism is no more than a preparation for a greater baptism to come, when God will pour out the divine Spirit on all the people of God.

Verses 17 and 18 could easily be understood as though there are two equally important aspects to all this: 1) harvest (i.e. reward) for some; 2) the fires of hell (i.e. punishment) for the rest. But John makes no mention here of hell; he is simply using imagery from harvest season.

I am inclined to agree with G.B. Caird in his comments on this text: "The object of the winnowing is not to collect enough chaff to have a glorious bonfire; it is to gather the wheat into the granary; the bonfire is purely incidental." (New Testament Theology, p. 360). We should, at the very least, note that according to Luke, John's message was "good news" (see 3:18). And when Jesus steps onto the stage, the goodness of that good news will be further magnified, while the judgment theme will recede even more into the background. In fact, the reason he will get into trouble when he preaches his very first sermon, is because his audience will nor hear the judgment themes for which they were all waiting (see Luke 4:14-30).

Luke then briefly tells how John himself got into trouble. He meddled in the affairs of powerful people (see 3:19). Jesus will do the same later on. In John's case it resulted in imprisonment and eventually beheading. In Jesus' case it will result in a crucifixion. Yes, there is good news proclaimed here, but it will come at great cost, not only for John but for Jesus, and not only for Luke's readers in the first century but for millions thereafter.

The Baptism of Jesus (3:21-22)

> *When all the people were being baptized, Jesus was baptized too. And as he was praying, heaven was opened and the Holy Spirit descended on him in bodily form like a dove. And a voice came from heaven: "You are my Son, whom I love; with you I am well pleased." (3:21-22)*

This is a short narrative, but it is packed with important points.

First, notice how Luke carefully separates John's ministry (ending the old era) from Jesus's ministry (starting the new era). He even reports John's imprisonment before backtracking and indicating that Jesus "was baptized too," leaving it in the passive voice so John is not even mentioned. Of course it was John who baptized Jesus, but even these small narrative strategies help Luke make his theological points.

Second, this introduces three consecutive texts about "the Son of God." Here the voice from heaven declares that Jesus is the Son of God (3:22). In the next incident, Luke traces Jesus's lineage back to God through Adam who (amazingly) is also called son of God (3:38). And then the temptations of Jesus will center around the tempter's words, "If you are the Son of God..." (4:3, 9).

Third, Jesus's baptism is in the context of prayer. This is an important theme in Luke's Gospel. In numerous stories, Luke mentions prayer when it doesn't appear in the other Gospels' versions: here, when Jesus appoints twelve disciples (6:12-13), at the Transfiguration (9:28-29), etc.

Fourth, God's Spirit empowering Jesus is presented here as a response to Jesus's prayer. Charles Talbert captures the significance of this:

> It is noteworthy that in the plot of the gospel Jesus found it necessary to receive an empowering for ministry before he embarked on his public career. He had been conceived by the Holy Spirit; he had been dedicated to God by his parents as a baby; he had personally identified with his parents' decisions about him and consciously assumed the yoke of the kingdom. Yet none of these could substitute for the necessary anointing-empowering given to him when he prayed after his baptism. What is needed for adequate ministry in the Lukan understanding is a prior empowering by God's Spirit. (*Reading Luke*, 41)

Fifth, even though Jesus here submits to the same baptism as all other Jews (see 3:21a), thereby committing himself like all others to live under God's rule as a faithful Israelite, everything else about this narrative sets Jesus apart as unique. For him the heavens open, onto him descends God's Spirit, to him speaks the voice of the Father. God is present as Father, Son and Holy Spirit, united as one God breaking through from the heavenly realms to bring salvation to the earth.

Sixth, the voice itself does so much more than affirm Jesus as "the beloved" (though it does that). The language clearly echoes three Old Testament texts:

- Psalm 2:7: Here, as in Luke 3:22, "The Lord" (Israel's God), speaks to "his Anointed" (the Messiah), saying, "*You are my son.*" Psalm 2 could well be titled, "God gets the last laugh!" It is a Psalm about evil kings and rulers mocking God and God's Messiah, who later discover that in the end God wins! It's a text that prefigures Jesus's own victory over the grave after mockers think they have spoken the final word. The allusion here to Psalm 2:7 says, Jesus will be mocked but finally vindicated as the Messiah.
- Genesis 22:2: In this text God directs Abraham: "Take your son, your only son *whom you love.*" God calls Abraham to sacrifice his own son, the miracle son through whom God's promises were supposed to be fulfilled! And then God provides an animal to take Isaac's place. It is a text that prefigures so much of what Israel's sacrificial system teaches: God will accept a substitute; indeed, God will provide it! Jesus too will be the beloved Son, through whom God's promises will be fulfilled. But an animal will not be given to take his place. On the contrary, his own atoning death will forever end the need for animal sacrifices. Jesus will be the final sacrifice.
- Isaiah 42:1: Here God presents his chosen Servant "*on whom his favor rests*" and here God empowers that Servant by God's Spirit for ministries of teaching, healing,

service, death and resurrection. The beloved Son will be the one Isaiah prophesied (see Isaiah 42:1-9; 44:1-5; 52:12 - 53:13, etc.). Jesus will be the Servant of the Lord.

The voice of God affirms Jesus as a beloved Son, but it does so much more. It commissions Jesus to be God's rejected and vindicated Messiah, the sacrificial and redeeming Lamb of God and the Spirit-empowered Servant of the Lord.

Jesus's Human Lineage (3:23-38)

> *Now Jesus himself was about thirty years old when he began his ministry. He was the son, so it was thought, of Joseph.... (3:23)*

The New Testament gives us two genealogies of Jesus, this one and the one in Matthew 1:2-16. The problem is that they are not the same. The same person (Joseph) cannot have descended through two completely different male lines from King David. Some interpreters claim that Matthew's genealogy provides Joseph's lineage and Luke's provides Mary's, but the texts sound as though both are claiming to give Joseph's. So what do we do with this discrepancy?

There are several theoretically possible ways of harmonizing the two lists (for example, if Joseph's line is given once through a birth father and once through a stepfather, or if each list includes between David and Joseph only those names that the other list leaves out). But such attempts sound a bit like harmonization desperation. Perhaps the best approach is to avoid imposing our own modern concept of "historical accuracy" on an ancient world that might have viewed it differently. It could well be that Luke's list aims to give us Joseph's "birth line" and Matthew's his "legal kingly line." Since Jesus inherits David's throne, the writer provides the legal line of Israel's monarchs as "Joseph's ancestry."

Our primary goal in reading Gospel texts should not be to cast doubt on, nor necessarily to defend, a modern concept of historicity. The meaning of the text should be our primary concern. Luke joins Matthew in presenting Jesus as Israel's king (a descendent of

David) and as a true Israelite (a descendent of Abraham). But unlike Matthew's genealogy, Luke's traces Jesus's line all the way back to Adam. In other words, Jesus, the Son of God, fully joins the human race on a mission to restore humanity to its rightful place as obedient stewards of God's creation. Jesus is, in a significant way, the "new Adam."

Luke will, of course, also present Jesus as the embodiment of God, but the fact that Jesus is called Son of God does not, all on its own, make the case that Jesus is divine. In the Old Testament, Solomon, Israel and a few others are ascribed the title Son of God. And here in Luke's genealogy, so is Adam (3:38). This of course does not mean Adam was divine, but perhaps it hints at the significance of Adam's (and our) essential role as image-bearers of God. G.B. Caird put it this way:

> God...created the human race for just that union of the human and the divine which Adam had failed to achieve and which was exemplified in Jesus. Thus...Jesus was more not less truly human because 'in him dwells the whole fullness of deity bodily' (Colossians 2:9)." (*New Testament Theology*, 320)

Jesus Is Tested in the Wilderness (4:1-13)

> *Jesus, full of the Holy Spirit, left the Jordan and was led by the Spirit into the wilderness, where for forty days he was tempted by the devil. (4:1-2)*

As we have seen, this section of Luke focuses on preparations for Jesus's ministry. Jesus's baptismal identification with Israel, the opening of heaven, the voice of the Father commissioning Jesus, the reception of the Spirit empowering Jesus – all these serve to prepare Jesus for what lies ahead. But so do the temptations narrated here. Jesus spends time in the wilderness preparing for his announcement of the kingdom's arrival, just as Israel spent time in the wilderness before entering the Promised Land. Ancient Israel spent 40 years there; Jesus spends 40 days (the number is at least symbolically significant). Just as Israel in the wilderness was tempted in times of hunger, tempted to compromise with political alliances, inclined to test God by looking for signs, Jesus is tempted in precisely these ways. Adam and Eve gave in to temptation in the garden. God's covenant people, Israel, was called to do better, yet fell into temptation over and over again. Now Jesus, the new Adam, the new faithful Israel, will face temptation and remain faithful to God and to his own calling.

The Three Temptations

There are various ways to interpret the significance of the three temptations. In his commentary on Luke, I. Howard Marshall focuses on "filial Sonship" – that is, the devil was tempting Jesus to take advantage of the fact that he was the divine Son of his heavenly Father. Will Jesus really trust his Father to "give him his daily bread" (see 11:3, 8), or will he take matters into his own hands (Temptation 1)? Will Jesus walk the hard road of obedience and suffering that his Father has mapped out for him (see comments on 3:22 and see 22:42), or will he compromise with the Satan's ways and dominate the world on the devil's terms (Temptation 2)? Will Jesus presume upon the promised protective care of his heavenly Father and turn it into his own advantage (Temptation 3)? The fact that the temptations center on the devil's words "If you are the Son of God" speaks in favor of this approach.

However, Donald Kraybill in his book, *The Upside-Down Kingdom*, takes a different approach, interpreting the temptations as the devil's enticements to bring in the kingdom in ways unfaithful to God's plan. Will Jesus become a "bread king," using his ability to provide abundant food as a way of gaining worldly acclaim (Temptation 1)? Will Jesus trade in the upside-down politics of the kingdom for the worldly ways of power and dominance (Temptation 2)? Will Jesus harness himself to the power of organized religion by making a spectacular soft landing in the temple square and gaining instant popularity with those whose religious focus is centered there (Temptation 3; see Malachi 3:1)? The fact that popular but misguided kingdom expectations in Jesus's day line up so well with the devil's temptations speaks in favor of this approach.

Perhaps we do not have to choose between Marshall's and Kraybill's alternative ways of reading the text. They are intimately connected. The sort of kingdom Jesus will proclaim and embody will be inaugurated precisely because Jesus will resist the temptations of popular economic, political and religious alternatives, and, as the obedient trusting Son of God, will trust his Father and walk the way of obedience and self-sacrifice marked out for him.

How did Jesus Resist Satan's Temptations?

Luke's text suggests important factors that strengthened Jesus to resist Satan's temptations.

- Prayer and dependence on God's Spirit: We remember that Jesus's baptism was in the context of prayer (3:21) and followed by the descent of God's Spirit (3:22). The Spirit leads and accompanies Jesus into the wilderness for his time of fasting and, presumably, prayer (4:1-2). Dependence on his heavenly Father and on God's empowering Spirit strengthens Jesus to withstand temptation.
- Knowing and understanding Scripture: Each time Satan tempts Jesus, Jesus responds with a Scriptural quotation. Jesus knows Scripture; Jesus is guided by Scripture; Jesus is strengthened by Scripture. And when the devil takes his cue from Jesus and tries to quote Scripture to Jesus (4:10-11), Jesus demonstrates that it is not enough to find a verse; one needs to discern which Scriptures apply to which people in which circumstances. In fact, the third temptation is not only a temptation to presume on God's protective care and thus test God, it is a temptation to rely on Bible verses taken out of context and misused for

personal advantage. Jesus knew the Bible, and he knew how to use it!

- Knowing one's identity and mission: Jesus heard his Father's voice call him the beloved Son. Jesus discerned the nature of his messianic mission, his role in bringing God's kingdom to earth. Clarity about these things prepared him to be the faithful, obedient trusting Son, and to stay the course when the devil enticed him with kingdom options more comfortable, more worldly, more devilish.
- All of this, of course, has a great deal to say to us as we prepare ourselves also to recognize and to resist the temptations Satan brings our way.
- John's ministry is complete. Jesus has been prepared in multiple ways for what lies ahead. The great showdown with God's enemy is over for now (see 4:13). After this, Jesus will step onto the world stage, and the drama of his life's work will begin.

Implications of the Text for Today

A wide range of implications flow from the diverse texts in this section. We have space to consider only a few.

Where is the straight and level road Isaiah prophesied and John was sent to build?

When Isaiah first prophesied about a voice crying in the wilderness, about the preparation of a straight and level road through the wilderness, the context was Israel's captivity in Babylon. Isaiah was announcing the good news that God would bring the exiles home, or more exactly, that God would come in person and lead them home. Israel's exile to Babylon did finally end, and some of the exiles returned to their homeland. But really they remained "in exile." They were still dominated by foreign powers. They still longed for that coming age of stability and peace, restoration and joy that the prophets had seen on the horizon. They set their hopes on a promised "Coming One."

John's announcement that it was time to build that road created quite a stir. Indeed, some thought John himself would be that Messiah. And he consistently pointed beyond himself to Jesus. But Jesus was not the kind of Messiah most people were waiting for. He did not take on the foreign oppressors; he called God's people to love them. Jesus "filled in valleys" by lifting up the least, the lost and the left out. Jesus "leveled mountains" by tearing down the barriers that separated rich and poor, clean and unclean, Jew and Gentile. The straight road John and then Jesus constructed ran straight through crooked hearts and lives and institutions of religion and politics.

Jesus is still about the business of creating that straight and level road. He does it by challenging us to "prepare the way of the Lord" in our lives, our churches and our world.

If you checked Google Maps, you would see that, on the literal level, Isaiah's prophecy has been fulfilled. There really is a fairly straight and fairly level road pretty much where the exiles needed it to be – from the ruins of Babylon through Baghdad and Jordan to Jerusalem. But it is hardly an open road on which captives find freedom and exiles find home.

Whatever happened to the dream? "Make straight in the desert a highway for our God!" That was the prophetic announcement. "For God!" God's people would walk that road, but the road was ultimately to be a way for God to move closer to God's plan for God's people and God's world. The road symbolizes forgiveness after judgment, redemption after captivity, peace after war, blessing after curse. Today that road through the desert exists, but where are those rejoicing captives finding freedom and their own homeland at either end of that long, long desert road?

It took the life, death and resurrection of Jesus to reinvigorate the hope and start the building project. And it takes the faithful, obedient, self-sacrificing lives and ministries of God's people to continue the project, until that day when God really does come in person, once more, to complete the project and bring all the exiles home at last!

Could Jesus really be tempted? Can we really resist temptation?

Bible students sometimes create theological arguments that cause us to ignore or misread Scripture. I have heard people argue that Jesus could not really be tempted. After all, he is God and God cannot be tempted (James 1:13). The temptation was not real because only one outcome was possible. If falling to temptation had been possible, God's whole plan of salvation might possibly have failed, and that is impossible. Case close: Jesus could not really be tempted.

A better approach is to take seriously what the text actually claims: Jesus was tempted! We may not know exactly how to fit that into our theological reasoning, but the point seems to have been very important to Matthew, to Mark, to Luke, to the writer of Hebrews. Jesus "has been tempted in every way, just as we are - yet he did not sin" (Hebrews 4:15).

Luke's approach is not to speculate about how it was possible for Jesus to be tempted. His approach is to show the magnitude of the temptations and then to make very clear that Jesus was able to resist them, and did! We should not say, "Because Jesus was God, he was not able to sin" but rather, "Because Jesus was the faithful, trusting Son of God, he was able not to sin." That makes Jesus a model for us, for we are assured in Scripture that, "God is faithful; he will not let you be tempted beyond what you can bear. But when you are tempted, he will also provide a way out so that you can endure it" (1 Corinthians 10:13).

We are all tempted in ways that focus on our own vulnerabilities. I have never been tempted to command stones to become bread, even when there were plenty of stones around (such as on a mountain hike), even when I was hungry. The reason is obvious: It would never have occurred to me that commanding them to become bread would have any effect! Jesus's situation and his ability to call down divine power in this way made the first temptation very real for him.

I have never been tempted to jump off a church steeple and pray for a soft landing. Come to think of it, I have never been tempted to embezzle money from a business partner – I don't have any business partners. Jesus's temptations were unique to his circumstances and his calling. Mine are unique to mine. Yours are unique to you. We are therefore called to be merciful and understanding of each other's unique circumstances and the temptations those circumstances bring with them. And we are all called to arm ourselves with precisely those spiritual weapons that enabled Jesus to ward off Satan's attacks, so we too can stand.

In what ways are we tempted?

Our temptations are not exactly the same as Jesus's were, nor the same as each other's are. Yet, we are tempted in all the ways humanity has always been tempted. For Adam and Eve, the temptation was to grasp for that which was "good for food and pleasing to the eye, and also desirable for gaining wisdom" (Genesis 3:6). The three temptations of Jesus are fairly closely parallel to these three. In 1 John, we are warned against "the lust of the flesh, the lust of the eyes, and the pride of life" (2:16). Ephesians warns us against the world, the flesh and the devil (2:3; 4:27; 6:12).

As we see in the narrative of Jesus's temptations, the devil schemes to make so enticing the things that lead us away from an obedient trusting relationship to God. The kingdom is a radical call to abandon widely accepted assumptions of our upbringing, of our culture, sometimes even of our religious tradition. Our lives are reoriented around the new values of God's reign. We must make choices that may well cost us prestige, acceptance and affluence in this world's system to invest our lives with Jesus for the kingdom of God.

Luke does not lay guilt trips on his readers for the times they give in to temptation. Rather he shows us our model, Jesus, as he successfully recognizes and resists Satan's advances. Let us keep our eyes fixed on Jesus, and then face temptation as he did, with prayer and dependence on God's Spirit, knowing and understanding Scripture, embracing our own identity and mission.

Personal Reflection Questions

- John's preaching is called "good news" (3:18) even though it warns of judgment and calls for changed lives. Do you believe contemporary preaching should resemble John's preaching, or rather focus on more positive and encouraging themes?
- After several centuries of sorting through the evidence and options, the church wrote creeds that clearly define Jesus as both fully God and fully human. Do you consider both these claims equally important to the gospel? Why or why not?
- Even the devil can quote Scripture! What dangers do you see in using Bible verses without paying close attention to their original contexts and original meanings? Are there times and places to ignore context and just "hear the Word" as it speaks personally to your needs?

Jubilee! (Good News to the Poor)

The Text: Luke 4:14-44 NIV

The Flow and Form of the Text

Some texts are incredibly significant. They narrate events of central importance to the ministry of Jesus. They function as lenses, bringing into focus the message of a particular Gospel. They challenge the contemporary church to recognize what it means to follow Jesus faithfully in life. The first half of this section (4:14-30) is one of those texts. And the second half (4:31-44) gives glimpses of what it means for Jesus.

We know from various summary statements that Jesus frequently ministered in the context of synagogue services – often he taught, sometimes he delivered people from demons, sometimes he performed healing miracles. This text, however, represents Luke's only window into what Jesus actually taught in a synagogue. And the message is radical indeed! Perhaps we could call it Jesus's "Kingdom Manifesto."

The flow of the text is fast-paced, though it also raises some tough questions that call for careful reflection. The first two verses and the last two verses of this section summarize Jesus's ministry and its enthusiastic reception. Everything between those two summaries shows us that alongside enthusiastic reception were opposite reactions – anger, rejection, even attempts on Jesus's life. The fact that it is Jesus's hometown synagogue, his relatives and friends, that reject him, prefigures the ultimate outcome of his ministry. He will be rejected by many of those he came to save!

The outline we shall follow as we interpret these verses is as follows:

Outline:

- Jesus and His Ministry Agenda (4:14-30)
  - Jesus Announces His Spirit-Empowered Ministry (4:14-15)
  - Jesus Reads the Scriptures (4:16-20)
  - Jesus Proclaims the Time of Fulfillment (4:21)
  - Affirmation and Critique (4:22-23)
  - Ministering to the Oppressed and to the Oppressors (4:24-27)
  - Jesus Rejected and Protected (4:28-30)
- Jesus's Authority in Word and Deed (4:31-37)
- Jesus's Multifaceted Priorities – Healing, Deliverance, Communion, Proclamation (4:38-44)

The Text Explained

Jesus and His Ministry Agenda (4:14-30)

This text is often referred to as Jesus's Nazareth sermon. But the sermon itself is far shorter than the text Jesus reads, and also than Jesus's response to the congregation's reaction to his sermon. A lot more is going on here than merely "Jesus's sermon." We will look at the text piece by piece.

Jesus Announces His Spirit-Empowered Ministry (4:14-15)

Jesus returned to Galilee in the power of the Spirit, and news about him spread through the whole countryside. He was teaching in their synagogues, and everyone praised him. (4:14-15)

What was it that led to Jesus's almost immediate and exceptional popularity? As N.T. Wright has argued, it was the fact that he went around doing miraculous healings and celebrating God's goodness with people on the fringes of society (*Simply Jesus*, 57). And these are the very things that in the end will also result in Jesus's rejection by powerful political and religious leaders.

Jesus returns to Galilee "in the power of the Spirit." Luke here is probably referring to the healing and deliverance ministries that are referred to in 4:23 and 35. Other texts in Luke and Acts seem to confirm this (see Luke 7:21-22 and Acts 10:38).

"Everyone praised him" – but not for long. Only a few verses later a synagogue crowd is ready to lynch him. How diverse are people's responses to Jesus! We sometimes imagine Jesus was rejected by those who did not understand what he was really saying and doing. The following verses suggest that the opposite is more likely. They understand – better than we do sometimes – and they reject him because they do not like what they hear and see! They expected a different kind of Messiah with an agenda more in tune with their own selfish priorities. As we shall see, this passage of Scripture is more challenging than we have often perceived. Perhaps when we see it more clearly, our own enthusiasm for this radical Jesus will also be tested.

Jesus Reads the Scriptures (4:16-20)

He went to Nazareth, where he had been brought up, and on the Sabbath day he went into the synagogue, as was his custom. He stood up to read, and the scroll of the prophet Isaiah was handed to him. Unrolling it, he found the place where it is written:

"The Spirit of the Lord is on me,
because he has anointed me
to proclaim good news to the poor.
He has sent me to proclaim freedom for the prisoners

and recovery of sight for the blind,
to set the oppressed free,
to proclaim the year of the Lord's favor."
Then he rolled up the scroll, gave it back to the attendant and sat down. The eyes of everyone in the synagogue were fastened on him. (4:16-20)

Ancient writers, Hebrew, Greek and Roman, often constructed texts using a reversing pattern called chiasm. We can clearly see it in this text:

A Jesus stands up (4:16)
B Jesus receives the scroll (4:17a)
C Jesus unrolls the scroll (4:17b)
D Jesus reads the Scripture (4:18-19)
C[1] Jesus re-rolls the scroll (4:20a)
B[1] Jesus hands back the scroll (4:20b)
A[1] Jesus sits down (4:20c)

This chiasm is artistically significant. It patterns the text in aesthetically pleasing ways and puts the focus on the center (the Scriptures). All else supports the importance of the text Jesus reads.

But perhaps the Scriptural text itself (part D above) is also constructed chiastically. It announces that God's Servant has been anointed with the Spirit (4:18a) for the following purposes:

A to proclaim good news to the poor (4:18b)
B to proclaim freedom for the prisoners (4:18c)
C and recovery of sight for the blind (4:18d)
B[1] to set the oppressed free (4:18e)
A[1] to proclaim the year of the Lord's favor (4:19)

Seen this way, the text highlights *proclamation* (A and A[1]), *deliverance ministry* (B and B[1]) and *healing ministry* (C), precisely the three things that typified Jesus's ministry as a whole, and his synagogue ministries in particular. But it suggests a few more things as well, though we must first examine the meaning of some terms before we can see these clearly.

First, who are "the poor" (4:18b)? At its heart, this term refers to those of "low status." For example, tax collectors and prostitutes would be counted among the "poor," even if they did not necessarily lack material resources. Their professions mean they would be rejected and despised; they would have no status in society. The same would be true for foreigners, those who practiced despised trades, those who were ceremonially unclean, perhaps even those who had lived their lives under the "curse" of childlessness (remember Elizabeth? See 1:25). And of course "poor" also includes those who were destitute, especially if those around them explain their "poverty" as God withholding divine favor.

When God's Anointed (God's Messiah) arrives, it is to proclaim good news to these people, not to enhance the reputations and the bank accounts of those who think God already favors them!

Second, what does it mean that freedom is announced to prisoners and to "the oppressed" (4:18c; 4:18e)? Though God does indeed sometimes rescue people who have been wrongfully imprisoned (see Acts 5:19, 12:6-11 and 16:26-29), we have no record of Jesus ever busting anyone out of prison – though his forerunner, John the Baptist, may well have wished he had (see 7:18-23). Rather Jesus will deliver people from Satan's bondage that comes in the form of demonic activity or physical ailments (10:17-19; 13:16) from the power of sin (5:24) and death (7:22). Luke's Gospel highlights all of these for the reader.

"Setting the oppressed free" means restoring God's creation to its original purposes, erasing the bondage that human rebellion against God has unleashed. And specific to the context of Jesus's pronouncement in Galilee, it means Israel's long exile is now coming to an end. In one sense, the original exile in Babylon ended five centuries earlier, seventy years (as prophesied) after it had begun. But in another sense, Israel had never again been truly free, as they were tossed back and forth between powerful empires. They longed for the promised Messiah to restore their fortunes. And Jesus now announces the time of fulfillment has arrived. Only it will not come as they had anticipated, and many will reject Jesus for that!

Third, what is "the year of the Lord's favor" (4:19)? *Every year* in Israel, on the Day of Atonement, the High Priest would make atonement for the people's sins. *Every seven years* the Day of Atonement included more than forgiveness of sins: it announced rest for the land, debts forgiven and slaves set free (Leviticus 25:1-7; Deuteronomy 15:1-18). *Every fifty years*, a trumpet blast would proclaim throughout the land. Not only were sins and debts forgiven and prisoners and slaves set free, but there was to be a complete redistribution of land and resources (Leviticus 25:8-55). Those who, in the intervening years, had become impoverished and lost their ancestral land would get it back – just like that! They did not have to buy it back or in any way deserve it. They simply got it back. This was called the *Year of Jubilee – the Year of the Lord's Favor*.

The sad truth is that Israel, as far as we know, never put into practice some of the more radical demands of God's law, and their subsequent experience of exile was God's judgment for their disobedience (Leviticus 26:33-34). Yet the prophets of Israel never lost sight of God's perfect plan to transform Israel into a model society based not on what individuals deserve, but on grace and generosity, and then, through Israel, to transform the whole of God's creation into such a place. And no prophet declared this more clearly than Isaiah, whose text Jesus reads this day in Nazareth. Isaiah foretold that one day God's Servant, God's Messiah, the one anointed with God's Spirit, would stand up and say: The time has come! This is the year of Jubilee! This is the year of the Lord's favor!

We begin to see how earth-shattering Jesus's announcement in Nazareth really is. It is astonishing, however, not only in what it says, but in what it *omits*. Everyone in the synagogue would have recognized that Jesus leaves out one line of Isaiah's prophecy. Isaiah's text says the Messiah would announce "the year of the Lord's favor, *and the day of vengeance of our God*" (Isaiah 61:2). By leaving off that last line, Jesus is in effect saying: The time of God's deliverance has come; but the time of God's judgment is not yet!

That goes against everything Israel anticipated. For them, it was clear: God's judgment would fall on their enemies, and that is when and why and how they would once more experience God's favor. Jesus comes to proclaim that the people will experience God's favor *even though* Israel's enemies will not yet undergo judgment. In fact, Jesus goes even further: he announces good news *even for Israel's enemies*. And he calls Israel to love them (6:27, 35).

Fourth, what does it mean to open blind eyes (4:18d)? By performing miraculous healings, Jesus is clearly doing something greater than what Israel was equipped or expected to do during the Year of Jubilee. He is accomplishing what the prophets promised God would do when God, in person, inaugurates the new age of fulfillment, the time of God's reign (see Isaiah 35:5; 43:8). "Recovery of sight for the blind" stands symbolically for the diverse healing miracles Jesus performs. But it does more. It also stands symbolically for another way that Jesus "opens blind eyes." Though Jesus really does come to fulfill the ancient promises, only those willing to have their eyes opened would recognize this. Jesus does not come to fulfill Israel's mistaken expectation that God would kill their enemies and restore their political fortunes. Jesus comes to embody and fulfill an entirely different vision of God's kingdom, to radically challenge Israel's assumptions.

Jesus will open the eyes of the blind – those who think they can see, but see everything wrongly, those who interpret the ancient promises, but are blind to their real meaning. Some whose eyes are opened will find in Jesus their Savior and Lord. Some whose eyes are opened will turn against Jesus. That is exactly what happens this day in Nazareth, and from now on, wherever Jesus goes.

And now, finally, we are ready to say what Jesus, and Luke the Gospel writer, want to communicate with the chiasm of Jesus's scriptural quotation. Here it is again. Jesus's mission:

A to proclaim good news to the poor (4:18b)
  B to proclaim freedom for the prisoners (4:18c)
    C and recovery of sight for the blind (4:18d)
  B[1] to set the oppressed free (4:18e)
A[1] to proclaim the year of the Lord's favor (4:19)

Jesus has come to proclaim God's Jubilee. It will, however, not be very good news for the rich and powerful, the self-satisfied and the self-righteous, the religious and political elite – unless they change their ways. It will be good news to "the poor": the low-status people on the margins of society, the least, the last and the left out, who will find in Jesus the grace of God and a new community that freely shares all God's good gifts. That is what A and A[1] are saying.

Jesus has come to bring deliverance. His faithful followers may languish in human prisons, but they will be set free from the powers of evil – from bondage to Satan, from sin and death, from their old status as despised outsiders. They will find freedom as a new community that celebrates the goodness of God. That is what B and B[1] are saying.

Jesus has come to open blind eyes. Yes, Jesus performs many healings in his earthly ministry, and he still does. But a far deeper need is to have the eyes of our hearts and minds opened, so we can understand and accept Jesus's announcement of a kingdom promising a far more radical restoration of God's creation than Israel anticipated, where we become participants in God's restoring work.

Up to this point in Luke's narrative, we have only listened in as Jesus reads the *Scriptures* in the synagogue of Nazareth. Luke now quotes the *sermon* Jesus preaches. It is perhaps the shortest sermon Jesus ever preached: nine words in Greek, only eight in our English translation.

Jesus Proclaims the Time of Fulfillment (4:21)

He began by saying to them, "Today this scripture is fulfilled in your hearing." (4:21)

Each part of this short sermon deserves comment.

Today: Jesus is claiming that the synagogue crowd in his hometown has just experienced what Israel's high priest in ancient times was expected to declare every fiftieth year on the Day of Atonement: The Jubilee has arrived. Only this time, they hear it from God's chosen servant, the one anointed by God's Spirit, announcing the great and final Jubilee that would fulfill all the ancient promises.

Yet this "today" actually refers not only to that one particular Sabbath day in Nazareth, but to the whole advent of Jesus's ministry. It is a "today" that would be repeated a week later in another synagogue and then again and again after that. "Today" means, "It is happening now!" And Luke uses that word often with great effect:

- "*Today* in the town of David a Savior has been born to you; he is the Messiah, the Lord" (2:11).
- "Everyone was amazed and gave praise to God. They were filled with awe and said, 'We have seen remarkable things *today*'" (5:26).
- "Zacchaeus, come down immediately. I must stay at your house *today*." A few verses later, "*Today* salvation has come to this house" (19:5, 9).
- "Truly I tell you, *today* you will be with me in paradise" (23:43).

"Today" for Luke is the time of fulfillment and salvation! It is a time of good news, a time of celebration, a time to respond.

This Scripture: Perhaps no other text in Israel's Scriptures more clearly states that God's Spirit-anointed Servant would one day come to judge and to save. By claiming to be the one to whom the prophet referred, Jesus is simultaneously claiming *all the Scriptures* bear witness to him – that he is the one through whom all the ancient promises will be fulfilled. This is a point Luke makes explicit at the end of his Gospel (24:27).

Is fulfilled: By quoting Isaiah's prophecy about salvation but omitting the last line that prophesied judgment, Jesus is saying: The time of salvation is now; the time of judgment is deferred. And so we learn that Scriptures can be fulfilled, and then later, be filled even fuller! Isaiah was announcing the full arrival of God's kingdom on earth, the new Jubilee for all of creation. And Jesus says: It is already and not yet. It is inaugurated now; it will be consummated at a later date.

In your hearing: Strictly speaking, Isaiah did not prophesy the deliverance of prisoners and slaves, nor the recovery of sight for the blind. He foretold the announcement of these. This day in Nazareth, Jesus fulfills the prophecy that the anointed one would proclaim these things. The synagogue crowd, Jesus's family and friends, are there to hear the proclamation, and thus the fulfillment of the prophecy. What remains is for Jesus to make good on the promise. And that is what the rest of Jesus's ministry is all about.

That is the sermon: nine words in Greek, eight in our English translation. How much more Jesus actually said that day, we will never know. Luke's text shifts now to the audience's reactions and Jesus's response.

Affirmation and Critique (4:22-23)

All spoke well of him and were amazed at the gracious words that came from his lips. "Isn't this Joseph's son?" they asked.

Jesus said to them, "Surely you will quote this proverb to me: 'Physician, heal yourself!' And you will tell me, 'Do here in your hometown what we have heard that you did in Capernaum.'" (4:22-23)

Verse 22 begins with what sounds like an unqualified positive response, but very quickly things turn bad. Jesus anticipates this, and in the end facilitates it. In other words, he sticks with the program he has announced, even when it becomes obvious that it will be critiqued and rejected.

The initial response, "All spoke well of him," echoes the response Jesus receives in other places, "Everyone praised him"

(4:15). When the text goes on to say that people "were amazed at his gracious words," one can begin to hear a slight shift in tone. Literally, they respond to his "words of grace." That can indeed be interpreted as "gracious words," but it can also mean something else. It can mean they are amazed that he speaks *only* "words of grace" and not *also* "words of judgment." In the end, that is what they will find most objectionable. Yes, they long to experience God's grace. But they want to see God's vengeance, not God's grace, raining down on their enemies.

The final phrase, "Isn't this Joseph's son?" suggests something like, "Who does he think he is?" Jesus responds to that with what must have been a well-known proverb, "Physician, heal yourself!" We cannot be sure how that proverb was used in Jesus's day, but it fits this context best if we understand it to mean something like, "If you are a doctor, you should be the first to benefit from your own healing powers." What that in turn implies is that your own family, your own relatives, your fellow villagers should be the next beneficiaries! Perhaps in our day, the proverb would have been "Charity begins at home." Jesus, if you are really going to fulfill the ancient promises, *make sure we are the primary beneficiaries!* Or to put it another way, as Jesus himself does, "Do here in your hometown what we have heard that you did in Capernaum."

And that is the big problem! Jesus sees in the response of the Nazareth synagogue precisely what he will see over and over again in his short ministry. People are much more inclined to grasp God's blessings for themselves than they are to share them with others. Jesus is announcing Jubilee, the time for radical redistribution, and they want to make sure they secure their own advantages. If they are beginning to compete with Capernaum, complaining when the neighboring town gets as much of God's grace as they do, just wait till God's grace is poured out on prostitutes, on tax collectors, on Samaritans, on Gentiles!

Ministering to the Oppressed and to the Oppressors (4:24-27)

"Truly I tell you," he continued, "no prophet is accepted in his hometown. I assure you that there were many widows in Israel in Elijah's time, when the sky was shut for three and a half years and there was a severe famine throughout the land. Yet Elijah was not sent to any of them, but to a widow in Zarephath in the region of Sidon. And there were many in Israel with leprosy in the time of Elisha the prophet, yet not one of them was cleansed—only Naaman the Syrian." (4:24-27)

Jesus diagnoses exactly what the problem is. His fellow townsfolk, like many others he will encounter in Israel, think that being God's "chosen people" means that they are chosen only for special blessing. Actually it means they are chosen for a special mission. And that mission is to pass on God's blessings to those not yet experiencing them.

Jesus cites two Old Testament miracle narratives to make this clear, one for a widow, one for an important official. What these two recipients have in common is that they are both foreigners, and that is the point Jesus highlights. Equally obvious, they are both low-status people: one a widow, one a leper. What is not said explicitly, but what everyone in Jesus's audience would have known, is that Naaman was a military officer in Syria's army. Even Israel's national enemies are objects of God's grace.

Soon Luke will be telling his readers about Jesus's own miracles on behalf of widows (7:12-15) and lepers (5:12, 13; 7:22; 17:11-14) and military officials on the "enemy side" (7:2-10). Jesus will pay special attention to those despised by others. As he claims, that is what God has always done!

When Jesus later calls his followers to love their enemies, he really does mean to say, "Yes, even the Roman oppressors!" Is it any wonder that Jesus's words provoke strong reactions? The synagogue crowd in his hometown is not ready for the radically counter-cultural claims of Jesus. Many a church-going crowd today is just as unready. Give the crowd in Nazareth credit for understanding what Jesus is actually saying. Today people find any number of ways of downplaying Jesus's claims, so that we do not feel called to love the outcast and the oppressor.

Jesus Rejected and Protected (4:28-30)

> *All the people in the synagogue were furious when they heard this. They got up, drove him out of the town, and took him to the brow of the hill on which the town was built, in order to throw him off the cliff. But he walked right through the crowd and went on his way. (4:28-30)*

What a shift from their initial enthusiasm. It is hard to imagine a pious group of synagogue worshippers turning so quickly into a lynching mob. Yet Jesus really does provoke strong reactions when his claims are truly heard – radical obedience from those who say "yes"; radical rejection from those who say "no"! The third option, taming Jesus into an innocuous teacher who explains how we can all get to heaven when we die, did not occur to people back then. That is a much later heresy. Back then, they got right down to the only two plausible options: try to rid the world of a dangerous troublemaker and false prophet, or else fall down before him, call him Lord and begin living as Jesus did.

The near murder that day prefigures the final rejection of Jesus, when those in power nail this dangerous troublemaker to a cross. And the fact that Jesus "walked right through the crowd" prefigures the empty tomb, where God speaks an emphatic "no" to the judgment against Jesus and a resounding "yes" to Jesus as Lord of all.

We have examined this text in detail because it is so important for our understanding of Jesus's mission and for focusing the agenda of Luke's Gospel. What remains in this section is to see how Jesus's ministry takes shape and how he begins to practice what he has been preaching.

Jesus's Authority in Word and Deed (4:31-37)

After Nazareth exhibited a "competitive spirit," trying to make sure they got as many miracles as neighboring Capernaum (see 4:23), it is ironic that Jesus returns to Capernaum to continue his ministry. There is some evidence that he actually relocated there and made that lakeside town his new ministry center.

In the synagogue, he teaches and casts out a demon. Luke's Gospel will later characterize Jesus as "powerful in word and deed" (24:19) and the crowds in Capernaum recognize that both Jesus's teaching and deliverance give evidence of his authority.

The demons reveal their nature as spiritual beings by correctly discerning an important component of Jesus's mission: Jesus has come to "destroy them." Jesus has indeed come to curb their power to "demonize" people (the Greek word is *daimonizo*), to block their ongoing attempts to spoil God's good creation and thwart God's purposes. The demons know not only Jesus's mission, but also his nature: The Holy One of God. By openly declaring this, they were claiming a competitive advantage in their conflict with him.

By silencing the demons, Jesus is doing two things. He is blocking their attempts to ward off his own power. And he is preventing them from prematurely and inappropriately bearing witness to his true identity. Jesus wants his true identity to be discerned in the context of faithful discipleship, not declared publicly by demons.

Jesus's Multifaceted Priorities – Healing, Deliverance, Communion, Proclamation (4:38-44)

In Nazareth, Jesus challenged those whose highest priority was to keep God's blessings for themselves. But that clearly does not mean that following Jesus never benefits those closest to us. Often it does. Here Simon, who will become a leading apostle, is blessed by the healing of his own mother-in-law.

Her response to the healing is to "serve." The appropriate response of all whom Jesus serves is to serve Jesus in return. We should certainly not read this text as if Jesus healed this woman simply because they needed someone in the kitchen to prepare the Sabbath meal! It is true that the word Luke uses (*diakoneo*) can mean "serving at tables." But that does not in the New Testāment mean anything like "women's work." In fact, it is the word Jesus applies to himself, the "one who serves" (22:27), and the word from which "deacon" is later derived.

At sundown (that is, when the Sabbath officially ends), the people bring many others for healing. Notice how scrupulously they observe the Jewish Sabbath traditions! Notice how carelessly (or subversively) Jesus ignores them by healing Simon's mother-in-law *before* the Sabbath has ended!

The final paragraph in this section features Jesus seeking solitude, presumably spending time communing with his heavenly Father. We will notice how often Luke emphasizes Jesus's times of prayer. But the people of Capernaum will have none of it. They want more ministry, more healings, more miracles – and thus they repeat the mistake of the Nazareth crowd: they want this Jesus to stick around; they want him to do more miracles for them! But Jesus has other priorities. He needs to go to other places; he needs to proclaim the message of the kingdom.

It is surprising that Luke mentions Jesus's synagogue ministries in *Judea* (4:44). His ministry before this and most of his ministry after this will be *in Galilee*. Jesus will not be boxed in by clamoring crowds wanting him to stick around and become their resident miracle-worker. He is starting a movement, a God movement. And the message must spread far and wide, first throughout Israel, and after Jesus's life, death and resurrection, throughout the whole world (see Acts 1:8).

Implications of the Text for Today

Church Attendance, Bible Study and Prayer

Luke tells us that it was Jesus's custom to attend synagogue services, and then, after his ministry began, to preach and teach there. Luke himself knows from personal experience how centrally important it is for the followers of Jesus to gather as communities of faith, for worship and fellowship, for instruction and prayer (see Acts 2:42-47). We are not told in this section that it was also Jesus's custom to study the Scriptures, but clearly he knows exactly where to find the very text he wants to read (see 4:17). Jesus, like all his fellow Jews, grew up learning the Scriptures, often by heart. And before this section is over, we find Jesus seeking a time of solitude to commune with his heavenly Father. Here, Jesus models three of the "disciplines" of the Christian life: gathering with believers, studying the Scriptures and prayer. The effectiveness of our own ministries is utterly dependent on these, as was Jesus's own.

Missional Living

The word "missional" was introduced into Christian vocabulary around 1998. It was intended to convey the notion that the church is not so much a "mission agency" sending out missionaries, but the church *itself* is sent on a mission. God is the one on a mission, and God sends the church into God's mission field. That could be across the world, but more often it is across our own cities or our own backyard fences.

Central to the concept of God's mission is the fact that we are always blessed in order to be a blessing, that we receive God's grace in order to pass it on. God's election is always for the benefit of *all the others*. When the gospel we preach is all about me and my own personal destiny, it is no wonder that we hoard God's goodness. When we recognize that our own calling is for the sake of the larger church and the church's calling is for the sake of the whole world, we capture the heart of God's mission – we become "missional" in the way that Jesus modeled and taught.

This section of Scripture highlights one of the greatest temptations of the church: the temptation to think it is all about us! The synagogue crowd in Nazareth made that mistake. The crowds in Capernaum did as well. Later, it will be the disciples. In Acts, there is evidence that the early church struggled with the same issues.

And who can doubt that this is one of the major problems with the contemporary church in North America? We are preoccupied with ourselves, our comforts, our buildings, our programs, our reputations. And the world is waiting for the one who said, "I must proclaim the good news of the kingdom of God to the other towns also, because that is why I was sent" (4:43). We are called to bring this one, his message and his kingdom to them.

Missional Readings of Scripture

Now that I have introduced the word "missional," let's use it to examine how Jesus uses Scripture, and how we should! The Bible is not a flat book from which we are invited to extract isolated verses that support favorite doctrines or personal convictions. Nor is it a bunch of jigsaw puzzle pieces scattered all over the place waiting for us to rearrange them into airtight systematic theologies and ethical systems. Those ways of treating Bible texts are rampant and sometimes vigorously defended. But their legacy is a selective literalism that cannot be practiced with any kind of consistency, and that often leads to an abuse of power, as Bible manipulators arrange the pieces in whatever ways support their own agendas.

We approach the Scripture far more faithfully when we recognize its storyline and live into it, finding our own calling within God's larger mission, God's ongoing project to restore creation to its original purposes, establishing the reign of God over all the earth. We participate now in God's mission as a symbol and a sign of what God will one day bring about in full, when God's will is done on earth as it is in heaven.

Jesus does not use a concordance and find a verse somewhere that says something similar to what he wants to claim. Rather, he discerns exactly what his own role is within the ongoing mission of God. Having discerned which text most clearly defines his mission, he allows its radical message to speak with power into his own context, even if that means adjusting the wording to capture God's intent.

In a provocative examination of Jesus's Nazareth sermon, César García (at the time of this publication, General Secretary of the Mennonite World Conference) concludes: "Jesus applied a located, communal, contextualized, theo-dramatic, imaginative, and devotional hermeneutic. This kind of approach led him to a specific and relevant message appropriate to his context" (*God Speaks Today: What does this mean in the midst of suffering and oppression?, 25*). García is saying, when Jesus uses Scripture, he speaks God's truth to the local situation, taking into account the communities Jesus addresses and their specific contexts. Jesus also discerns how specific texts function to define and further the ongoing drama of God's work in the world. And he does it in ways that draw on and inspire human imagination to participate faithfully in God's mission.

Jesus invites us to read and apply Scripture in similar ways. The outcome will not be a system of doctrines or a code of ethics. It will be a faithful people living under God's reign and bringing about God's will on earth as it is in heaven.

A Few More Lessons from this Text

This text is so loaded with theological and practical implications, all we can do is comment briefly on several that have not already been addressed.

- **We live in the time of Jubilee.** If Jesus announces that his ministry is enacting Jubilee, we should believe and live and act as if it were true, even if the world does not believe it, even if evidence is rampant that things are not yet as they should be, as they one day will be. Jubilee has begun – but God has not yet fully implemented it. Meanwhile, we set captives free, we heal, we restore, we proclaim the good news.
- **Our actions symbolize the time of fulfillment.** Yes, Jesus came to proclaim Jubilee. But he only ministered in one village at a time, in one small corner of the world, for a

few short years. Our ministries will also be very limited. But they bear witness to the watching world that God is restoring creation, setting the oppressed free, healing the sick, making things right. Our actions on behalf of God's kingdom will not save the world, but they witness to the fact that God's mission has begun and one day God will bring it to completion.

- **Self-centeredness is one of the greatest barriers.** Living missionally is living for God and for others. Nazareth and Capernaum had a hard time looking beyond themselves and their own interests. The church has struggled in the same way ever since. How will cities and provinces/states and nations ever look past their own interests, if God's people do not model what that is like and why it matters?
- **We are anointed by the same Spirit that empowered Jesus.** One great Old Testament promise was that one day God's Spirit would empower a deliverer to proclaim Jubilee. But an equally great promise was that God would one day pour out this same divine Spirit on *all God's people!* That happened on the Day of Pentecost and has been happening ever since. The same Spirit that empowered Jesus to preach and teach with authority, to deliver and to heal, to reach out to those on the margins of society, to love even the enemy, now lives in each one of us. We join Jesus in proclaiming Jubilee. Let us make sure we also, in the power of God's Spirit, practice what we preach, as Jesus did.

Personal Reflection Questions

- In the ancient world, God's people always read and studied Scripture communally. People did not have copies of the Scriptures in their own homes. Many early Christians (many Gentiles, at least) would not have been able to read. But they studied Scripture together. What do you believe are the most effective ways of studying Scriptures today? Do you see the advantages of reading and studying Scripture in community? What are they?
- In the passage we just studied, Jesus models, and Luke endorses, a particular way of approaching Scripture. It does not rearrange individual verses into systems of doctrine and ethics. Rather it discerns the drama of Scripture, the narrative of God's work in the world. And it invites us to find and take our place in that ongoing story. What would it mean for the church to approach and apply Scripture in similar ways?
- This text is not only about discerning and proclaiming what Scripture teaches. It is also about actually *doing* it – setting people free, associating with those on the edges of society, reaching out beyond ourselves so that God's grace can touch others. How can you do what this text teaches, concretely, today?

Living for God's Reign

The Text: Luke 5:1 - 6:49 NIV

The Flow and Form of the Text

I am calling this section "Living for God's Reign." The New Testament word usually translated "kingdom" (*basileia*) is not so much about the territory over which God rules; it is about God's active *reign*. And that becomes the main theme of Jesus's teaching. Yet Luke has so far included only one reference to the "kingdom" God is now establishing. In 1:33 the angel Gabriel told Mary that "his (that is, Mary's unborn child's) kingdom will never end." God's reign is established, according to the Gospels, when Jesus is enthroned as the world's true Lord.

In this section of Luke, we see glimpses of what happens when Jesus begins to reign. He calls people to discipleship, he restores people to wholeness, he teaches what it means to live under God's reign and he claims an authority that will be rejected by those invested in worldly kingdoms.

In the previous section, we looked in some detail at Jesus's ministry agenda – proclaiming release to captive people. Now his ministry broadens as he releases people from sin, from false priorities and misunderstandings and from lifestyles centered around self. Jesus also begins to instruct the crowds, and especially a growing group of disciples, in the ways of God's kingdom.

Luke's Gospel opened with portraits of pious Jews faithfully upholding time-honored traditions and carefully obeying the Law of Moses. Now we see Jesus doing what might well have appeared to be the opposite: playing fast and loose with time-honored traditions, even justifying acts that would have technically violated Mosaic laws (see 6:3-4). Various incidents in this section show Jesus in conflict with religious authorities. And sometimes he deliberately provokes their reactions by claiming authority they thought was theirs, by ignoring traditions they thought were binding and by challenging their conclusions about what really matters to God.

Simeon already prophesied Jesus would "cause the falling and rising of many in Israel, and be a sign that will be spoken against" (2:34). In this section, we see the opening volleys of a conflict that will crescendo until Israel's leaders are bargaining with Pilate to have Jesus killed.

Outline:

- Jesus Recruits Simon (5:1-11)
- Conflict Narratives (5:12 - 6:11)
  - Jesus Cleanses a Man with Leprosy (5:12-16)
  - Jesus Forgives and Heals (5:17-26)
  - Jesus Consorts with Tax Collectors and Sinners (5:27-32)
  - Fasting and Feasting (5:33-39)
  - Jesus and the Sabbath (6:1-11)
- Jesus Designates Twelve Apostles (6:12-16)
- The Sermon on the Plain (6:17-49)
  - Introduction to the "Sermon" (6:17-20a)
  - Blessings and Woes (6:20b-26)
  - Loving Enemies (6:27-36)
  - Judging and Discerning (6:37-45)
  - Wise and Foolish Builders (6:46-49)

The Text Explained

Jesus Recruits Simon (5:1-11)

The very last verse of this text indicates that not only Simon, but also some of his fellow fishermen, followed Jesus that day. But the text is so centrally focused on Simon himself, that it seems appropriate to interpret the text from his perspective.

According to Luke, this is not the first meeting between Jesus and Simon. Jesus has already healed Simon's mother-in-law (4:38-39). But this meeting is the one that changed Simon's life forever. He is called to discipleship and commissioned to a new kind of "fishing ministry."

A group of fishermen are cleaning up after a night of fishing – a futile night of fishing, but we learn about that only later. Jesus commandeers Simon's boat and thus turns him into a captive audience as he teaches the crowds on the shore.

And then comes the dramatic encounter. Simon and his companions caught nothing all night, and now Jesus sends them back out on the lake to try again. I wonder how excited Simon feels to take fishing advice from this carpenter! But he has seen Jesus do amazing things, so he takes the risk and heads back out to sea, and soon has two boats full of fish.

Simon recognizes the miracle and is suddenly aware of his own unworthiness. His words, "Go away from me, Lord; I am a sinful man!" (5:8), lead to a response that could be paraphrased like this: "Leave you? Now that you've shown you trust me, that you are willing to obey, that you need my help, that you do not deserve my grace? On the contrary: I'm not leaving you; I'm inviting you to join my team! Are you coming? I'll teach you a whole new business – bringing people into the kingdom!"

Simon's call is also his commissioning. Actually, it is always that way. When we truly encounter Jesus, it is never only about experiencing a miracle or receiving forgiveness for our sins. It is always a call to discipleship and a recruitment into the mission of God.

One final point: As Charles Talbert points out, this text is about the futility of "fishing" with merely human resources. We need to be empowered by God's Spirit. When that happens to Simon, his first "catch" for the kingdom numbers 3000 (Talbert, 61; see Acts 2:41)!

Conflict Narratives (5:12 - 6:11)

The following four sections address diverse topics, but their common thread is the growing conflict between Jesus and those who feel threatened by Jesus's activities and claims. As we shall see, Jesus pursues his God-given mission, no matter whose toes he steps on!

Jesus Cleanses a Man with Leprosy (5:12-16)

At first glance, there may not seem to be much conflict in this short narrative. But Jesus provokes his critics by choosing to heal this leper by touching him. Often he does not do this. Lepers, of course, were considered ceremonially unclean, not to be touched. Jesus ignores these regulations. Indeed, when Jesus heals lepers, the texts regularly report that he "*cleanses*" them. The biggest issue is ceremonial cleansing, identifying with and restoring those pushed to the margins of society, whether by prejudice or by regulations in the Mosaic Law.

The last words of 5:14 also strengthen this story's status as a conflict narrative. One possible translation is that Jesus sends the man to the priest "as a testimony to them." Jesus bears witness to the inferiority of the priestly system. They function as health inspectors only. They can certify lepers as clean; they are powerless to make them clean. But the same words can just as well be translated "as a testimony against them." This makes the same point with a stronger focus on how Jesus and his ministry far outstrip the capabilities of the priestly system's role. So we should not interpret Jesus's commission to "offer the sacrifice" as Jesus fitting comfortably within his own religious culture. At multiple points, he is bearing witness to/against it and thus subverting it.

Three more points:

- As Bible footnotes regularly indicate, the word for "leprosy" actually cover any number of serious or minor skin diseases and conditions, not necessarily the debilitating disease we call leprosy today (Hansen's disease).
- The man's words to Jesus, "If you are willing, you can make me clean" (5:12) model the attitude we should have when we bring our requests to God. We trust God's ability to act on our behalf; we do not presume to know or prescribe what God should do.
- Jesus's (not very successful) injunction to silence is designed to give himself space for both teaching and private prayer (see the larger context). Healing miracles are a part of Jesus's ministry, but they are neither the whole of it, nor even the main focus.

Jesus Forgives and Heals (5:17-26)

Each of the character groups in this text plays a significant role. The large crowds make it a challenge to get a paralyzed man into Jesus's presence. The Pharisees and legal experts facilitate the primary conflict by, at least within their hearts, accusing Jesus of blasphemy. The man's friends show persistent faith that is rewarded by Jesus's miraculous interventions. Jesus addresses multiple topics (forgiveness of sins, charges of blasphemy, persuasive evidence, claims about his authority and finally a healing miracle). The only character who seems entirely passive, until he stands up in 5:25, is the man who is forgiven and healed.

We should probably not read 5:17 as if it implies that God sometimes granted to Jesus and sometimes withheld from him the power to heal. It speaks more to Jesus's own discernment that sometimes he should express his ministry through miraculous healings and at other times through teaching or other aspects of kingdom work. Healing was not always Jesus's first priority. Even here, where "the power was present," we are told Jesus is teaching, and we notice that before he heals, he pronounces sins forgiven.

We must note the logic of Jesus's "proof that he can forgive." He does not claim it is harder to heal than to forgive. The whole episode assumes that forgiving is harder, for it is something only God can do, even though others can heal. The issue is not which is harder *to do*, but which is harder *to say*, and that in turn means, "to say and bring about what is claimed." Anyone can utter the words "Your sins are forgiven," but to actually bring about the forgiveness by means of those words – well, one would need to be God to accomplish that! Jesus heals to demonstrate that his words indeed do what he says they will do. When the crowd sees the man healed at Jesus's word, he wants them to know God's power is every bit as active in his words of forgiveness.

The response of the man and of the crowds is to praise God – a strong theme in Luke, and the appropriate response of all who experience and witness God at work.

And it is really God at work, not merely Jesus! We should not overlook the real implication of the Pharisees' objections and Jesus's responses. Jesus really is blaspheming – unless, of course, Jesus really is God! Here, the Pharisees choose the first option, and Jesus (and after him, Luke) argue for the second. Thus, the battle lines in this growing conflict are being drawn. Yes, they concern healing miracles; yes, they concern forgiveness of sins. But at the deepest level they are about identity: Who is this Jesus? Is he an imposter, a false teacher? Or is he God in the flesh, now present among God's people to restore them and ultimately God's whole creation?

Jesus Consorts with Tax Collectors and Sinners (5:27-32)

Levi would have been an outsider within his cultural, ethnic and religious context. He worked in a despised profession where uncleanness was automatic (always dealing with unclean products and Gentiles). Tax collectors were regularly judged (perhaps occasionally misjudged) to be scoundrels and cheats. And perhaps worst of all, they were traitors. They worked for the hated occupying power, collecting taxes from their own people to pay the Romans.

And yet, Jesus invites Levi to be one of his disciples! What better evidence is there that Jesus will accept *anybody*? Levi, in turn, invites Jesus. His banquet includes his friends (tax collectors and sinners, of course); and it includes Jesus who violates all the rules of his religious environment by joining such people and eating with them, signaling he identifies with and accepts them.

Levi's "party evangelism" of course raises the hackles of the guardians of good behavior, but their complaints simply open the door for Jesus to make his intentions unmistakably clear. He has come to welcome and restore sinners. Those who think they do not need his help are (ironically, of course) declared "healthy." The truth is they will need the doctor's prescriptions every bit as desperately as anyone, only they do not yet recognize their need.

Luke wants his readers to see in this text a glimpse of the true nature of the church: "a fellowship composed of social outcasts restored to community, and sinners forgiven by grace who have left all to follow Jesus" (Talbert, 64).

Fasting and Feasting (5:33-39)

Jesus makes it clear there are times for fasting and times for feasting. In this way, he points to the heart of both activities. They are not merely religious rituals, nor are they merely about food. Both are expressions of the already/not yet kingdom of God. In times when its presence is celebrated, feasting is appropriate! Luke's Gospel highlights this side. In fact, Jesus will later be called a glutton (7:34), and he will be critiqued often for feasting with all the wrong people. Some interpreters note that food appears, in one way or another, in every chapter of Luke. Around Jesus, people celebrate, or at least, they are invited to do so.

But neither Jesus nor Luke after him abolish the practice of fasting. In times when Jesus's followers keenly feel his absence, fasting is appropriate. And fasting really did begin again for Jesus's followers when he returned to his Father. Yet feasting continues as well, for Jesus never really abandoned them. Instead, he sent his Spirit. So until Jesus comes again, we both feast and fast, discerning the times and doing both as memorials to a kingdom already inaugurated but not yet consummated.

The imagery of the wineskins and the patching of clothes is designed primarily to say some things fit together appropriately and others are really a mismatch. Discern with care! It also implies that old forms cannot accommodate the new things that God is now doing.

Yet the final words of the passage suggest something else as well. "The old is better" suggests that what Jesus is bringing is actually "the old"; it is what God originally intended. For all their attempts to preserve traditions, it was really Jesus's enemies who were the innovators, introducing all sorts of religious regulations and restrictions incompatible with what God had always intended.

The conflict of perspectives in this text is obvious. But Luke also hints at the conflict's outcome. Jesus refers to a bridegroom "being taken away" (5:35). He is not going off on his honeymoon. The violent "taking" of the bridegroom is fulfilled later when Jesus is arrested, hauled off to court and finally killed.

Jesus and the Sabbath (6:1-11)

Two separate "Sabbath controversies" are narrated back to back as Luke brings this "conflict section" to a close. In the first, Jesus defends his disciples' right to "harvest grain" on the Sabbath. The issue here is neither traveling on the Sabbath, nor is it stealing food; the issue is harvesting, even if only the palm of the hand is used for threshing! In the second, Jesus himself provokes the confrontation, inviting a man with a shriveled hand to stand up between the conflicting parties, while Jesus claims authority to violate his enemies' rules in order to restore life.

In these two narratives, Jesus claims the right, not only to violate Pharisaic rules, but to determine when even God's own law needs to be relativized, to determine when human need trumps religious rules. Ultimately, the issue is what brings life! That is more important than everything else; that was God's whole purpose in giving the Torah in the first place.

We should not overlook the parallels between 5:24 and 6:5. In the first, Jesus (as Son of Man) claims the right to forgive sin. In the second, Jesus (as Son of Man) claims the right to interpret the law. In one fell swoop (OK, I guess, in *two*), he relativizes everything the religious leaders of his day claim they are authorized to regulate. No longer the priests, but Jesus, will determine who is forgiven and who is not. No longer the Pharisees, but Jesus, will determine what the law means and how it should be applied.

The conflict reaches fever pitch. In the final incident, the whole purpose of the Pharisees' presence is to look for evidence against Jesus. And when he readily provides it, they begin to plot his demise.

Jesus Designates Twelve Apostles (6:12-16)

> *One of those days Jesus went out to a mountainside to pray, and spent the night praying to God. When morning came, he called his disciples to him and chose twelve of them, whom he also designated apostles: Simon (whom he named Peter), his brother Andrew, James, John, Philip, Bartholomew, Matthew, Thomas, James son of Alphaeus, Simon who was called the Zealot, Judas son of James, and Judas Iscariot, who became a traitor. (6:12-16)*

As so often noted in Luke, Jesus is again at prayer. Perhaps he is seeking his Father's guidance concerning whom he should choose to train as disciples and commission as apostles. Or perhaps he knows whom he will choose and is praying for them, and for the decisions they will need to make to accept the call.

The word "apostle" means "sent forth," and the use of that word here indicates one of the main things Jesus will do to these 12: he will commission them as traveling ministers to carry on his work. Yet their roles will be broader than just preaching and healing. They will be the guarantors of historical continuity between Jesus's ministry and the early church's embodiment of it after Pentecost. And they will be guardians of the authentic teaching of the church as they pass it on to others, to people like Luke, for example, who in turn will pass it on to the Christian church.

An important fact to notice: Jesus selects exactly 12! Beyond doubt, Jesus intends to symbolize the re-founding and restoration of faithful Israel (see 22:30). Birth lineage in one of the 12 tribes is not the basis for a covenant relationship with God; joining those who gather around Jesus is what counts.

Peter, whom Luke will clearly portray as leader of the apostle group, is listed first, as he is in every list of disciples in the New Testament. And Judas the betrayer is here and everywhere else listed last. The ominous note sounded by Luke's words, "who became a traitor" (6:16), reminds us that the conflict we have just experienced between Jesus and his enemies exists even within the group of disciples.

The Sermon on the Plain (6:17-49)

Introduction to the "Sermon" (6:17-20a)

The next 33 verses present us with Luke's version of a sermon better known as "The Sermon on the Mount," based on Matthew's much longer version. Luke's version is delivered "on the plain" and is much shorter. Luke's Gospel incorporates in various other places much more of the material in Matthew's version. Neither version should be considered a transcript of what Jesus said on one particular occasion. Both contain diverse teachings that Jesus no doubt presented many times and in various forms.

Yet the gist of this sermon and many others is not difficult to determine. It is: "This is how kingdom people live!"

Jesus usually presented his sermons in public, but the real addressees are often the disciples; that is certainly the case here (see especially 6:20). Jesus is not instructing the world how it is to structure society. He is instructing disciples how to live the life of the kingdom in a world out of step with God.

Blessings and Woes (6:20b-26)

> *"Blessed are you who are poor,*
> *for yours is the kingdom of God.*

Blessed are you who hunger now,
for you will be satisfied.
Blessed are you who weep now,
for you will laugh.
Blessed are you when people hate you,
when they exclude you and insult you
and reject your name as evil,
because of the Son of Man.

"Rejoice in that day and leap for joy, because great is your reward in heaven. For that is how their ancestors treated the prophets.

"But woe to you who are rich,
for you have already received your comfort.
Woe to you who are well fed now,
for you will go hungry.
Woe to you who laugh now,
for you will mourn and weep.
Woe to you when everyone speaks well of you,
for that is how their ancestors treated the false prophets."
(6:20b-26)

A series of four "blessings" is exactly matched by a series of four "woes," and between the two parts is a call to rejoice.

The main point is that people who live to secure their own advantages in the present age (being rich, well-fed, full of laughter and enjoying a good reputation) will lose out when, one day, the tables are turned. On the other side, those who identify with the Son of Man (Jesus) and who participate in God's reign may well experience the opposite now (hunger, deprivation, weeping and rejection), but "in that day," they will rejoice.

We should guard against extremes here. This does not imply that in this present life, Jesus's followers will always get the short end of the stick, nor that those rejecting Jesus will always do well. But we also cannot assume the opposite: that those living right will always be well off, and that those who are deprived must have done something wrong. Nor should we assume that tables are turned only in the life to come. Life does not deal out rewards and punishments that uniformly, nor does God!

What Jesus promises is that where there are inequities, those who participate in God's reign can look beyond present injustices to final justice, even as they work for it in this life. We need not despair if life is not yet fair. God's kingdom will prevail and our ultimate welfare depends on living in conformity to its values and expectations.

Some readers of both Matthew and Luke's versions read them as though Luke speaks of "material blessings and woes," whereas Matthew's speaks only of "spiritual blessedness." Again we should avoid extremes, not least because these two spheres are not as easily separated as we often assume. To take one example: When Luke refers to people as "poor" (see 6:20), that need not mean that they are economically disadvantaged. They are often those lacking status, those shunned by society, those at the end of their rope for one of many reasons. Meanwhile, when Matthew refers to people as "poor in spirit" (see Matthew 5:3), he does not refer to something "purely spiritual." In the Bible, humans are depicted as "always both spiritual and embodied." And God's reign affects all of life. Neither Luke nor Matthew wants to divide us artificially into separable parts; neither claims that blessings are *either* spiritual *or* physical.

A few more comments:

- To declare someone "blessed" (in Greek, *makarios*) is not simply to announce some sort of sacramental blessing, nor is it to declare them happy (as some translations word it). It is rather to assure them that if this life, and especially their allegiance to Jesus, involves hardship and loss, they can rejoice in the assurance that God will make things right, if not in this life, then certainly in the next.
- "Woe to" should not be read as "a curse upon" but rather as "alas for." Jesus characterizes people who live only for what this life can offer, and he laments for them and their misplaced priorities.
- Finally, we are reminded of Mary's song and its reference

to God bringing down the mighty and lifting up the fallen (Luke 1:52). God's plan is to level the playing field, not to create a new set of oppressors. And if the justice and equality Jesus envisions are only occasionally evident, still these glimpses serve as assurances and foretastes of what God will one day bring about. Jesus invites his followers to trust in God's promises, especially as they experience foreshadowing of what is yet to come in the communities they form around the values of God's reign.

Loving Enemies (6:27-36)

> *"But to you who are listening I say: Love your enemies, do good to those who hate you, bless those who curse you, pray for those who mistreat you. If someone slaps you on one cheek, turn to them the other also. If someone takes your coat, do not withhold your shirt from them. Give to everyone who asks you, and if anyone takes what belongs to you, do not demand it back. Do to others as you would have them do to you.*
>
> *"If you love those who love you, what credit is that to you? Even sinners love those who love them. And if you do good to those who are good to you, what credit is that to you? Even sinners do that. And if you lend to those from whom you expect repayment, what credit is that to you? Even sinners lend to sinners, expecting to be repaid in full. But love your enemies, do good to them, and lend to them without expecting to get anything back. Then your reward will be great, and you will be children of the Most High, because he is kind to the ungrateful and wicked. Be merciful, just as your Father is merciful." (6:27-36)*

The call to love enemies in both verses 27 and 35 highlights the main point of this text. There may be many other worthy motivations for treating all people well – planting seeds of peace, deflecting hostility, bearing witness to a better way – but the motivation Jesus highlights here focuses on the nature of God! God loves enemies; we are to do the same. We are children of God if we bear

God's likeness, and that centers on love and mercy.

When Jesus refers to enemies, he does not mean merely those near to us who get on our nerves. In his world, he meant also the despised Samaritans and the oppressing Romans. He meant those who curse you, strike your cheek and steal your property (see 6:28-30).

We must be careful to interpret deeply and apply broadly. The text calls for *more than merely literal obedience.* Imagine someone saying, "If someone slaps me on one cheek, I'll turn the other; Jesus said I should. But if they kick me in the shin, I'll kick them back; Jesus never addressed that situation!" That would be an extreme example of taking a text *literally*, but not taking it *seriously*. To take these instructions seriously is to grasp the radically counterintuitive ways of God's kingdom, adopting attitudes and values that fly in the face of this world's sense of "dishing out what people deserve." And after we have grasped those kingdom attitudes and values, we watch for radically practical ways of embodying them, whether people slap our cheek, kick our shin or mistreat us in any other way. Love and mercy are the operative priorities.

It goes without saying that we need a supportive Christian community to live so out of step with the values of this world. That same believing community can help us discern appropriate concrete actions that embody the values Jesus calls for here.

In the middle of this text is Luke's version of the so-called "golden rule" (6:31). Normal human self-care (indeed even human selfishness) can be turned in a positive direction by caring for others, even enemies, as diligently as we naturally care for ourselves.

Verse 35 assures us that this way of living is always worth it in the end, if not in this life, then in the next.

Judging and Discerning (6:37-45)

This section is broadly about judging and discerning, though it contains diverse sub-sections.

> *"Do not judge, and you will not be judged. Do not condemn,*

and you will not be condemned. Forgive, and you will be forgiven. Give, and it will be given to you. A good measure, pressed down, shaken together and running over, will be poured into your lap. For with the measure you use, it will be measured to you." (6:37-38)

Jesus first warns his disciples against judging and condemning. The combination of the two assures us that this does not rule out careful discernment (see below). A number of aphorisms (wisdom sayings; proverbs) are cited that make the point: You get what you deserve! Of course we already know this is no guarantee that there will always be a fair payout in this life. The point is rather that one never loses out in the end when one generously treats others better than they deserve; God will see to that!

He also told them this parable: "Can the blind lead the blind? Will they not both fall into a pit? The student is not above the teacher, but everyone who is fully trained will be like their teacher." (6:39-40)

These verses invite Jesus's disciples to learn from him, to become like him, to practice what he teaches here. But Luke may well also have meant that in the later life of the church, those who have walked with Jesus have the role of training others to follow this teaching.

"Why do you look at the speck of sawdust in your brother's eye and pay no attention to the plank in your own eye? How can you say to your brother, 'Brother, let me take the speck out of your eye,' when you yourself fail to see the plank in your own eye? You hypocrite, first take the plank out of your eye, and then you will see clearly to remove the speck from your brother's eye." (6:41-42)

Here it becomes obvious that the prohibition against judging does not mean we avoid careful discernment. It is hypocritical blatantly to violate Jesus's teaching and then meticulously hold others accountable to follow Jesus's teaching. But when we do take Jesus's teachings seriously and seek diligently to live by them, we really can live as a mutually discerning and supportive community, where one aspect of love and mercy is helping each other experience restoration and learn faithfulness.

> *"No good tree bears bad fruit, nor does a bad tree bear good fruit. Each tree is recognized by its own fruit. People do not pick figs from thorn bushes, or grapes from briers. A good man brings good things out of the good stored up in his heart, and an evil man brings evil things out of the evil stored up in his heart. For the mouth speaks what the heart is full of."* (6:43-45)

The careful discernment we practice when we help remove each other's specks is matched by just as careful discernment when it comes to the "good" and "evil" that show up in the Christian community. The focus is probably on false teachers who can so easily lead a community away from its true center, the person of Jesus and his call to live the kingdom life. Jesus's imagery suggests that a "tree" (a person) is either good or bad, depending on what is in the "heart" (the control center). The "fruit" here might be the words one speaks, the quality of life one lives, or even the sort of community that emerges when people practice what these false teachers are advocating.

Wise and Foolish Builders (6:46-49)

> *"Why do you call me, 'Lord, Lord,' and do not do what I say? As for everyone who comes to me and hears my words and puts them into practice, I will show you what they are like. They are like a man building a house, who dug down deep and laid the foundation on rock. When a flood came, the torrent struck that house but could not shake it, because it was well built. But the one who hears my words and does not put them into practice is like a man who built a house on the ground without a foundation. The moment the torrent struck that house, it collapsed and its destruction was complete."* (6:46-49)

This concluding section first makes crystal clear that what our mouth professes does not count for much if we are not obedient to what Jesus says. Calling Jesus "Lord" is not enough; Jesus must *be* our Lord.

Then it uses two builders as examples of two kinds of people who hear Jesus, those who obey and those who do not. Likely Jesus is thinking here of Psalm 1. His sermon, just like the Psalm, begins with pronouncements of blessing on those who hear and obey. And his sermon ends, just like the Psalm, with images of those who are firmly rooted and those that the wind blows away. In Psalm 1, the images are a planted tree and chaff. Here they are houses with and without proper foundations. But the point is the same. Are we or are we not listening to and then practicing what God and God's Word teach – back then, through the Torah; in this text through Jesus's own words; today, through the teaching, interpretation and embodiment of Scripture in our Christian communities?

Implications of the Text for Today

The Call of Simon in Many Versions

The Gospels contain quite diverse ways of narrating the call of Simon Peter. Mark and Matthew report that Jesus summons him to follow, and he does. In these versions, there is no introduction, no explanation, no reason to suspect Simon had ever met or even heard of Jesus before (see Mark 1:16-18; Matthew 4:18-20). Luke's narration, by contrast, not only provides evidence that Simon has been in Jesus's presence prior to his call, but the call narrative itself contains many facets of Simon's growing awareness of who Jesus is, what he teaches, what he can do and how he relates to people (see comments on 5:1-11 above). In John's version, several others already follow Jesus, and one of them, Andrew, fetches his brother Simon, whom Jesus promptly renames Cephas/Peter (see John 1:40-42).

We should resist the temptation to create a composite picture that erases the uniqueness of each Gospel's telling. Rather, each narrative should be allowed to make its own unique contribution. When we read that way, we find glimpses of the multiple unique ways Jesus calls each of us, and the challenge of each Gospel speaks to our own changing circumstances and needs.

Jesus Provokes Conflict

A book that fascinated me as a young Bible student was John R.W. Stott's *Christ the Controversialist.* Stott points out how Jesus *provokes* controversy by speaking and acting in ways *he knew* would provoke reactions, and sometimes precisely *in order* to provoke reactions.

This section of Luke's Gospel reveals several ways Jesus directly challenges and clashes with his religious culture. Two of the prominent issues involve Jesus's direct claim that he has the prerogative to forgive sins (5:24) and interpret the Torah (6:5). But equally provocative are the ways he interacts with people – with the wrong people and in the wrong ways, according to the norms of his religious culture. One did not go around touching lepers or feasting with tax collectors. One did not choose the Sabbath as the time to heal, nor the synagogue service as the place to do it – unless one was Jesus, deliberately challenging the status quo, introducing a whole new way of thinking about God's will and God's ways.

That of course raises provocative questions for Jesus's followers. When are we more on the side of the religious establishment than on the side of the radically innovative Jesus, the one willing to provoke controversy if that is what it takes to be faithful? Where are we trying to pour new wine into old wineskins when the "wine" of the gospel needs new forms? When do we try to patch old garments with new cloth, not discerning carefully when and where "the old is better" (see 5:39 and the comments on it above)?

Meal Fellowships that Celebrate and Challenge

One of the primary functions of "meal fellowship" in the Jewish context was to signal solidarity. That could take the form of creating bonds of friendship, or it could deteriorate into competitions for status and honor by associating with all the "right" people and avoiding all the "wrong" ones. When Jesus feasts with tax collectors, he sends a powerful signal that God's people can and should forge bonds of acceptance, not only with like-minded people, but across the boundaries that separate social classes. And by provoking the critique of his enemies, Jesus demonstrates he is more interested in honoring the outcast than preserving his own reputation.

In a Roman, and especially Greek, context, meal fellowship had other functions as well. A Greek meal was sometimes called a "symposium" (literally translated "drinking party"). It combined eating and drinking with verbal sparring, with debate and challenge.

When Luke narrates various episodes where Jesus is sharing table fellowship, both of these emphases combine. Sometimes the most provocative thing Jesus does is simply to eat with all the "wrong" people. Sometimes the most provocative things are what he says, either because he challenges fellow guests or the host (we will encounter many such texts in Luke!) or because he faces down their challenges, turning the tables on them and their skewed perspectives.

If meal fellowship plays such significant roles in Jesus's ministry and particularly in Luke's Gospel, should Jesus's followers not find creative ways of using meal fellowship to forge bonds of acceptance among believers and with those not yet committed to Christ? And would we not do well to move some of our conflicts to the context of "table fellowship" where the edges of our conflicts can be softened by the sharing of a meal?

My wife and I, for a period of time, had a very difficult time speaking kindly to each other in a certain set of circumstances on certain topics. Our home fellowship group gave us the best advice we could have imagined. They said, "In such times, call on us. We will provide childcare. You two go to your favorite restaurant, and if you need to argue it out, do it there." They were serious. And we took them seriously. Many a conflict was either avoided or turned into a productive conversation over our favorite pizza and Bavarian soda.

Hermeneutics

That is a big theological word, sometimes provoking the question, "Herman who?" Hermeneutics is the study of how to move faithfully from what Bible texts *say* to how they should be *applied*. Sometimes we oversimplify things, assuming that anything a text says should just be "applied literally" and we will surely get it pretty much right. There are dozens of reasons to doubt that this is an adequate approach, and thousands of texts for which it really does not work at all.

This section of Scripture has important hints on how to do it better. Jesus cites what I call the "David precedent" (see 6:3-4), reminding us the Bible is not a flat book: some principles take precedence over others. Meeting genuine human need trumps meticulous attention to the fine points of ancient laws. Jesus revises "rules governing the Sabbath" (6:9), reminding us that our approach to Scripture must always be Jesus-centered. Jesus is the lens through which we discern what the Bible really teaches. The specific instructions in Jesus's sermon that point beyond themselves to underlying attitudes and priorities (6:29) remind us that simply "doing what the words on the page say" is usually too simple, and too little. The deeper issues the passage addresses should be our primary focus.

Our aim is to take all the teaching of Scripture with utmost seriousness, and then to recognize where we take things even more seriously by not taking them literally. Jesus taught his followers by example and by instruction that a genuine discerning hermeneutic provides more reliable guidance on how to apply God's word faithfully, than does an oversimplified literalism.

Personal Reflection Questions

- Am I willing to identify with Jesus who courageously challenges the status quo around him – both the status quo of the world and the status quo of religious institutions? Are we as communities of believers willing to do that?
- What happens around our dining room tables, or in the fellowship halls of our church buildings, or in restaurants in our city? Are we forging bonds of Christian fellowship? Are we welcoming the outsider to become a friend? Are we sharpening our understanding of what Jesus asks us to be and do?
- How can we move beyond oversimplified approaches to Scripture, so that we can rightly discern the Bible's deeper messages of hope and challenge, rather than focusing on sometimes questionable lists of do's and don'ts?

Good News of the Kingdom

The Text: Luke 7:1 - 8:56 NIV

The Flow and Form of the Text

I have selected "Good News of the Kingdom" as a title for this section. It is taken directly from 8:1, though that deserves a few more comments. Actually, 8:1 refers to Jesus "proclaiming the good news of the kingdom of God." In the original language, however, "proclaiming the good news" is actually one word, a word I am tempted to translate as "good-news-ing"! Jesus not only *talked* about the kingdom, he *embodied* it. He not only *announced* good news, he *was* the good news. He healed, he raised the dead, he welcomed the outcast, he calmed storms, he made people whole.

In this section of Luke, Jesus does indeed talk about the kingdom, but even more frequently, he draws people into an experience of it, as they are welcomed by Jesus and transformed in meeting him.

And there is more. While the kingdom is consistently called "the kingdom of *God*," this section shows us in multiple ways that it is about the kingship, the loving restorative reign, of *Jesus*. None of the Gospel writers ever say explicitly, "Jesus is God." But they all challenge the perceptive reader to connect the dots. Yes, of course, Jesus is a human person. Yes, of course, Jesus embodies the faithful remnant of Israel. Yes, of course, Jesus is in some way distinct from the God of heaven. That is obvious by the fact that Jesus communes with God, prays to God, carries out the commission his Father gives to him. But in some mysterious sense, Jesus is really God, the actual embodied presence of God on earth. And various texts within this section drop hints in that direction. We will watch for them as we explore this section, using the following outline.

Outline:
The Faith of a Centurion (7:1-10)
Jesus Raises a Widow's Son (7:11-17)
Jesus and John the Baptist (7:18-35)
Jesus Anointed by a Sinful Woman (7:36-50)
Women Participate in Jesus's Ministry (8:1-3)
The Parable of the Sower (8:4-15)
A Lamp on a Stand (8:16-18)
Jesus's Mother and Brothers (8:19-21)
Jesus Calms a Storm (8:22-25)
Jesus Restores a Demon-Possessed Man (8:26-39)
Jesus Raises a Dead Girl and Heals a Sick Woman (8:40-56)

The Text Explained

The Faith of a Centurion (7:1-10)

In this text, Jesus commends the Gentile centurion's faith in the highest possible terms (see 7:9). But Jesus is not assessing faith as if it were some nebulous, mystical inner quality; he is commenting on a whole set of attitudes, behaviors and convictions this centurion evidences in his life and relationships. These include:

- His loving concern for a mere servant, an impressive show of compassion coming from a high ranking military official (see 7:2, 3).

- His generous good works on behalf of others; he built a house of worship for people who to him were foreigners worshiping another God (see 7:5). As a military officer of Rome, he himself was required to worship the emperor.
- His clear recognition that anything Jesus would do for him would be undeserved grace. Compare the Jews' view that he *did* deserve such help (7:4) with the centurion's conviction that he *did not* (7:6).
- His sensitivity to Jewish scruples: aware that Jews would not normally enter a Gentile's home, he proposes Jesus heal without coming (7:6-7).
- His great faith in the healing power of Jesus: not only is he sensitive to Jewish scruples, he actually believes Jesus can heal just by saying the word (7:7).
- His clarity about Jesus's divine authority: he compares his own delegated authority ("I am a man under authority," 7:8) to that of Jesus. The centurion's own word has the authority of Rome's empire behind it, so when he speaks, people move! And he knows Jesus's spoken word has heaven's authority behind it, so when Jesus speaks the healing word, it comes to pass.

In the end, the centurion's attitude to himself is right (he deserves nothing from Jesus); his attitude to those in need is right (he cares about a mere servant); his attitude to foreigners is right (he loves the Jews, built them a synagogue, cares about their religious scruples); his attitude to Jesus is right (he trusts Jesus to act with divine authority, even at a distance). That is what Jesus calls an amazing faith. And we remember again that in Greek "faith" and "faithfulness" are always exactly the same word.

Faith, for us, should also be more than a mystical inner quality! It is nothing less than "faithfulness" – living with the attitudes, behaviors and relationships that please God.

Jesus Raises a Widow's Son (7:11-17)

It would be easy to put the focus of this text on the young man Jesus raises from the dead, speculating about the causes of his death, wondering what became of his life. But that would miss Luke's point completely. He puts all the focus on the grieving widow. This miracle is for her!

The person who died is referred to as "the only son of his mother, and she was a widow" (7:12). In Jesus's world, women were always under the care and protection of a man, first their fathers; then when they married, their husbands; then if they were widowed, their sons. This widow has just lost her last protector: her only son has died. Notice the focus of the text: "And a large crowd from the town was with *her*. When the Lord saw *her*, his heart went out to *her* and he said [*to her*], 'Don't cry'" (7:12-13; I added italics to make the focus clear and one more "to her" that the NIV translators left out). When the great miracle happens, we read: "Jesus gave him back *to his mother*" (7:15; see also 1 Kings 17:23). She is the one who suffered loss; she is the recipient of the miracle.

There is also value in reading this text as a complement to the previous one about the centurion. When Jesus preached in Nazareth (see 4:16-30), he referred to Elijah who was sent to minister to a foreign widow. Jesus has just done a great miracle for a foreigner (the centurion); now he does a great miracle for a widow. The Jews who believe God cares only about them have not been reading their Bibles correctly. No wonder they fail to recognize Jesus as the one God sent to make things right. Those pious and powerful religious leaders who thought the Messiah would come to enhance their positions and prestige were also not reading their Bibles. Jesus came to minister to the most needy, and to create a community of care that would spill over in love even for the enemy.

The present text ends with expressions of praise to God (7:16). We have seen many of these already in Luke (see 1:64, 68; 2:13, 20, 28; 4:15; 5:25, 26). Those who experienced this miracle may not have fully understood Jesus (they call him [merely] a prophet), but they could recognize God at work, and they raised their voices in praise and rejoicing.

Jesus and John the Baptist (7:18-35)

Luke informed his readers already in 3:19-20 that John is in prison for courageously confronting King Herod. In the meantime, we have learned that Jesus came "to proclaim freedom for the prisoners" (4:18). And yet John still languishes in prison! Perhaps he has really begun to doubt that Jesus would make good on the promises, even that Jesus was the one for whom his own ministry had been preparing. His faith seems to be growing weak, or at least, his patience. Unless, of course, his decision to send messengers to ask Jesus about these things is more for *their* sake than *his* own. We cannot be sure.

Jesus does not launch into a theological defense of any claims about himself. Rather, he does the work of the kingdom and invites his observers to draw appropriate conclusions. When he describes his own works, he echoes a variety of texts from Isaiah that describe what things will be like when God restores the people of Israel and the rest of the world. In particular, he echoes the words he quoted in Nazareth: he is proclaiming good news to the poor – or, as I'm tempted to translate it – the poor are being "good-news-ed" (see 8:1 and my comments under the "Flow and Form" of this section). The poor are not only *hearing* good news; they are *experiencing* its effects!

Jesus's final line to John's messengers is "Blessed is anyone who does not stumble on account of me" (7:23). In this context, it probably means, "Blessed are those who recognize who I am and what my ministry is all about, even if they themselves are not the ones who benefit most from what I do (like John in prison, for example)."

After the messengers return to John, Jesus speaks to the crowds about John and his ministry. John is a prophet indeed, but more than just an ordinary prophet. He is the one the Scriptures foretold would prepare for God's own coming (7:26-28). When Jesus asks whether people would go out into the desert to seek "reeds" or "people dressed in fine clothes," he probably means something like this. People would not go out into the desert to look for what is always there (like reeds). Nor would they go to look for what is never there (people in fancy clothes). Rather, they go to see if in fact what they have been promised has finally arrived. It has arrived, says Jesus. It arrived when John did his preparatory work there, and it continues in Jesus's own ministry of bringing the kingdom and its good news!

After so strongly affirming John, Jesus adds that paradoxical line, "The one who is least in the kingdom of God is greater than he" (7:28). As closely tied as John is to Jesus, he still belongs to the old era of preparation. Those who now join Jesus and his kingdom movement belong to the new era of fulfillment.

Verses 31-35 use the imagery of two groups of children, each refusing to play the other group's games. One group wants to mourn; the other wants to dance. At the very least, this text says what 5:33-39 already said: there are times when fasting is right and times when feasting is better!

But perhaps we are also invited to identify who is calling people to fast or to feast. Perhaps it is the religious establishment. They reject both John and Jesus; John because he does not dance enough, Jesus because he does not mourn enough. You just can't please people whose minds are already made up. If they intend to reject God's messengers, they will make up their excuses as they go along.

Or maybe we should turn that around. Maybe John is calling people to fast (repent, be transformed), and Jesus is calling them to feast (welcome the sinner; rejoice in God's goodness). Are we heeding the call – both parts of it? The right call is the one consistent with the need of the hour and the roles God calls us to play in God's kingdom.

"Wisdom is proved right by all her children," says Jesus (7:35). That means all of John's followers and all of Jesus's followers are getting it right, if they learn to discern when the time is right to abstain, and when it is right to celebrate.

Jesus Anointed by a Sinful Woman (7:36-50)

Simon the Pharisee makes a major miscalculation the day he invites Jesus to a banquet and forgets all the usual courtesies. It was unthinkable to welcome a guest without providing water to wash his dusty feet, without honoring him with a greeting kiss and without anointing him with oil. It seems Simon is too intent on discrediting Jesus to pay attention to normal courtesies.

Where Simon leaves out all that should have been done, a sinful woman goes far beyond normal courtesies. Washing Jesus's feet with her tears, drying them with her hair, kissing them fervently (the Greek word is pretty strong here!) and lavishly applying perfume far exceeds what was considered appropriate or even decent.

Yet when Simon tries to discredit this woman, along with trying to discredit Jesus (see 7:39), it all backfires. Jesus defends the woman, discredits Simon and shocks everyone in the room by welcoming this woman's expressions of heartfelt love, interpreting them as evidence of a repentant faith-filled heart and a forgiven life.

Jesus's parable is simple enough. If two people's debts are forgiven, the one whose debt had been greater will respond with greater love. And the implication is also obvious: This woman, described by the narrator as "one who lived a sinful life" (7:37), had experienced a great debt of sin forgiven. Simon, by contrast, had not. No wonder the woman responded with fervent expressions of love.

Yet the ending also leaves a question unanswered. Which came first: the forgiveness or the love? The NIV translators sneak an answer into the text, but it is not in the original. The text does not specify, "*As her great love has shown*," but "Her many sins have been forgiven, *because she loved much*." This more literal translation sounds as though the love came first and the forgiveness afterwards. The fact that Jesus pronounces her forgiveness in 7:48, after her act of love, seems to confirm this reading.

However, the most natural reading of the parable is that the forgiveness came first and love was the response, as 7:47 confirms.

The NIV translators got it mostly right, but perhaps they leaned a bit too far one way. God always provokes our love by first reaching out to us in grace and forgiveness, but then inviting us into a lifelong love relationship that recognizes our ongoing need of forgiveness. So Jesus's pronouncement that her sins are forgiven in 7:48 is probably not the first time she heard Jesus say that, nor the last.

The final verse is a pronouncement of salvation and peace. Both words have a broad meaning in the New Testament and both probably borrow their meaning from the well-known Old Testament concept of *shalom*. We cannot narrow salvation and peace in the New Testament to an assured final destiny with God. They include wholeness in life, acceptance in a loving community and an ongoing experience of God's goodness.

Jesus will pronounce the same words for another risk-taking outcast in 8:48. If only Simon realized he also needed forgiveness, the dinner at his home could have introduced him as well into the upside-down kingdom Jesus is making real for all who turn to him.

Women Participate in Jesus's Ministry (8:1-3)

This text mentions both men and women, that is, "the Twelve" (whom we know to be all men because of 6:13-16) and "also some women" (8:2). Yet this short narrative deserves a section of its own, and it invites us to focus on the women.

We have seen multiple times how carefully Luke balances references to men with references to women. In Luke's second volume, Acts, he will also carefully document the ministry of women in various places, even though the primary missionaries are men (see Acts 16:40; 21:9).

Luke's model, of course, is Jesus himself, who welcomed and associated with women as freely as with men – something unheard of in his time and place. The women Luke names in this text travel around the countryside with Jesus; that would have been unthinkable in many Jewish circles. Although several New Testament passages indeed place some restrictions on the ministries of women, the larger cultural and biblical contexts strongly suggest these were based on extenuating circumstances in specific places, not on any principle the New Testament promotes. At any rate, the goal of the gospel is clear: that barriers are removed between slave and free, Jew and Gentile, male and female (Galatians 3:28). Luke does his part to bring about this reality within the Christian community, following the model of his Lord.

In the present text, Luke highlights diverse women, including a formerly demon-possessed woman and a woman married to a leading official. He also mentions "many others" (8:3) and affirms them here for following Jesus and participating in his ministry, both by traveling with him and providing financial support.

The Parable of the Sower (8:4-15)

There are three parts to this text: the sower parable itself; Jesus's explanation for why he speaks in parables; an interpretation of the sower parable. We will examine the first and third of these and then come back to the middle one.

Clearly, this is one of Jesus's parables that functions as an allegory: where features of the story symbolize particular aspects of his teaching. Jesus tells us what each aspect represents: the seed (the Word of God), the four soils (the four kinds of hearers), the birds (the devil), the thorns (life's worries, riches and pleasures).

We are not told, however, whether the sower represents anyone in particular, nor exactly what Jesus is referring to by "the harvest." I believe the parable applies no matter who is preaching the Word. The first sower would be Jesus, but Luke himself sows God's Word by writing this Gospel. So also do preachers and teachers, or for that matter, all of us who share the good news. And the harvest, presumably, is the goal of the proclamation: leading people to "believe and be saved" (8:12), endure times of testing without falling away (8:13) and reach maturity by living for kingdom values rather than the pleasures of this life (8:14).

We must not overlook another important aspect to this parable: this is a parable about the kingdom. Luke has explicitly told us the topic of Jesus's itinerant ministry is God's kingdom (8:1). And between the sower parable and its interpretation, he refers to "the secrets of the kingdom of God" (8:10). It is easy to read the parable as only about the personal spiritual journey of individuals: whether or not they believe, persevere, single-mindedly follow God's ways and thus reach final salvation. This text does challenge individuals, but it is also a strong word of encouragement for the community gathering around Jesus that this kingdom he announces is really coming to pass.

The movement certainly had humble beginnings. And then there were setbacks, like John's imprisonment. No doubt even Jesus's own followers sometimes echoed the words John the Baptist conveyed through his messengers to Jesus: "Are you the one who is to come, or should we expect someone else?" (7:20). With this parable, Jesus encourages his listeners: they can be assured of a spectacular final harvest that exceeds all expectations, even though many do not receive the word of the kingdom or receive it but do not persist when things get tough. The word of the kingdom will achieve its goal: the kingdom will finally be established and those who stick with Jesus will finally be victorious, no matter what setbacks they face along the way.

That then helps us understand the short section between the parable and its interpretation (8:9-11). Jesus knows that hard-hearted people will reject the message of the kingdom. Some will hear but not really hear, see but not really see. They will be like the first three groups of people to which the parable refers. By using parables, Jesus chooses a method of communication that requires genuine "hearing" (see 8:8), and sometimes, private interpretations (see 8:11). Those intent on missing the point have the freedom to do that! Jesus wants willing followers, not people badgered into believing.

A Lamp on a Stand (8:16-18)

> *"No one lights a lamp and hides it in a clay jar or puts it under a bed. Instead, they put it on a stand, so that those who come in can see the light. For there is nothing hidden that will not be disclosed, and nothing concealed that will not be known or brought out into the open. Therefore consider carefully how you listen. Whoever has will be given more; whoever does not have, even what they think they have will be taken from them." (8:16-18)*

Parables are designed both to reveal and to conceal (see comments above). Jesus intends for people to "consider carefully how they listen" (8:18a), and he promises that those who do will understand more and more. That is the meaning of the promise to "be given more" in 8:18 – Jesus is not talking about economics! As for those who do not listen with "hearing ears," they will eventually understand less and less (see also 8:10). But the final goal is never to keep anyone in the dark. Jesus knows people's hearts need to be transformed before they can truly hear, so he uses a communication method that forces his hearers to "consider" their choice.

Not only is full revelation Jesus's goal, it is guaranteed! In the end, all secrets will be revealed. That is good news for those who side with Jesus, for along the way, there will be dark times indeed. But it is sobering news for those who reject Jesus. Neither this text nor the parable of the sower before it need be interpreted as referring solely to final salvation and a final judgment; at the same time, these are realities toward which Jesus's ministry ultimately points.

Jesus's Mother and Brothers (8:19-21)

> *Now Jesus' mother and brothers came to see him, but they were not able to get near him because of the crowd. Someone told him, "Your mother and brothers are standing outside, wanting to see you."*
>
> *He replied, "My mother and brothers are those who hear God's word and put it into practice." (8:19-21)*

This text joins other texts in Luke that present faith and obedience as more important realities than family relationships (see also 1:45; 11:27, 28; 14:26; and my comments). People in Jesus's day emphasized family relationships more strongly than in many Western cultures today. For Jesus to prioritize relationships among his followers over family relationships was radical indeed.

This does not imply Jesus rejects his own physical family. They can be members of his true family by hearing God's Word and putting it into practice. Luke portrays Jesus's mother Mary as one who does precisely that.

Jesus Calms a Storm (8:22-25)

The miracles of Jesus so far in Luke have been miracles of restoration: people are restored to sanity, to health, even back to life! Such miracles fix things that have gone wrong in the old creation. But Jesus also performs another kind of miracle: he exercises power over nature itself. He walks on water, multiplies loaves and (as in this text) tells wind and waves to cease. After his resurrection, he will walk through closed doors. Such miracles prefigure a restored creation in which all needs are met and storms no longer threaten – where our resurrection bodies transcend the limitations of our present bodies.

Yet, it does not seem the disciples actually expect Jesus to rescue them. They are completely taken aback. What then were they expecting him to do when they woke him up in a panic? A good guess is that they were remembering Jonah's story. There, too, experienced sailors panic in a storm, and then remember Jonah sleeping in the bottom of the boat. They wake him so he will pray to his God (Jonah 1:6).

Since the Old Testament clearly teaches only God has power to control wind and waves, the disciples no doubt expect Jesus to "pray to his God," that is, to call down God's power in their present need. To their amazement, he does not pray to God; he acts as

God. It is as if Jesus were saying, "Why should I cry out to God; you just did!"

Their final sentence highlights the primary function of this text – to raise the ultimate question: Who is this? Luke himself has no doubts. Over and over again, he alludes to the astonishing fact that this Jesus is none other than God, present to heal and save.

Jesus Restores a Demon-Possessed Man (8:26-39)

Everything about the man we call the Gerasene demoniac and his environment is unclean. For Jews, Gentile territory was by definition unclean. This man lives in the tombs, also unclean. And he is near a herd of pigs, also unclean. Worst of all, of course, he himself is inhabited by a legion of unclean spirits. Luke highlights all these things in order to magnify the full healing Jesus provides.

Besides his uncleanness, this man is anti-social. His townspeople have tried in vain to control him. Finally the demons drove him into the wilderness. There he lived, naked and alone.

Jesus restores him fully! Before the narrative ends, the demons are gone. The man himself is found dressed, sitting at Jesus's feet (the posture of a disciple). He wants to accompany Jesus; instead, Jesus sends him as a missionary to his own village. That is the story of the man's healing.

But this text also has two subplots. The first has to do with the pigs. We may wonder why Jesus would allow demons to bargain with him for the right to enter pigs, and perhaps we wonder again why Jesus would allow such a colossal waste – a whole herd of pigs drowned! (The fact that Jews did not eat pork did not mean Gentiles should not!)

Here knowledge of some first-century circumstances comes in handy. This was the region where Rome stationed its Tenth Legion and they raised pigs for their daily rations. In fact, the Tenth Legion had chosen a pig for its mascot. First-century Roman coins documenting this still exist. Connections between the Roman legion and this text are unmistakable. We remember the demons claim their name is Legion. Luke reports that the herd of pigs rushes down the steep bank. The Greek word that Luke chose can mean "rush" (something pigs do), but it is often used for what armies do ("march in formation"). How is that relevant?

When God delivered Israel from the Egyptian Empire, their song of victory was, "Horse and driver he has thrown into the sea" (Exodus 15:1, 21). Now God is signaling the ultimate defeat of Rome's imperial pretensions with (appropriate to the circumstances) pigs rushing to their own destruction. As often happens in the New Testament, evil brings about its own destruction by miscalculating the greater power of God exhibited through Jesus the great warrior, the one who defeats evil – not with swords, but with a word.

The other subplot in this text is its christology – what it implies about the identity of Jesus. The legion of demons calls Jesus "Son of the Most High God" (8:28). That is a high title to be sure. But it is worth noting what the narrator of Luke's text does at the end of the text. Jesus tells the restored man, "Tell how much *God* has done for you." In obedience he "told all over town how much *Jesus* had done for him" (8:39). So was it Jesus who did it, or was it God? The perspective of Luke is that if it was Jesus, then it was God – for Jesus is not merely "God's Son" (as high a title as that is!); Jesus is God!

Jesus Raises a Dead Girl and Heals a Sick Woman (8:40-56)

By wrapping two stories together, Luke's purpose goes beyond presenting events in chronological order. He could, after all, have narrated only one of the two incidents, or inserted both in different places. Their combination suggests:

- Jesus cares equally for a prestigious synagogue leader and a very needy woman. One had high status in society; the other was (at least as long as she had a bleeding problem) an outcast. They are equally important to Jesus, and it fits Luke's portrait well for Jesus to interrupt his ministry to the man, so that he can first minister to the woman.

- Jesus calls for radical trust in his ability to heal. Imagine how impatient Jairus would be. His daughter lies dying at home, and on Jesus's way there, a woman who, by all the rules of their society should not have been in the crowd at all, interrupts Jesus. And when Jairus's greatest fear becomes reality (his daughter dies in the meantime), Jesus says, "Don't be afraid; just believe, and she will be healed" (8:50). Keep believing, after the girl has died? Indeed, Jesus's healing word is sufficient even to raise the dead.
- And then there is the puzzling correlation in 8:42 and 8:43: Jairus's daughter is 12 years old and the woman has bled for 12 years. Given that 12 is almost always a significant number in Scripture (12 tribes, 12 disciples, etc.), it is hard to believe that these back-to-back references are coincidence. Yet no obvious significance emerges. Maybe that in itself should keep us humble. We do not always know all that the text aims to communicate. So we keep studying and sometimes say, "We cannot be sure!"

A few more comments on each of these incidents.

The woman's bleeding problem left her unclean, untouchable. In fact, she would have been required to shout, "Unclean! Unclean!" and keep clear of people. Instead, she pushes through the crowd and touches Jesus. By all the rules of the day, Jesus would now be considered unclean. Instead, Jesus's cleansing power neutralizes and counteracts any power to make unclean.

Telling her story in the presence of the crowd becomes a large part of her full healing. Now all would know that she is to be welcomed back into the community. And hearing Jesus say to her, "Daughter, your faith has healed you. Go in peace," would have led to even greater restoration. Twelve years of humiliating isolation and shunning necessitate this radical reintegration. Jesus calls her "daughter": she is now part of the family! Jesus affirms her faith: she is now a model to follow rather than an outcast to avoid. Jesus pronounces her healed: the word here really means "saved" (completely restored). And Jesus invites her to (literally) "walk into peace": the Greek carries the connotations of that wonderful Old Testament word *shalom*, where everything has been restored to the way it should be.

Concerning the raising of Jairus's daughter: this is certainly a test of his faith. But it is, of course, also a testimony to the resurrection power of Jesus: the girl really dies and he really raises her to new life. This is not a near-death experience, not a coma, not a trance. And yet, her resurrection is nothing like the resurrection of Jesus, still to come.

Our own final resurrection from the dead is guaranteed, not by the resurrections Jesus performed, but by the one he experienced. Jairus's daughter and the widow of Nain's son were merely raised back to their old mortal life. Jesus rose with the incorruptible body of the new creation. That is what guarantees our own final resurrection.

Implications of the Text for Today

Jesus and Gentiles

This section began with a portrait of a remarkable Gentile, the centurion who, through intermediaries, asks Jesus to come heal his servant. As noted above, the text is about this man's amazing faith. But we can also see it as a contribution to Luke's portrait of Jesus in relation to Gentiles.

Jesus came to save the whole world! That is why he concentrated his ministry almost exclusively on his own people, the Jews. That sounds like a paradox, but it is not. God elected Israel, right from the start when he called Abraham, to be the means by which God's salvation would reach the whole world. Now that the world's redeemer had arrived, Israel needed to be prepared to bring the good news to the rest of the world. Jesus's ministry on earth was primarily about that. And in Luke's second volume, Acts, the gospel spreads from an originally Jewish Christian community to the farthest reaches of the Roman Empire. The community of Jesus invites Jews to accept the gospel and confess Jesus as the promised Messiah, and it invites Gentiles, steeped in pagan idolatry and worship of the emperor, to turn to the living God by accepting Jesus as their Savior.

By affirming the faith of a Gentile in 7:9, Jesus is foreshadowing the day when Gentiles will become fellow heirs alongside Jews in the family of God. And through the fact that this centurion never actually meets Jesus, Luke's Gospel affirms two more points:

- The Jews really did play the role of being "intermediaries," bridging the gap between the needs of a pagan world and the God of Israel who came to redeem and restore the Gentiles along with the Jews. God called Israel to be a "kingdom of priests." In 7:1-10, Jews play the role of priests, intermediaries who bring those without access to God into an experience of God's grace.
- And the use of intermediaries also makes visible one of the clearest expressions of this centurion's faith: he understands how delegated authority works. Those authorized from above are able to speak with authority to those who do their bidding. The centurion understands this, for he is himself a military commander. But more importantly, he understands Jesus stands under the authority of his heavenly Father, so when Jesus speaks the word, it accomplishes its purposes, even if others speak that word on Jesus's behalf. What an encouragement as we become Jesus's mouthpieces in a world that needs God's presence.

Christology

Each Gospel is, first and foremost, about Jesus – who Jesus is, what Jesus accomplishes. In this section, we catch glimpses of the multi-faceted portrait Luke paints of Jesus.

Jesus speaks with divine authority (7:1-10); he is master over death (7:11-17; 8:51-56); he is "the one who is to come" (7:19-23); he is "friend of tax collectors and sinners" (7:34); he pours out God's grace and receives extravagant love in response (7:36-50); he builds an inclusive community (8:1-3); he inaugurates a kingdom that cannot fail (8:4-15); he promises that one day all God's goodness will be revealed (8:16-18); he creates a new family around himself (8:19-21); he does what only God can do: forgive sins (7:48-49), calm storms (8:22-25), restore broken people (8:26-39, 42-48).

Above and below and alongside all of the above, Luke drops multiple hints that Jesus is not just a great man; Jesus is the presence of God living on earth, doing the works of God and beginning the great project of restoring God's creation. And central to his mission is inviting and preparing people to be God's servants and co-workers in that great project.

Resurrections as Resuscitations

The raising of Jairus's daughter is not comparable to Jesus's own resurrection. Jesus is described in Scripture as the "firstborn from among the dead" (see Colossians 1:18). All prior "resurrections," those in the Old Testament and those performed by Jesus, were restorations back to a mortal life that would eventually end in death once more. Jesus's resurrection was a resurrection to an incorruptible life that will never end. And it really was Jesus's human body that was resurrected and transformed. We as humans can now rejoice and say, "One of us has already made it!"

The resurrection of Jairus's daughter, like that of the son of the widow in Nain (see 7:11-17), is at most a symbol and foreshadowing of the great resurrection at the end of the age, the one that Jesus's resurrection in the middle of history guarantees and begins. Jesus said of Jairus's daughter, "She is not dead, but asleep" (8:52). It is appropriate for us to say the same of all those who die in the Lord. The sleep of death is not terminal; we are guaranteed one day to rise again.

Personal Reflection Questions

- How has this section of Luke's Gospel fleshed out what it means to experience the kingdom of God? Who are the people who experienced good news, either by hearing it, or by benefiting from the rescue and restoration it brings?
- Where do you experience the church sharing Jesus's and Luke's concern for creating an inclusive community, where all are equally honored, welcomed and served – where we experience the fulfillment of God's challenge in Galatians 3:28, that "there is neither Jew nor Gentile, neither slave nor free, nor is there male and female, for you are all one in Christ Jesus"? How can the church move closer to fulfilling this ultimate goal of God's kingdom?
- This section of Luke narrates at least six explicit miracles, plus references to many more. But the miracles often focus on aspects other than merely the "divine power" unleashed – aspects like inclusiveness, compassion, restoration to society, etc. And alongside all these miracles, Jesus also teaches about the coming of God's reign and what this means for his disciples. How can we as congregations find balance between these various components in our own congregational life – emphasizing proclamation and discipleship training, doing the works of the kingdom and expecting God to do miracles? Are some of these receiving all our focus so that others are being neglected? Are we truly open to all the ways that God may want to work among us? How can we grow in this?

Christology and Discipleship

The Text: Luke 9:1 - 10:42 NIV

The Flow and Form of the Text

Luke retains his strong focus on God's kingdom in this section. It continues to be the main theme of Jesus's teaching (9:11) and the two groups of missionaries he sends out (see 9:2, 60; 10:9, 11). Moreover, Jesus defines being a disciple as one "fit for the kingdom" (9:62). Jesus promises that those around him will indeed catch glimpses of this kingdom, already present, though not yet in its coming fullness (9:27).

Yet this section does not explain in detail what Jesus means by "kingdom of God." Rather, it highlights two other closely related themes: Who is this Jesus? And what does it mean to be Jesus's disciples?

So far, Luke has introduced Jesus in many ways: as the promised Messiah (2:11, 26; 4:41), God's own Son (1:32, 35; 3:22; 4:41; 8:28), the world's Savior (2:11), the authoritative Son of Man (5:24; 6:22). Luke has even alluded to the fact that Jesus is "the Lord God" embodied truly, though mysteriously, in a human person (1:17, 43, 76; 2:11; 3:4).

In this section, Luke's major addition to his christology centers on the coming passion: the Son of Man not only comes with God's authority; he comes to do God's will, which will include suffering, death and resurrection (9:22, 44). Jesus explicitly predicts these things; indeed, he converses about them with Moses and Elijah on the Mountain of Transfiguration, indicating that these events will bring about a new "exodus" for the people of God (9:31).

Luke has also introduced Jesus's disciples in various ways. They are uniquely called to follow him, trained to catch people (5:10, 11), appointed to be apostles (6:13). They are the ones who receive special instruction in the ways of the kingdom (6:20-49), the ones entrusted with its secrets (8:10).

The relationship between Jesus and these disciples is the major focus of this section of Luke's Gospel. It features two separate mission trips: one involving the twelve apostles (9:1-9), the other an expanded group (10:1-20). The disciples serve as Jesus's ministry helpers (9:13-17). Though they are sometimes credited with great insight (9:20), often they struggle to understand who Jesus is, how to follow and serve him faithfully, and what to make of his puzzling predictions of suffering and death (see especially 9:45).

Occasionally in this section, Luke highlights other characters: crowds on the hillside, Moses and Elijah on the mountain with Jesus, a father seeking deliverance for his demon-possessed boy, an expert in the law, Martha and Mary. But the narratives that feature these characters all seem designed to help Jesus's disciples, then and now, to grasp who Jesus really is and to learn about faithful discipleship and service.

Outline:

Jesus Sends out the Twelve (9:1-9)
Jesus Feeds the Five Thousand (9:10-17)
Peter Declares that Jesus is the Messiah (9:18-20)
Jesus Predicts His Death and Resurrection (9:21-27)
The Transfiguration (9:28-36)

Jesus Heals a Demon-Possessed Boy (9:37-43a)
Jesus Again Predicts His Death and Resurrection (9:43b-45)
Greatness in God's Kingdom (9:46-50)
Samaritan Opposition (9:51-56)
The Cost of Following Jesus (9:57-62)
Jesus Sends Out the Seventy-Two (10:1-20)
Special Revelation for Jesus and His Disciples (10:21-24)
The Parable of the Good Samaritan (10:25-37)
At the Home of Martha and Mary (10:38-42)

The Text Explained

Jesus Sends Out the Twelve (9:1-9)

Jesus sends his twelve disciples on a mission. He previously designated them as "apostles," that is, "sent out ones" (6:13); now they will enact that calling. Jesus sends them to do exactly what he has been doing – driving out demons, healing the sick, proclaiming the kingdom. They also go with Jesus's power and authority – and his vulnerability! The Son of Man has no place to lay his head (see 9:58) unless those receptive to his message welcome him in. He tells the disciples to follow him in this. Stay wherever people will welcome you! Let them provide for your physical needs. That is the main point of his instruction to "take nothing" (9:3).

If we compare passages where Jesus sends missionaries (see 9:4; 10:4; 22:35-36 and parallels in other Gospels), we see the instructions are not identical. Different situations require different kinds of preparations and securities. But the main point remains constant: go in Jesus's name, with Jesus's authority, to do Jesus's work and proclaim Jesus's message; and do it in Jesus's way. That is also the mission of the church. And just as the disciples did in 22:35, so we can testify that when we carry out this mission, our needs are also always met (see also 12:31).

Jesus makes it clear that those who reject the apostles are actually rejecting Jesus and his message of the kingdom. The consequences of doing so will be spelled out more clearly in the next chapter. Here Jesus simply tells the disciples to "shake the dust off their feet" when they leave towns that reject their message. This was a significant symbolic gesture, communicating three things: 1) Be warned; 2) We are absolved of responsibility for the consequences; and 3) You are no longer faithful Jews. All three meanings are evident in Paul's later use of the same symbol in Antioch of Pisidia (see Acts 13:46, 51).

The third of these is particularly provocative. When Jews traveled abroad and then re-entered their own territory, they would ceremoniously shake the dust off their feet to symbolize leaving the filth of Gentile places outside the "Holy Land." By performing this symbolic act against *Jewish villages*, the disciples would be communicating on Jesus's behalf that such a village had just "opted out" of the covenant; it had declared itself to be "Gentile." This is the second time we've seen a ritual previously reserved for Gentiles practiced on Jews: recall John baptizing Jews, proselytizing them anew into the covenant people of God (see comments on 3:1-6).

These symbolic acts, John's baptism and the disciples shaking dust off their feet, powerfully enact one major feature of Jesus's ministry. He came to call Israel to repentance and faithfulness, and to bring about a clear division between those do not respond and those who do. Those who reject him would be viewed as outside the covenant Jesus is now renewing. Those who accept him would be the faithful minority of Israel that would carry on Israel's mission to be a blessing to the whole world by inviting Gentiles into full covenant participation in the people of God.

The effective mission of Jesus's disciples must have created quite a stir, for news of it even reaches Herod's palace (9:7-9), and leads to all sorts of speculation about what kinds of powers are here at work.

Jesus Feeds the Five Thousand (9:10-17)

The main points of this narrative are that Jesus has compassion for people who are hungry, acts miraculously to feed them and recruits his disciples to help with the distribution and cleanup.

The text provides warrant for Jesus's followers giving food to the hungry, even if when we do so it is usually through more ordinary channels – like donating to food banks, providing emergency aid or inviting hungry people to share our dining room tables.

Yet there may be more meaning to Jesus's miracle than this. Perhaps Jesus is casting himself in the role of "the new Moses" once again providing "manna" in the wilderness. Or maybe Jesus is playing the role of the Good Shepherd in Psalm 23 by providing food for the hungry "flock." Or Jesus is pointing toward the next time he will take bread, give thanks and break it, prefiguring the Last Supper that Luke describes in similar terms. Or Jesus is providing a foretaste of the coming banquet in the kingdom of God, where all who follow him share in the abundance God provides. Bible interpreters have defended all of these views.

My own view is that many of these additional meanings are more obviously present in other accounts of this event (which appears in all four Gospels). Luke's point is probably more basic: Jesus feeds hungry people.

At Jesus's "table," there is no opportunity for washing ceremonies, no jockeying for positions of honor (see 14:10), no dividing up along lines of ethnicity, social class or religious persuasion. The groups of "about fifty" (9:14) are for the sake of care and fellowship, certainly not segregation. All are welcome to dine with Jesus. That should be our experience and commitment. And where there is not enough food to go around, we trust Jesus and share what we have.

Peter Declares that Jesus is the Messiah (9:18-20)

> *Once when Jesus was praying in private and his disciples were with him, he asked them, "Who do the crowds say I am?"*
>
> *They replied, "Some say John the Baptist; others say Elijah; and still others, that one of the prophets of long ago has come back to life."*
>
> *"But what about you?" he asked. "Who do you say I am?"*
>
> *Peter answered, "God's Messiah." (9:18-20)*

As we've come to expect whenever he narrates major events or turning points, Luke again tells us Jesus is at prayer. At this significant juncture, Jesus will reveal to his disciples deeper levels of his own identity and mission. One will confess Jesus as God's Messiah, and Jesus will talk to them explicitly about his coming passion and the challenging call on their lives to "take up the cross."

Already in 9:7-8, we heard diverse speculations about Jesus's identity. Now, in response to Jesus's question about popular opinions, the same options are listed: John the Baptist, Elijah, another ancient prophet; someone must have come back to life! When Jesus asks his disciples (the question is addressed to "you" plural), Peter, on behalf of the group, identifies Jesus as "God's Messiah."

Jesus has not, thus far, acted the way most of his contemporaries expected the Messiah to act. His compassionate ministries, his consorting with sinners and tax collectors, his gathering of a motley crowd of followers – all these were quite contrary to what various groups in Israel expected. Some thought the coming Messiah would be a military leader, some a religious reformer, some a prophetic voice. Peter here seems prepared to say something like this: "You are not what we expected the Messiah to be like, but we acknowledge you are the one who was to come. Now please help us understand what that actually means." And that is precisely what Jesus does, probably to the great surprise of those he now addresses.

Jesus Predicts His Death and Resurrection (9:21-27)

> *Jesus strictly warned them not to tell this to anyone. And he said, "The Son of Man must suffer many things and be rejected by the elders, the chief priests and the teachers of the law, and he must be killed and on the third day be raised to life."*
>
> *Then he said to them all: "Whoever wants to be my disciple must deny themselves and take up their cross daily and follow me. For whoever wants to save their life will lose it, but whoever loses their life for me will save it. What good is it for someone to gain the whole world, and yet lose or forfeit their very self? Whoever is ashamed of me and my words, the Son of Man will be ashamed of*

> *them when he comes in his glory and in the glory of the Father and of the holy angels.*
>
> *"Truly I tell you, some who are standing here will not taste death before they see the kingdom of God." (9:21-27)*

Jesus first commands silence about his identity. That is not because he rejects Peter's point of view. He accepts it. But he does not want it publicized; not yet, at any rate. That might partly be because he has much work to do before his messianic claims become public knowledge. Or maybe premature publicity about his messianic identity could only lead to massive misunderstanding, given the diverse expectations people had. Maybe Jesus wants others to discern his true nature in the context of faithful following, as Peter and the other disciples have done, rather than having them merely decide for or against claims other people are making.

Next, Jesus explicitly predicts what he has only alluded to thus far. He will be rejected and killed by powerful people. After that, God will raise him back to life. He is not talking about the immortality of the soul or anything else that Greek philosophers sometimes speculated about; he is talking about actually being raised back to life, with a transformed resurrection body. Such a "resurrection" is categorically different from the kind Jesus had already enacted for the widow in Nain (7:11-17) and for Jairus the synagogue ruler (8:49-56). Their children were merely raised back to their old mortal lives. Jesus was predicting something completely different for himself.

The Jews were unique for their widespread belief that God really did intend to raise the dead. But they believed it would happen only at the end of history as we know it. The idea that it would happen to one person in the middle of history was unprecedented. But that is what Jesus is claiming. He would be rejected by Israel's powerful Jewish leaders, but God would overturn their wrong verdict about him by raising Jesus back to life, not to the old mortal life destined to end in death again later, but into the resurrection life that inaugurates God's new creation.

Jesus's next words concern what it means to follow a Messiah who will be rejected and killed: being prepared to face exactly the same thing. Following Jesus means full identification with him, even when that leads to rejection and death. We are called to trust God for vindication as Jesus did, no matter how God chooses to bring that about, whether in this life or the next.

And Jesus's final word is one of assurance. Those standing around Jesus, if they will faithfully follow this Messiah destined for death and resurrection, for rejection and vindication, will see God's kingdom. They may not live long enough to see the final arrival of God's eternal kingdom, but they will experience its reality in relation to this Jesus who is already inaugurating God's reign. And he will, after his resurrection, lead his followers into an ever greater experience of God's kingdom, until it is fulfilled at the end of the age.

Three more points are important in this context:

- Luke alone among the Gospel writers speaks of "taking up the cross *daily*" (9:23). This is not a once and for all decision to follow Jesus. This is a continuous submission to God's will, come what may.
- To "take up the cross" does not mean to suffer per se. It might involve suffering. But its meaning is something else. When Jesus faced the prospect of crucifixion, his prayer to the Father was "Not my will but yours be done" (22:42). That is the essence of cross-carrying. The cross is not at its heart a negative symbol. It is a positive symbol for a commitment that says, "I submit to God's will and accept all the challenges and the blessings that will entail."
- Following Jesus is not the bad news that comes after the good news of God's free grace. Receiving God's grace and responding in discipleship are inseparable aspects of the gospel itself. To take up the cross and follow Jesus is the means by which our lives are saved (9:24); it assures us we will be on Jesus's side when he comes in glory (9:26); it enables us to experience God's kingdom in the meantime

(9:27).

The Transfiguration (9:28-36)

Once more, Luke reports Jesus is praying (see 9:18). This time, prayer forms the context in which he and his disciples experience something special. They receive a vision (they see Moses and Elijah) and an audition (they hear God's voice from heaven). Jesus and the two visitors from the past appear to the disciples in blinding splendor, perhaps prefiguring the glory of the resurrection Jesus foretold in 9:22 or the "seeing of the kingdom" he promised in 9:27. Yet the central feature of the text is the focus it puts on Jesus. Moses was indeed a great lawgiver and prophet. Elijah was a fearless prophet as well. The Old Testament speaks of both as preparers for the one who was to come (Deuteronomy 18:15, 18; Acts 3:22; 7:37; Malachi 4:5, 6). Perhaps they even stand symbolically for the Law and the Prophets that testify of Jesus. But when all is said and done, Jesus stands there alone and the voice from his Father points to him, calls him the beloved Son and charges the disciples to listen to him.

There is a unique feature in Luke's narrative of this event. Other Gospels tell the same story, but only Luke says that the three men conversed about Jesus's impending "exodus" (9:31), the Greek word sometimes translated "departure." It helps define Jesus's death and resurrection as the "new exodus," God's new intervention to lead God's people out of slavery and oppression and send them on a journey to the Promised Land. The first time God accomplished a great exodus, it was out of Egypt. The same language is used much later in the Old Testament to speak of Israel's return from Babylonian captivity. But the Law and the Prophets alike (Moses and Elijah here!) speak of a great exodus yet to come. God will one day intervene to bring to an end all suffering and slavery, whether at the hands of powerful empires or the supernatural powers of sin and death. It is that exodus that Jesus will inaugurate in Jerusalem. And it is that exodus that Jesus will one day bring to completion when God's kingdom is fully established, on earth as it is in heaven.

In this context, "Listen to him!" takes on layers of meaning. It means that Jesus's disciples, then and now, learn the ways of God's already/not yet kingdom from the life and teaching, death and resurrection of Jesus. And it means that as we take up our own crosses and follow Jesus, we too experience a foretaste of the exodus that begins now and leads us onward to the Promised Land.

Jesus Heals a Demon-Possessed Boy (9:37-43a)

This text reminds us how challenging it is to understand what is going on when people exhibit "demonic" symptoms. The text creates the impression that this boy has epilepsy, and indeed some translations use that word to describe his condition. Luke refers to the cause as an impure spirit, and yet he says, not that the boy is delivered, but that he is healed (using a clearly medical term). In one sense, all uncleanness, all sickness, all spiritual oppression is demonic – it stems from the evil one and the influence of evil in our fallen world.

Why Jesus's disciples were not able to bring about this boy's healing/deliverance is not explained. They successfully healed and delivered during their mission trip examined above (9:1, 6). Whatever the reason for the disciples' failure here, Jesus finds it exasperating. We hear in his response (9:41) a longing for the ultimate deliverance (the final exodus; see 9:31) he will soon accomplish in Jerusalem.

This text reminds us of the resurrection Jesus performed at Nain in 7:11-17. There Jesus raised and returned an only son to his mother. Here Jesus heals and returns an only son to his father.

Jesus Again Predicts His Death and Resurrection (9:43b-45)

In this text, Jesus again predicts his coming passion, though he is not explicit about what it will involve. Despite Jesus's challenge to the disciples to follow him, despite the voice from heaven calling them to listen to Jesus, despite all they have heard and experienced, they are having a hard time keeping up with Jesus. They simply do not know what to make of all this.

We are not told whether God hid these things from them, whether it was "demonic blinding" or whether their own human frailty resulted in their non-understanding. Commentaries have presented all three views. I suggest it is rarely easy to separate out the influences on our lives. We are always frail and imperfect humans. God's enemy always aims to blind us to what God is doing and saying. And God sovereignly chooses if and when and how to make things more plain. Meanwhile "we know in part" (1 Corinthians 13:12), we hear Jesus challenge us to follow faithfully even when the road leads to a cross (9:23) and we hear the heavenly voice call us to "listen to Jesus" (9:35). In due time, what we need to understand God will reveal.

Greatness in God's Kingdom (9:46-50)

> *An argument started among the disciples as to which of them would be the greatest. Jesus, knowing their thoughts, took a little child and had him stand beside him. Then he said to them, "Whoever welcomes this little child in my name welcomes me; and whoever welcomes me welcomes the one who sent me. For it is the one who is least among you all who is the greatest."*
>
> *"Master," said John, "we saw someone driving out demons in your name and we tried to stop him, because he is not one of us."*
>
> *"Do not stop him," Jesus said, "for whoever is not against you is for you." (9:46-50)*

Of all the things the disciples might be preoccupied with at this moment, arguing about who is greatest seems the least appropriate. Jesus calls his disciples to rethink greatness. The world's kind is not worth pursuing. The kind Jesus endorses is its polar opposite. Truly great people do not claim greatness for themselves. True greatness consists in welcoming children. Indeed, it consists in being like children, in being "the least among you" (9:48). Greatness rolls out the red carpet for the least, the children – those who model the stance of Jesus himself.

If clamoring for greatness is not bad enough, now the disciples become gatekeepers, making sure nobody outside their group is allowed to act in Jesus's name. How ironic: just nine verses back they themselves were unable to drive out a demon; now they want to prevent someone else from doing it in Jesus's name. Jesus's response is a strong word for all who would rather keep the boundaries tight and the "wrong" people out: "Whoever is not against you is for you" (9:50).

Samaritan Opposition (9:51-56)

Sometimes Luke's Gospel teaches about discipleship through direct words of instruction (9:23-26); more often it teaches about discipleship by showing the reader how Jesus's own disciples get it wrong and have to be corrected. They compete to be "greatest" (9:46-48); they maintain exclusive boundaries (9:49-50); now they respond to rejection with threats of violence. Again Jesus will correct them.

I suppose we should credit James and John with great faith: apparently they really believe if they called down the fires of God's judgment, it would happen! But their proposal is completely misguided. Jesus has already instructed his disciples how they should respond when villages do not receive the message of the gospel (see 9:5), and it does not involve retribution. He has already told them he himself will be rejected and God would be the one who vindicates him in the end (9:22). He has already told them they are to "take up the cross" as they follow after the way of Jesus. James and John's zeal in this text is admirable, but as the history of Christianity has so often demonstrated, zeal without an unwavering commitment to the way of Jesus – the way of suffering love – can go badly wrong.

This text signals the beginning of Jesus's journey to the cross: "As the time approached for him to be taken up to heaven, Jesus resolutely set out for Jerusalem" (9:51), the place of the final confrontation. The next ten chapters narrate that journey.

Luke does not write a travelogue (meaning we do not see a day-to-day account of progress toward Jerusalem); he rather uses the symbolism of a journey to teach about following Jesus. Luke reminds us more than once that Jesus is heading for the destiny he has disclosed to his disciples (see 13:22; 17:11; 18:31; 19:11, 28). And we will remember along the way that the disciples are called to follow in faithful discipleship. How ironic that, as the journey begins, the disciples imagine they should call down God's judgment on those who reject Jesus. The whole journey is designed to teach the opposite: Jesus came to save precisely such people.

The Cost of Following Jesus (9:57-62)

Jesus has been very clear in this chapter that discipleship can be costly. It involves taking up a cross. It inverts this world's value systems. It suffers wrong without retaliation. Now, as Jesus interacts with three would-be disciples, the cost is again in the forefront.

The enthusiasm of the first ("I will follow you wherever you go") is countered with a sobering word: then you will be trading in the security of a home for a life of trusting God to provide places for you to stay! The conditional commitment of the second ("First let me take care of important business") is countered with an uncompromising challenge: nothing takes priority over the call of the kingdom. The divided loyalties of the third ("Let me pay attention to other relationships first") is countered with a strong warning: turning back puts one's entire commitment at risk.

We should not read this text as if it said: don't pay attention to future housing needs; boycott your parents' funerals; leave home without saying farewell. Rather these are deliberately exaggerated scenarios designed to say above all else: our allegiance to God's kingdom and the costly discipleship that it entails is our highest allegiance.

Jesus deliberately chose provocative scenarios to make the point. The Son of Man in fact had many places to lay his head, but on his journeys, he did not always have reservations in advance, and perhaps at times, when village after village rejected his message, he did sleep under the stars (see 9:53, 56). In Jesus's time, burying the dead took precedence over studying the law, serving in the temple, bringing the Passover sacrifice and observing circumcision. By juxtaposing "burial" with "discipleship," Jesus is saying discipleship is your highest calling; we may have many other duties, but they never take precedence over following Jesus. And in a communal and family-oriented society like that of the first century, prioritizing a relationship with Jesus over family was radical indeed (see also 8:21; 11:27, 28). But it is what Jesus called for back then – and today.

Robert Karris in his book, *Invitation to Luke*, put it this way: "Following Him is not a task which is added to others like working a second job.... It is everything. It is a solemn commitment which forces the disciples-to-be to reorder all their other duties" (130).

Jesus Sends Out the Seventy-Two (10:1-20)

This missionary trip is a mission to Jews, just as the first had been (see 9:1-6). Yet this second missionary trip foreshadows and symbolizes the future Gentile mission. It does so by virtue of its sheer magnitude (six times as many missionaries are sent forth); and it does so by the specific number of missionaries. Both 70 and 72 (manuscripts vary as to which number is original in the text) were proverbially used to number the "nations on earth." Even the call for prayer for more future missionaries (10:2) points in this direction. Jesus is still preparing Israel for its mission, but one day, the gospel he now preaches to Israel will be proclaimed to the ends of the earth as Gentiles are invited to join the people of God.

The instructions for this mission trip are similar, though not identical, to those for the first trip. Again the call is for minimal provisions; they are to trust God to meet their needs through those who welcome them and the message of the kingdom. Again Jesus hightlights the possibility of rejection and instructs the missionaries how they should respond. Again they are to warn those villages that reject the message. That is part of the meaning of "shaking off the dust" (see comments on 9:5).

What is different here is that Jesus spells out that a final judgment awaits those who do not accept Jesus and the message of the kingdom. And that judgment will be all the more severe the more opportunities and evidence people have received (10:12-15). The reference to Sodom is particularly interesting, for the judgment that fell on Sodom in the days of Lot was "fire from heaven," precisely what James and John wanted to call down on a village that rejected Jesus (see 9:54). Jesus's point is that we never respond with vengeance. Final accounting is always in God's hands, the one who knows when and where and why and how to hold people accountable in ways consistent with God's love and justice.

When we are active in God's mission (and the call really is on all of us to be that!) we need the assurances that Jesus in 10:16-19 gives us. We are involved in something so much bigger than ourselves, bigger even than our mission projects and agencies. People are not so much accepting or rejecting us; they are accepting or rejecting Jesus and the heavenly Father who sent him. And when miracles occur, we do not delight in the miracles for their own sake; rather we recognize Jesus is using us to push back forces of evil and spread the restorative kingdom of God.

The reference in 10:19 to treading on snakes reminds us of what is sometimes called the *protoevangelium* (the first announcement of good news). Way back in Genesis 3:15, God told Eve her seed would ultimately crush the serpent (elsewhere identified as Satan) under its heel. Jesus, of course, is the ultimate victor over Satan's power, but over and over again, the New Testament makes clear Jesus does not win the battle unilaterally. He empowers his followers and his church to join in that battle against evil and to participate in his victory over it (see Romans 16:20; Ephesians 1:18-23; Revelation 12:7-11).

The final verse of this section again addresses the matter of priority. That we are recipients of God's grace, and therefore destined to share life with God eternally, should fill us with wonder and amazement, far beyond anything we might count as missionary success. This is not about a shift in priorities from service to selfishness – far from it. It is about a shift in perspectives, from our current victories that symbolize Christ's victory over evil, to the ultimate arrival of that final victory at the end of the age.

Special Revelation for Jesus and His Disciples (10:21-24)

This important passage reminds us that God's revelation is not something guaranteed to the intelligent or well-educated, but a gift God gives to those whose hearts are right (10:21). It reminds us that ultimate truth is not captured in doctrinal correctness, but in the revelation of God to us through Jesus (10:22). It assures disciples of Jesus that they are especially blessed, not because they are greater than kings or more insightful than prophets, but because they are living in the time when God's purposes are being fulfilled through Jesus (10:23-24). If there is an overriding concern here it is this: true blessedness belongs to those who stick with Jesus and learn from him.

The Parable of the Good Samaritan (10:25-37)

This passage is well-known, so I will summarize its most important points. The occasion for Jesus's famous parable about the good Samaritan is a conversation between a legal expert and Jesus. The man is trying to test Jesus, but in the end, Jesus turns the tables on him.

After the man correctly identifies the two greatest commandments, he wants to justify himself. Apparently, he believes he is fully devoted to loving God, and that he truly loves his neighbor. The problem is his very narrow definition of "neighbor" – it certainly does not include Samaritans.

Jesus puts his finger on the man's problem by changing the question. The issue is not "Who is my neighbor?" – as though we have the right to put boundaries around that. The issue is "Who is being a neighbor?" (see 10:36). When people need our help, we are called to "be neighborly" to them, no matter who they are. That is the main point, though Jesus seldom limits his parable lessons to "one main point."

When Jesus speaks of a priest and a Levite passing by the injured man, the legal expert might well have responded, "That figures!" Pharisaic lawyers were not great supporters of the priesthood and all the Levitical ceremonies. But when Jesus declares that the one who stopped was a Samaritan, certainly the lawyer's jaw would have dropped. A hated, despised Samaritan?

I can imagine, by the time Jesus finishes his parable, the Pharisee has felt outrage at pretty much everyone under consideration: the contemptible robbers, the hateful Romans who cannot even keep the roads safe, the uncaring priests and Levites, certainly the Samaritan, and probably even Jesus – who has the audacity to make a Samaritan into the hero of the day.

Yet, despite his hatred and outrage, he may still be thinking, "I love my neighbor." He assumes he gets to define neighbor – someone from his own ethnicity, social class and theological convictions. Jesus's whole point is that, by definition, neighbor love is the opposite of that: it does not pay attention to ethnicity, social class or theological convictions. It does not draw narrow boundaries around those I consider part of my community. It seeks to *be a neighbor* by concretely caring for those in need, whoever they are.

At the Home of Martha and Mary (10:38-42)

It is clear that in this text Jesus chides Martha and affirms Mary. What is less clear is what exactly the problem was. Suggestions include:

- Was it Martha's intemperate mood? "Calm down, you could learn from your quiet, peaceful sister."
- Was it her busyness? "Don't you know a contemplative life pleases God so much more?"
- Was it her priorities? "Physical needs are important, but

spiritual disciplines are much more important."
- Was it her pride? "That magnificent spread might feed your ego; but Jesus delights more in Mary's humility."
- Was it her gender stereotyping? "Just because you prefer the kitchen doesn't mean Mary shouldn't get a theological education."

There might be truth in more than one of these. But I think the main point is that Martha thought her sister should have made the same choice she herself did. Mary chose a theological education (that's what sitting at a teacher's feet meant). Martha chose to prepare a meal. Both were good choices – and still are. The challenge is to discern which choice is appropriate in a given situation, based on our opportunities, our gifts and our calling. And the challenge is to let others make a different choice than we do without criticizing them.

One more thing. The previous passage named the two greatest commands: love God and love your neighbor. The parable of the good Samaritan helps us understand what "love your neighbor" means. I think the Mary and Martha incident helps us understand what it looks like to "love God." We love God with heart and soul and strength and mind when we invest our gifts and pursue our callings, whether in the kitchen or at Jesus's feet.

Implications of the Text for Today

The Cost of Discipleship

This section of Luke highlights the cost of discipleship using language like "denying self," "taking up the cross," "losing one's life" and "no turning back." And Luke supplements these calls with warnings that, when we carry out Christ's mission, we may well be rejected just as Jesus often was.

How transparent should we be concerning the cost of discipleship when we invite others to follow Jesus? Do we invite people to accept the "good news" of salvation, and later try to convince them also to take on the "bad news" of discipleship? That is never the approach Jesus takes, nor for that matter, any writer of the New Testament.

As paradoxical as it may seem, the dominant message of Scripture is that salvation is a "costly free gift." We could never earn it; it can only be provided by God. But gifts need to be received, and Jesus explains with great clarity what that "receiving" entails. It means changing loyalties; it means abandoning sinful ways; it means following, whatever the cost. These are not ways of buying or qualifying for the free gift. These are the means of receiving it.

Why do we so often speak of "good news," and then talk about it in ways that sound much more like "bad news"? Taking up the cross is not a heavy burden but the way we follow Jesus through death to eternal glory. Losing one's life does not sound pleasant, but Jesus explains it is the way ultimately to save it. Jesus says clearly that any costs are far more than repaid in Christ's kingdom (18:29, 30). Salvation is always by grace – costly grace!

Adopting the Upside-Down Values of the Kingdom

This section of Luke gives multiple glimpses into the strange upside-down ways of God's kingdom. We value and welcome children, and they become models for us. Greatness is found in being a servant. Mistreatment and rejection are accepted as inevitable; we never pay back. Obligations our culture places on us are simply abandoned, if that is what the call of Jesus entails. Treasured family relationships take a back seat to Jesus and the family of disciples gathering around him.

No wonder the disciples were often baffled by Jesus's words. No wonder the church in every age has found ways of playing down the radicalness of Jesus's demands. Sometimes it has even found clever theological maneuvers that simply wipe out what Jesus said, imagining Jesus's instructions were meant only for the first disciples, for the first century, for the Jews, for a future millennium or a few special Christians.

Jesus's sayings are often paradoxical; admittedly, they often involve hyperbole; always, they are directed at issues relevant to his world. But their challenge is always also meant for us. We must hear and apply, not explain away and avoid. Those most committed to live by the values of Christ's upside-down kingdom are also those most likely to confess that there is no better way to live!

Narrow Boundaries or Wide Open Doors?

In 9:50, Jesus challenges the narrowness of the disciples by saying, "Whoever is not against you is for you." Later in 11:23, Jesus will say, "Whoever is not with me is against me." So which is it? Both, of course.

The context of the two sayings helps us understand how that is possible. In this chapter, fellow servants of God are doing Christ's work in Christ's name. One group has no business trying to stop the other! In Luke 11, the context is the great spiritual battle between Jesus and God's enemy, Satan. Jesus's opponents accuse him of colluding with Satan. Jesus points out how absurd that charge is and insists he is the stronger one, out to plunder the strong one's (Satan's) house. Those who oppose Jesus will find themselves on the enemy's side, or as Jesus puts it: "Whoever is not with me is against me."

This is a good example we could apply to many texts. Two statements appear to contradict each other, but when we observe their appropriate contexts, they prove to be fully compatible claims; indeed, often they each provide support for the other.

Because Jesus and those acting in his name are part of a spiritual battle against God's archenemy, we cannot afford to draw narrow boundaries around ourselves and our ministries. We collaborate with all who name Jesus, for only in this way can we effectively stand against the real enemy, the one with whom no compromise or collusion is possible.

On a Journey with Jesus

The journey motif Luke introduces in 9:51 he will sustain through chapter 19, when Jesus arrives in Jerusalem. Or perhaps, we should say through 23:26, where Jesus walks the last steps toward his crucifixion.

As disciples, we are called to follow Jesus. He modeled the journey for us; we follow after. For this very reason, the earliest Christians were called "people of the way" (see Acts 9:2). The Christian life is a pilgrimage. We are "marching to Zion." Along the way, we may face rejection as Jesus did. But we journey on, sharing life with our traveling companions, keeping our eyes fixed on Jesus who leads us beyond all rejection and suffering to glory on the other side.

Finding People of Peace

Years ago, I was introduced to The Church on Brady, then led by pastor Tom Wolf. The church took literally Jesus's instructions to the 72 missionaries. In each neighborhood where they wanted to do kingdom ministry and share the gospel, they would seek the "person of peace" (a literal translation of Jesus's words in 10:6). The person might or might not be a believer. But he or she cared about the welfare of the neighborhood and was willing to allow ministers of the gospel to become collaborators in bringing God's goodness to the neighborhood. Thus a "beachhead for the gospel" was established.

We are not necessarily required to mimic the missionary strategies Jesus outlines for the 12 and the 72 in the first century. But collaborating with peace-loving people is an appropriate way to "seek the peace of the city" (see Jeremiah 29:7). God will help us discern when the time is right to call people to allegiance to Jesus.

Personal Reflection Questions

- Do you (or does your congregation) struggle with the paradox that salvation is God's free gift, and yet it costs us everything? How do you find an appropriate (though perhaps paradoxical) position between two extremes: 1) viewing "costly discipleship" as the means by which grace is earned; and 2) treating "costly discipleship" as something completely optional? What resources does Luke provide in this section for living with the paradox?
- We speak sometimes of God's "upside-down kingdom"; perhaps instead we should speak of God's "right-side-up kingdom" in a world that has turned everything upside down. As you aim to live by the values of God's kingdom within this world, where do you experience its pressures to conform? How can we discern how to live in tension with, or even protest against, the priorities of our world?
- As you reflect on the Martha and Mary incident, where do you find it difficult to let other believers follow their own convictions and priorities? How do we resist the temptation to do as Martha did – complaining about her sister who made different choices than she did? How does Jesus's response to Martha help us as a Christian community accept one another with our own unique callings and giftedness?

Prayer and Diverse Responses to Jesus

The Text: Luke 11:1-54 NIV

The Flow and Form of the Text

The first 13 verses of Luke 11 deal with the theme of prayer: Jesus prays; he teaches his disciples a model prayer; he tells a parable about prayer; he uses human fathers as a teaching tool to convince his hearers that our heavenly Father gladly gives us all we need and more.

It is less clear what holds the rest of the chapter together. I have decided to use the three different responses to Jesus that Luke mentions in 11:14-16 as the overarching themes. Some hearers are amazed, some attribute Jesus's power to Satan and some test Jesus by asking for signs. Much of the rest of the chapter deals directly with Jesus's rejoinders and critiques of these diverse ways people respond to him and his teaching.

We will examine the first 13 verses in more detail than usual, with special focus on 11:5-8, the parable of the friend at midnight. Many readers assume it teaches persistence in prayer; however, contemporary translations have almost uniformly abandoned that interpretation. Let us assess alternative ways this parable is now understood and translated and why.

The well-known material before and after the parable contains important instructions on prayer and why we can trust God to hear and answer prayer. We will see how these instructions contribute to and benefit from the new way of reading the "friend at midnight" parable.

The remainder of the chapter also contains important themes that help us understand right and wrong responses to Jesus and his ministry.

Outline:

Jesus Teaches about Prayer (11:1-13)
- The Lord's Prayer (11:1-4)
- The Friend at Midnight (11:5-8)
- Ask, Seek, Knock (11:9-13)

Three Responses to Jesus (11:14-16)
Jesus and the Powers of Evil (11:17-26)
Who is Blessed? (11:27-28)
The Sign of Jonah (11:29-32)
The Lamp of the Body (11:33-36)
Alas for the Pharisees and the Experts in the Law (11:37-54)

The Text Explained

Jesus Teaches about Prayer (11:1-13)

The Lord's Prayer (11:1-4)

> *One day Jesus was praying in a certain place. When he finished, one of his disciples said to him, "Lord, teach us to pray, just as John taught his disciples." (11:1)*

We learn from the disciples' request that John the Baptist either "taught his disciples to pray" or (more likely) "taught his disciples a model prayer." The first alternative is unlikely; faithful Jews did not need to learn to pray – they grew up praying. Likely John taught his followers a specific prayer that defined his repentance and preparation ministry. Now Jesus's disciples want Jesus to teach them a new model prayer, one that corresponds to Jesus's ministry and his priorities. That is the context in which Jesus teaches his famous prayer of the kingdom, commonly known as the Lord's Prayer.

When we understand the disciples' request for a model prayer, it makes sense that they memorized and preserved it, paving the way for Christians to pray that same prayer ever since. Jesus likely intended for that to happen when he gave this prayer to his disciples.

To slavishly pray only the exact words Jesus first used is neither possible nor necessary. We do not know what those original words were! What we have is a Greek translation passed down in more than one form before being written down (compare Matthew 6:9-13). The church has never felt obligated to exactly replicate either of the two forms preserved in the Gospels. Usually we have added lines at the end, and sometimes people have suggested (quite legitimately, I would say) the Lord's Prayer can also be used as a grid for various components of prayer, rather than merely as words to repeat.

Yet we should not completely rule out another aspect of this chapter's first verse. "Teach us a prayer" seems to be the main concern of the disciples. But teaching readers "to pray" is also extremely important to Luke. That is why he so often presents Jesus as a model of prayer. We do not usually know the content of Jesus's prayers, but we know he prayed fervently and often and in a wide variety of situations. We know it because Luke keeps telling us. But let us also note this: "fervently and often" does not mean the same as "persistently and long," as we will soon see!

One more point: this is the only time in all the Gospels that anyone asks Jesus to teach! That the topic is prayer further demonstrates how important that theme is for the writer of this Gospel.

> *He said to them, "When you pray, say:*
> *'Father,*
> *hallowed be your name,*

your kingdom come.
Give us each day our daily bread.
Forgive us our sins,
for we also forgive everyone who sins against us.
And lead us not into temptation.'" (11:2-4)

Jesus is teaching his followers to address God as "Father." Though the word "our" is not included in Luke's version, it becomes clear soon enough that this is a community prayer. This is a family praying about the family's needs. That is why the pronouns later are all plural – "our bread," "our sins," "we," "us." The followers of Jesus constitute brothers and sisters who together call God "Father."

"Hallowed be your name" is not quite the same as "glory to God" (or some other expression of praise and adoration). While praise is an important component of prayer, the phrase "hallowed be your name" really is a petition. It means "those things must be done which bring honor to your name." We are asking God to do that which brings honor to God's name, with the implication that we will actively participate in those action, so that by our actions, we too will honor God.

"Your kingdom come" is not merely a request for God's kingdom to arrive in a future divine intervention. Jesus himself inaugurated God's kingdom through his own coming, his teaching and ministry (see 11:20), and of course, especially his death and resurrection. And so, we are praying God's kingdom will come more and more.

And how does God's reign come? The rest of the petitions in this prayer help us answer that. God's reign comes when we recognize God as the one who provides for our needs, when we trust God for forgiveness and learn to forgive one another, when we experience God's help in times of testing. In other words, God's reign is established among us when we experience God's goodness, live God's priorities and experience God's active participation in our lives and in our world.

Matthew's version of the Lord's Prayer includes the line: "Your will be done on earth as it is in heaven" (Matthew 6:10). While that line is not included here, it is the true intention of what Luke does include. The burden of our prayer and the passion of our lives is to participate in the active coming of God's kingdom, until God's will truly is done on earth, as it is already done in heaven. And since that will never be fully the case until Jesus comes again, our kingdom prayer also expresses our longing and hope that one day Jesus will return to complete the kingdom project his earthly life inaugurated and in which his followers participate.

Jesus's model prayer not only gives us words to say. It also tunes our hearts and focuses our priorities. As we long for, pray for and work toward the coming of God's reign, we truly honor God's name, trust God to meet our needs, learn forgiveness, strive for purity, resist temptation – in short, we live the kingdom life for which we pray.

The Friend at Midnight (11:5-8)

> *Then Jesus said to them, "Suppose you have a friend, and you go to him at midnight and say, 'Friend, lend me three loaves of bread; a friend of mine on a journey has come to me, and I have no food to offer him.' And suppose the one inside answers, 'Don't bother me. The door is already locked, and my children and I are in bed. I can't get up and give you anything.' I tell you, even though he will not get up and give you the bread because of friendship, yet because of your shameless audacity he will surely get up and give you as much as you need." (11:5-8)*

Jesus is teaching about prayer and uses a parable about a request for bread from a sleeping friend as a teaching tool. In Jesus's parable, the friendship between these two men would already no doubt motivate the sleeper to give the needed bread, but even if it would not, something else would – "his *anaideia*." There are two big problems. Nobody knows for sure what this Greek word means; and until we figure that out, we cannot be sure *whose anaideia* is referred to here.

I indicated above that this parable was traditionally understood as a call for persistent prayer; that is, the man at the door motivated the sleeper to get up, and the strategy he used was persistence. Today hardly any interpreter believes that is the point of Jesus's parable. And more and more contemporary translations are abandoning that way of wording the parable in English. The problem is they cannot agree on any one alternative. What has happened?

A researcher named Alan Johnson discovered there was no evidence that the crucial word, *anaideia*, would have been understood to mean "persistence" until at least 300 years after Christ. It must have meant something else. But what? Here there is a lot of disagreement. Contemporary translations now often abandon "persistence" in favor of words like boldness, brashness, impudence, importunity, shamelessness or some combination of the above (for example, shameless audacity or brash persistence). Sometimes they create a paraphrase, such as "because you are so bold" or "because you are not ashamed to keep asking."

It seems likely that *anaideia* is composed of "an" (a prefix used in Greek for "not") and "*aidos*" (a word meaning shame). The possibilities then are that it means "shameless" (acting without regard to the shame incurred) or "not wanting to experience shame" (motivated by the desire to avoid shame). If it is the first, it refers to the man who is asking: he asked "shamelessly." If it is the second, it refers to the man in bed: he gets up so as not to lose his good reputation.

The most likely proposal, in my view, is the one the NIV Bible (2011) prints in its footnotes as an alternative – "yet to preserve his good name." A form of this is also found in the footnotes of other translations and in the main text of at least two. This way of interpreting *anaideia* makes it clear it is the *anaideia* of the sleeper, not of the bread requester, that is in view.

Here are the reasons I prefer the second option (for more, see my book *Double Take*, pages 135-141):

- In Jesus's culture, it would not have been shameful to request bread at midnight from a friend. People did not usually have large stores of food at home; there were no 24-hour grocery stores, no fast food drive-ins. It was the responsibility of the entire village to provide hospitality for a guest, so if one family did not have food to offer a guest, they would borrow from neighbors or friends.
- The sleeper really would ruin his reputation if he answered in the way the parable proposes he might have. If he refused to get up and give bread, the requester would not go home disappointed; he would go to the next neighbor to borrow bread, and there he would certainly report how impossibly his sleeping friend had responded. By morning the whole village would know about it!
- The parable as a whole centers around the sleeper, not the bread-requester. A literal reading of the Greek says, "Suppose one of you has a friend and he goes/comes (same word in Greek) to him." The NIV translation assumes the first person introduced is the requester, and so translates it, "Suppose you have a friend, and you go to him at midnight." But the first person introduced is much more likely the sleeper, so we could, if we wished, make that clear by translating it, "Suppose you have a friend and he comes to you at midnight." It seems likely the hearer is supposed to try to imagine himself or herself, not as the requester, but as the one expected to supply food. That makes it exactly parallel to 11:11: "Which of you fathers, if your son asks for a fish...?" Jesus's point is, because we, as humans, cannot imagine ourselves doing such a thing, we can be confident that God would not do that.
- The whole parable invites us to imagine the unimaginable. That is what the expression "Which of you?" implies. When the Greek speaker said, "Which of you?" the expected response was "No one, of course." That is exactly what happens in 11:11-12, and what we should assume is

happening in 11:5. Jesus is saying it is unthinkable that anyone would stay in bed instead of giving the needed supplies. Why? You would ruin your reputation if you did that.

- Jesus tells what would have been a very imaginable story in their world about traveling late at night (normal in summer), about arriving and expecting to eat (normal in their culture), having no food available (normal in a warm country without refrigerators), going to the neighbor (normal for the reasons already given). Everything is very imaginable, except for the one thing we in our culture could easily imagine doing – telling him to go away, because we have already gone to bed. But in their world that valued hospitality above convenience, it would be unthinkable.

So what does Jesus's parable mean? It does not mean we pray to persuade a grouchy, sleeping God to get up. Persistence does not guarantee an answer. So what does motivate God to act? Our boldness? On the contrary. We do not bank on the quality of our praying. We put our confidence in the generosity of a faithful God. We do not trust in faith; we trust in our Father. To paraphrase what Jesus is saying with this parable:

> *It is unthinkable, isn't it, that a scenario like this would unfold? It is midnight and you are in bed. Your friend comes and tells you about his need for bread. ("A traveler has arrived, and I have nothing to offer!") Can you imagine yourself saying to your friend, "Go away! I'm in bed with my children. I'm not getting up to give you anything"? Of course not. Why not? Well, he's your friend, and besides, you would never do that because of the shame factor. By morning, your reputation would be ruined!*

God will generously meet our legitimate needs. The primary motivator is that we are God's children and, according to Jesus's parable, his friends. But if that were not enough, God would act anyway: God's reputation is at stake!

Remember the Lord's Prayer, recorded just before this parable. It begins with a petition that God act for the sake of God's own honor. Only after that do we ask for daily bread.

The key to answered prayer does not lie in our successful prayer techniques; it lies in the nature of God.

Ask, Seek, Knock (11:9-13)

> *"So I say to you: Ask and it will be given to you; seek and you will find; knock and the door will be opened to you. For everyone who asks receives; the one who seeks finds; and to the one who knocks, the door will be opened." (11:9-10)*

We sometimes see these verses as teaching persistence (to go along with the traditional view of the parable we just examined). Ask, and ask and keep on asking – and it will be given to you. Seek, and seek and keep on seeking – and you will find. Knock unendingly – and eventually, the door will open. But in Greek, an imperative (seek) followed by a promise (and you will find) almost always implies a conditional statement: "If you seek, you will find."

Those who ask really do receive, if the giver wants to give what is best. Those who seek find, if they search for the things God intends for them to find. Those who knock really do have doors opened for them, if those doors are the ones God wants them to walk through. If persistent praying guaranteed we could get whatever we wanted, even if it were outside God's will we would be wielding a very dangerous power indeed.

> *"Which of you fathers, if your son asks for a fish, will give him a snake instead? Or if he asks for an egg, will give him a scorpion? If you then, though you are evil, know how to give good gifts to your children, how much more will your Father in heaven give the Holy Spirit to those who ask him!" (11:11-13)*

Jesus again asks us to imagine the unimaginable, reinforcing the same point as the parable of the friend at midnight. Even you earthly fathers, evil as you are, would not think of giving snakes and scorpions to your children, when they ask for food. You would not deceive them with look-alikes (the fish they ate looked quite a lot like a snake, and a rolled-up scorpion really could look like an egg!). You would not put them in danger (remember Jesus granted his missionary teams special protection against "snakes and scorpions"; see 10:19). Shouldn't it then be obvious that God can be trusted to meet our needs and ultimately give us the best gift of all, the Holy Spirit (11:13)?

So this section closes with grand promises about the generosity of a loving God, who does all things for the sake of the honor of God's name. God's hallowed name is our highest concern (see 11:2), and it gives us confidence that God will do what is right and best. In that light, the pressure tactics we sometimes use in prayer seem quite out of place.

Three Responses to Jesus (11:14-16)

> *Jesus was driving out a demon that was mute. When the demon left, the man who had been mute spoke, and the crowd was amazed. But some of them said, "By Beelzebul, the prince of demons, he is driving out demons." Others tested him by asking for a sign from heaven. (11:14-16)*

As I indicated in the introduction to this section, there are three different reactions to Jesus that Luke reports in rapid succession here:

- Many are amazed.
- Some credit Jesus's power to Satan.
- Others want to test him by demanding a sign.

In the material that follows, Jesus will respond at length to those reactions: to the Beelzebul charge in 11:17-26; to the amazement in 11:27-28; and to the demand for signs in 11:29-32.

Verse 14 reports the incident that led to the crowd's amazement. A man who was mute because of demonic influence is delivered and healed.

The charge that Jesus casts out demons in demonic power (11:15) does not seem particularly logical, as Jesus will point out. But it shows people will go to great lengths to avoid the conclusion that Jesus's life and ministry are authorized and empowered by God, that Jesus's ministry is "God at work."

Asking for a sign (11:16) was probably motivated by more than mere curiosity or hankering after something supernatural. It may well have represented a malicious strategy to have Jesus officially labeled a false prophet. Jesus was teaching things his enemies considered false. If he now used signs to bolster his authority (his fake authority, from their point of view), he would deserve the death penalty (see Deuteronomy 13:5).

There is a lot at stake in these responses to Jesus. Let's observe how he reacts to them.

Jesus and the Powers of Evil (11:17-26)

Some observers charge Jesus with casting out demons in satanic power. In 11:15, Beelzebul is called "the prince of demons"; here we get just the name, which mimics that of a pagan god mentioned in 2 Kings 1:2, 3, 6 and 16. The name meant "lord of the flies" but it was then later modified to "lord of dung." Presumably, Jesus's critics use it as an alternate name for Satan.

It would, of course, be illogical for Satan to drive out Satan, as Jesus points out in 11:17-18. That would be a recipe for disaster. In 11:19, Jesus says his present opponents will be judged by their own followers: if their followers indeed cast out demons (as Jesus seems to concede), it must be in God's power, for that is the only power that can defeat Satan. But if they do it in God's power, then they are on the same side of the cosmic battle as Jesus himself. And that, in turn, implies that those now rejecting Jesus are on Satan's side.

The most important saying in this section is Jesus's own alternative explanation of his authoritative ministry: he is bringing in God's kingdom (11:20). In saying this, Jesus makes clear that God's kingdom is not merely some future heaven, or some internal piety or some moral teaching. It is the powerful in-breaking of God which defeats the powers of evil and restores creation to God's original purposes.

Verses 21-26 expand Jesus's teaching about his own participation in God's victory over the powers of evil. Jesus is the "stronger one" (11:22) who renders the "strong one" (Satan) powerless. Mark's version refers to "plundering Satan's house" (Mark 3:27). Luke's version describes a military victory.

I recall the tour I enjoyed recently of the longest fortress in the world, the "Burg" in Burghausen, Bavaria. More than a kilometer long and containing multiple levels of security, it was so impregnable, it stopped Napoleon's armies. Satan's fortress and his weaponry are more powerful than those that stopped Napoleon. But Jesus is infinitely more powerful than Napoleon – and Satan.

Jesus's parable assures us he is about the business of dismantling Satan's weapons and his power. The end result is a redistribution of what Satan has amassed, the victims he has held captive, the possessions he and those on his side have hoarded. Jesus came to decimate the power of evil and make God's good gifts available to all in need. And so God's kingdom advances, as Jesus wields the "finger of God" (see 11:20) to rescue, free and heal this fallen and suffering world.

Verse 23 appears to contradict an earlier saying of Jesus: "Whoever is not against you is for you" (9:50). But that was in the context of narrow-minded disciples trying to keep God's authority inside their own small circle. Against that attitude, Jesus will always call for openness and acceptance.

Here, in the context is spiritual battle, Jesus says, "Whoever is not with me is against me." There are two sides, and one cannot participate on both of them. This is a call to examine our response to Jesus. In the end, we do not want to find ourselves fighting against the one who will rule God's creation.

Verses 24-26 point out that the deliverance Jesus brings must result in true conversion, true discipleship, a brand new life. Those who experience God's gracious intervention, whether that be in healing, in deliverance or in any other way, are called to participate in the kingdom work Jesus is doing. A response of apathy makes us vulnerable to those things from which Jesus already freed us. Indeed, "the final condition of that person is worse than the first" (11:26).

Who is Blessed? (11:27-28)

> *As Jesus was saying these things, a woman in the crowd called out, "Blessed is the mother who gave you birth and nursed you."*
> *He replied, "Blessed rather are those who hear the word of God and obey it." (11:27-28)*

The "amazement" Luke refers to in 11:14 is here expressed: an unnamed woman blurts out a double compliment – for Jesus's mother, but of course also for Jesus. How blessed must that person be who gave birth to, and who nurtured, someone as great as you, Jesus! Surprisingly, perhaps, Jesus challenges the claim. It is not that he is denying Mary's blessedness, a theme Luke has been at pains to develop (see comments on 1:42, 45, 48). Mary is indeed blessed, but she is blessed for a different reason than this woman claims. Mary is blessed because she is a model of one who heard God's Word and who obeyed. And that means that every other person can share in that same blessedness. Jesus creates a family of brothers and sisters and mothers (8:21). Each of us, regardless of gender, or family status, regardless of the fame or infamy of our parents or children, can be blessed – by hearing God's Word and doing it.

In Jesus's world and in Luke's world, this would be a powerful word for women in particular. Their blessedness does not depend on the men they are attached to (father, husband, son), but on their own personal response to the call of God.

The Sign of Jonah (11:29-32)

Luke does not explain the "sign of Jonah" as Matthew's Gospel does (see Matthew 12:40). In Luke, there is no clear focus on the three days of Jesus's death matching the time Jonah spent in the belly of a fish, nor on the rescue each of them experienced. Here the focus seems to be on Jonah's role as a prophet calling for repentance. It is as if Jesus were saying, "You want a sign from me? Actually, I have come to call you to repent. Do that and you will find all the evidence you need that my ministry is not some sinister demonic plot; it is an extension of God's kingdom."

Verses 30-32 make one basic point: with greater opportunity, there is greater responsibility. Jesus brings wiser teaching than even Solomon. Jesus's call for repentance is more authoritative than Jonah's was. If people then responded, how much more should those who hear Jesus now. If even Gentiles responded then, how much more surely should the people God called and prepared to bring the good news to them.

The Lamp of the Body (11:33-36)

The connection between 11:33-36 and what precedes may be the reference to an "evil generation" (11:29) and an "evil eye" (11:34). Or perhaps, having spoken of a surprising group of outsiders who will rise up to testify against unfaithful insiders, Jesus is calling insiders to make sure their own testimony is shining brightly.

Lamps are designed to illuminate their surroundings. They cannot do that if they are hidden. So also our eyes "bring to light" our surroundings, but they cannot do that if they are not healthy. There may also be hints in this passage that Jesus is comparing himself to the light-giving lamp. Lamps are not normally things we look at, but things we see by. Yet 11:33 indicates the lamp in view draws attention to itself. That sounds like a call to see Jesus, recognize his life-giving, light-shedding ministry and then let him light up our world, our lives and our own witness.

Alas for the Pharisees and the Experts in the Law (11:37-54)

The final section of this chapter is a long critique of those religious leaders who have not only taken their stand against Jesus, but have been leading people astray with their example and teachings. It is a strong indictment of the Pharisaic errors, though we should not conclude that all Pharisees practice all the faults Jesus here critiques. There are also well-meaning and sincere (though sometimes still misguided) Pharisees around Jesus. Both he and Luke would have known that.

Though strong critiques are included here, we should think of this more as a lament than as vindictive condemnation. The word "woe" can just as well mean "alas for." Jesus laments a whole host of Pharisaic faults.

The Pharisees pay a great deal of attention to detailed cleansing ceremonies; Jesus does not (11:37-38). Jesus critiques "externalized religion" and calls for clean hearts (11:39-40). He also calls for generosity (11:41), justice and love (11:41-42) in place of greed (11:39) and picky calculations (11:42).

Jesus critiques Pharisees for their status-seeking; they draw attention to themselves and their own honor (11:43). They give the impression that they are helping people, but actually they are defiling them unawares (like unmarked graves that made people unclean; 11:44).

Next Jesus turns to legal experts (some of these would have been Pharisees, others not). They are critiqued for prioritizing law over people and for using the law to their own advantage (11:45-46).

Next comes a critique of them and their ancestors for rejecting and killing God's prophets and then claiming to honor them by decorating their tombs. Jesus indicts this generation for rejecting God's true messengers (like John the Baptist and, of course, Jesus himself), just as their ancestors did those of old (11:47-49). He returns to the theme from 11:30-32: with greater opportunity comes greater responsibility. Those who reject Jesus now are demonstrating an even greater unfaithfulness than those who rejected the prophets from Abel to Zechariah in earlier times. Note that these two names represent the first faithful martyr (Abel; Genesis 4:8) and the last one, according to Jewish ordering of the Old Testament books (Zechariah; 2 Chronicles 24:20-21). (It looks in English as if Jesus is referring to martyrs "from A to Z," but this is pure coincidence; Z would not represent the last letter of either the Hebrew or the Greek alphabet.)

Finally, Jesus indicts the legal experts for refusing to enter God's kingdom and for trying to stop those who want to enter. Their rejection of Jesus, and their influence on others to do the same, is clearly in view (11:52).

Now that we have heard Jesus's reaction to a diverse set of responses to his teaching and ministry, we hear once more his enemies' response to him. They try to trap him, so that they can lay official charges against him (11:53-54).

So ends a long chapter with multiple important themes. Learning what it means to trust God and express it in appropriate prayer is central to our life with God, as is learning to avoid the failures of those who reject Jesus. When we have our priorities in the wrong places, when we take advantage of others and lay heavy burdens on their backs, when we reject God's messengers, we are called to hear again the sign of Jonah (Repent!). The one who brings this sign offers us participation in a kingdom that will ultimately bring down the power of evil, establishing God's rule of justice and peace.

Implications of the Text for Today

How Then Should We Pray?

Generations of Christians have heard the key to effective prayer is being persistent enough. Two parables in particular have seemed to provide biblical justification for that view. I have argued above that few interpreters today still interpret the parable of the friend at midnight as a call to persistence. When we reach 18:1-8, we will encounter another parable often so interpreted. Again I will argue that there are more appropriate ways to read the text.

But that does not eliminate the idea that the Bible teaches praying with persistence. Jesus prays fervently for three hours in Gethsemane before concluding that God's plan is clear and unavoidable (Mark 14:35-41). Paul prays three times for the "thorn in his flesh" to be removed and eventually hears God's response: "No, but I will give you grace to deal with it" (2 Corinthians 12:7-9). Elijah prays seven times before the promised rain falls (1 Kings 18:44). Daniel prays for three weeks while the heavenly messenger with God's answer battles through enemy territory to get that answer to Daniel (Daniel 10:13).

And many texts in the Gospels portray people of faith demonstrating it with a measure of persistence. Four friends tear open a roof to get their friend into Jesus's presence (Luke 5:19). A woman worms her way through a crowd, from which she is supposed to keep her distance, because she believes Jesus can heal her (Luke 8:42-44). Bartimaeus is undeterred when a crowd tries to hush his calls for Jesus's help (Mark 10:48). And of course, Paul calls Christians to "pray without ceasing" (1 Thessalonians 5:17).

Multiple texts call us to fervent and often repeated prayer. But other texts warn against thinking we can persuade God to act by our "much speaking" (Matthew 6:7-8).

In my view, if we pray persistently because it works, that can be an expression of faith. But if we pray persistently to see if we can get it to work, that usually leads to misplaced trust. (We trust our prayer techniques and our own faith, rather than our generous God.) And it often leads to distorted pictures of God (as if God needed to be persuaded to do the right thing). Finally, it often leads people to blame others whose prayers are not answered, or to carry guilt feelings themselves, when their own prayers are not answered as they wish.

"Prayer without ceasing" is about continuous communion with God and constant dependence on God; it is not about trying to outlast God, get God to change his mind or "prove our seriousness" to a God who already knows what we need and knows our hearts as well.

Multiple Causes of Illness and Infirmity

In 11:14, Luke tells us Jesus drives out a "demon that was mute." Only after the man was delivered of that spirit could he speak again. This of course raises questions about the relationship between physical infirmities and the power of evil. In one sense, Satan's power really is behind all suffering and evil. Satan is the one whose destructive work infects all of creation. Yet there are certainly many situations where a specific incident of illness or infirmity cannot be linked to any specific "demon." That should be clear even from Luke's own Gospel.

In Luke 1, we read about another man who was mute, but that had nothing to do with Satan's power. It was God's punishment (or at least a form of discipline) on the priest Zechariah. In every age, there are numerous sick, disabled or injured people whose condition has nothing to do with specific demons or with God's punishment. They are simply the unfortunate victims of things that go wrong in a fallen world. Whatever the cause, God does at times provide surprising miraculous interventions, whether or not we specifically pray for them. More often people's conditions are alleviated by medical interventions. And often people have no options but to live with physical challenges in their lives, until the day when all God's promises are fulfilled.

Jesus's healing miracles, the times he made the blind to see, the deaf to hear, the mute to speak and the lame to walk, were signs and symbols, foretastes of the world to come. When it happened to a man in 11:14, "the crowd was amazed." Why of course! They had just witnessed how God, through Jesus, demonstrated mastery over evil forces, and thus also prefigured a healed creation.

The Center of the Law

In this chapter, Jesus critiques the Pharisees for not prioritizing "justice and the love of God" (11:42). Already in the Old Testament, we find multiple indications that a narrow focus on the details of the law is far less important than such things as faithfully walking with God (Jeremiah 7:21-23), steadfast love and knowledge of God (Hosea 6:6), doing justice, loving kindness and walking humbly with God (Micah 6:8) and, when we fall short in these priorities, coming to God with a broken and contrite heart (Psalm 51:16, 17).

The New Testament continues this theme. Love is highlighted everywhere, most centrally in Jesus's unequivocal statements that loving God and loving neighbor are central to the whole law (Matthew 22:37-39; Mark 12:29-31; Luke 10:27). For Paul, it is love that fulfills the law (Romans 13:8) and that supersedes spiritual gifts in importance and permanence (1 Corinthians 12:31 - 13:13). For James, love is the "royal law" (James 2:8). For John, love encompasses everything old and new (1 John 2:7-11).

In his teaching, Jesus highlights the more important matters of the law – "justice, mercy and faithfulness" (see Matthew 23:23) and in this section of Luke, "justice and the love of God" (Luke 11:42). Faithful Christian practice does not consist of compiling and fulfilling long lists of dos and don'ts. The law's many details were never designed to become final authorities on every aspect of human behavior. They were designed to support the higher priorities God establishes for our relationships with God, with each other in the faith community and with neighbors – including our enemies – in a hurting world. Where specific aspects of the law conflict with God's highest priorities for our lives, they can be safely set aside, as Jesus demonstrated with respect to cleansing ceremonies (11:38) and Sabbath rules (6:1-5).

Burdens of the Law

In 11:46, Jesus critiques legal experts for loading people down with burdens they could hardly bear. Yet the legal experts themselves were always able to find ways around the more demanding expectations of God's law. An example of what they did has been preserved in literature outside the New Testament, as reported by Leon Morris:

> On the Sabbath, they taught, a man may not carry a burden "in his right hand or in his left hand, in his bosom, or on his shoulder." But he may carry it "on the back of his hand, or with his foot or with his mouth or with his elbow, or in his ear or in his hair or in his wallet (carried) mouth downwards, or between his wallet and his shirt, or in the hem of his shirt, or in his shoe or in his sandal" (*Shabbat* 10:3). Multiply this by all the regulations of the Law and ordinary people have a burden beyond bearing even to know what they might do and might not do. But there is also a multitude of loopholes for a lawyer who knew the traditions which enable him to do pretty well what he wished. (205f)

Jesus, by contrast, opposed loading laws on people's backs. In fact, he modeled a significant disregard for the things that did not matter much, like countless washing ceremonies (11:38). At other times, he counseled conformity with the rules but urged people not to neglect the far more important things (11:42). Jesus came to set people free, not only from sin, not only from satanic oppression, not only from abusive religious leaders, but even from the burden of the law itself.

Personal Reflection Questions

- Have you experienced pressure from others to pray more persistently or guilt for not meeting your own highs standards of "prayer persistence"? How does the first part of this chapter help reshape your thinking about prayer and "how it works"?
- What do you see as advantages or as dangers when people try hard to discern spiritual forces behind physical events – like claiming to know that "Satan caused this infirmity" or "God is the one who designed this for you"? What are the positives and pitfalls of concluding that sometimes things "just happen" – directly or indirectly claiming that there is no rhyme or reason to what we experience?
- In your experience, does the church overemphasize "legal obedience" – burdening participants with heavy loads, as Jesus said the legal experts did in their day? Or has the church swung to an extreme on the other side, where God's law is scarcely considered, as each of us does what seems right in our own eyes? What are the keys to finding an appropriate balance between rules and freedom? Between personal decisions and community accountability?

Living Faithfully, Serving and Waiting

The Text: Luke 12:1 - 13:9 NIV

The Flow and Form of the Text

The first 12 verses of this section introduce a series of loosely connected topics, but weaving through them is the theme of "final accounting." God is the one who will judge rightly – will make all things right in the end. For that reason, we live with integrity, we witness with courage and we serve generously in this life. God is the one who aids us now and guarantees our future. We have no reason to fear!

And so the theme of the rest of this section is introduced. We are called to live faithfully while we serve God and others, and while we wait for God to make all things right. Faithfulness is expressed in many ways, but Luke emphasizes the generous sharing of our resources. Serving is also expressed in many ways, but this section of Luke emphasizes watchfulness, obeying our master and serving our fellow servants. Waiting does not mean trying to figure out when the master of the house will return. We are not on the lookout for signs that relieve us of the need to be faithful at all times. Waiting means confidently trusting God will make all things right and will richly repay us for sacrifices we made along the way.

Throughout this section, we need to remember God's kingdom is both "already" and "not yet." We live by its values today; we experience its fullness in eternity. We enjoy God's generous care already; we know the final reward is coming.

Throughout this passage, we see glimpses of the historical crisis Jesus saw up ahead for the people of Israel. If they choose to confront Rome's military might, they could expect only disaster. And this becomes a symbol of the greater folly of opposing God and God's kingdom; there is also disaster at the end of that road for those who reject Jesus and the Holy Spirit Jesus will send.

Apart from occasional times someone poses a question or comment, this section consists entirely of Jesus's teaching. There are warnings and encouragements, instruction and new revelation, parables and imagery and symbolism. All this material is embedded in the journey that began at 9:51. As Jesus makes his way toward Jerusalem, where he will be killed and rise again, he teaches his disciples what it means to take up their crosses and to anticipate the glory that will be theirs, when the discipleship road reaches its final destination.

Outline:

Warnings and Encouragements (12:1-12)
The Parable of the Rich Fool (12:13-21)
Do Not Worry (12:22-34)
Watchfulness and Service (12:35-48)
Not Peace but Division (12:49-53)
Interpreting the Times (12:54-59)
Repent or Perish (13:1-9)

The Text Explained

Warnings and Encouragements (12:1-12)

Luke introduces various audiences: there are thousands in the crowd (12:1a), yet Jesus first addresses his disciples (12:1b). Later, individuals in the crowd demand Jesus's assistance (12:13), so Jesus turns his attention back to the crowds (12:16, 54). Later still, he turns back to teach the disciples (12:22). It is hard to keep track of which audience Jesus is addressing, as Peter himself acknowledges (12:41). Luke apparently envisions multiple audiences on the stage at the same time, with the spotlight shifting from one character group to another. All are listening in, even when they are not directly addressed.

Jesus's initial teaching of the disciples has diverse components:

Do not be two-faced like the Pharisees. Live lives of integrity and openness. True, some things remain undisclosed for now, but that is only because the time is not yet right for open proclamation (12:1-3).

The only one whom disciples should "fear" is God, the one who will preside at the last judgment (12:4-7). If we are confident of God's final judgment in our favor, we can with courage face even those who have the power to take our present lives. Notice the quotation marks around "fear" above. Just two verses after Jesus tells his followers whom to fear, he says, "Fear not!" (12:7). There is an appropriate "fear" (awe, respect, deference) that recognizes the awesome power of God, and God's right to final judgment. And that kind of "fear" casts out fear of mere mortals (see Psalm 56:11). Yes, God has the power of life and death, but if we belong to Jesus, God is always on our side. The one who cares about every sparrow and counts the hairs on our head can be trusted to take care of us, even when persecution is inevitable!

"Hell" in 12:5 is actually a reference to "Gehenna" (in Greek *geenna*; in Hebrew *gehinnom*, translated "Valley of Hinnom"). This was a valley where pagan peoples had once performed child sacrifices (see 2 Kings 23:10). The Jews considered it permanently desecrated and therefore selected it as an appropriate location for the largest garbage dump in the region. Jesus uses Jerusalem's dump as a symbol for the final destiny of those who reject Jesus.

> *"I tell you, whoever publicly acknowledges me before others, the Son of Man will also acknowledge before the angels of God. But whoever disowns me before others will be disowned before the angels of God. And everyone who speaks a word against the Son of Man will be forgiven, but anyone who blasphemes against the Holy Spirit will not be forgiven." (12:8-10)*

Our present response to Jesus will have eternal consequences. If we acknowledge Jesus, he will acknowledge us; if we disown Jesus, he will disown us. And then comes the puzzling verse about the "unforgiveable sin." It sounds as if it is a minor infraction to blaspheme against Jesus; just don't try it against the Holy Spirit! But that is not likely what this text means.

In Acts 3:17, this same writer Luke refers to his fellow Jews as "acting in ignorance" when they rejected Jesus. But now that God had raised Jesus from the dead and poured out the Holy Spirit, the apostles are calling them to change their verdict about Jesus. In other words, they can be forgiven *now* for *previously* speaking against the Son of Man. But if they reject the Holy Spirit's prompting to change their previous verdict about Jesus, they will be rejecting, fully and finally, Jesus himself – and he is the only means by which their sins can be forgiven.

If that is what Jesus's reference to "blasphemy against the Holy Spirit" means, then what he is really saying is this: people can be forgiven of anything through Jesus, except for the sin of refusing to receive that forgiveness.

12:11-12: This section ends with assurances for Jesus's disciples that in times of difficulty the Holy Spirit will be present to help them.

The Parable of the Rich Fool (12:13-21)

Jesus's teaching is interrupted by someone who tries to draw him into a family dispute about an inheritance. Justice is, of course, an important theme for Jesus, and likewise for Luke, the evangelist. The complainer naturally assumes Jesus will judge fairly. What he does not take into account is that "fairness" is trumped by "generosity" in the values of God's kingdom. So Jesus addresses the underlying problem – greed. He challenges the very idea that we are justified in claiming for ourselves what is rightfully ours. Rather we should share with others.

The parable that follows makes that very point. A successful (but greedy) farmer has a problem. He does not have large enough granaries to store his bumper crop. Jesus then builds into the parable a soliloquy – that means the parable teller divulges what the central character is thinking. In Jesus's parables, a soliloquy usually signals the perspective of that character is dead wrong. That is the case here. What might seem like good business practice Jesus harshly critiques; the character's thinking is completely inconsistent with the values of God's kingdom.

The farmer's plan to replace his granaries with larger ones signals his greed; he is hoarding for himself what Jesus would have expected him to share with others. But he is probably also aiming to do something else. He is trying to manipulate the market, storing grain when it is plentiful (and thus prices drop) so that he can take advantage of market conditions (and of the poor) when crops are poor and prices high.

In Jesus's parable, the voice of God breaks into the self talk of the greedy farmer. He might well have used great "business wisdom," but he is called a fool. He thinks he is planning for his future ("plenty of grain laid up for many years, take life easy") but God says he is not planning well enough nor far enough ahead. Life is uncertain, and his eternal destiny is on shaky ground!

When God's voice says, "This very night your life will be demanded from you," it is not self-evident what form of demise awaits him. Some interpreters think a tenant revolt will end the life of this greedy manipulator; others read it as God's hand of judgment. I think it is deliberately left open-ended, so that it can apply to both of the above possibilities. For that reason, it also applies to all who succeed in living comfortably with their hoarded wealth, but will one day have to give an account before God.

This passage began with Jesus refusing to cast present judgment (12:14) and it ends with the warning that God will one day demand final accounting (12:21). We will observe throughout this whole section of Luke how present and future judgments are often contrasted and sometimes combined. The implication of this passage is that we are to live by the radically counter-cultural (and counter-capitalist) values of God's kingdom in this in-between time. When we do, as Jesus has already made clear, we need not fear people, and our proper "fear" of our final Judge will leave us with no reason to fear at all (see 12:5-7).

Do Not Worry (12:22-34)

Instead of hoarding (see previous section), followers of Jesus trust God to meet all their needs. Only when we learn to trust can we truly "seek God's kingdom first" (see 12:31). And when we seek God's kingdom first, our trust in God is met with God's gracious provision.

Jesus lists (and sometimes explains) multiple reasons worry is either unnecessary or misguided. Yes, we have legitimate physical needs, but worrying about them is not the way to take them into account. We should not read this passage as though worry is *condemned*; this is not about adding guilt trips to our worries. Rather, Jesus is supplying words of assurance, helpful perspectives, reality checks, and along the way, some very practical advice.

12:22-23: Jesus's first point is that the mundane matters of food and clothing are not our ultimate concerns. That does not mean they are unimportant, and certainly it does not mean that we should be unconcerned when we or others do not have enough to eat. Rather, those of us who have enough to spare should guard against hoarding food (see previous passage) and overstocking our wardrobes. There are more important things in life.

12:24: We are more valuable than birds! We are God's own children (see the references to "Father" in verses 30 and 32). If God cares for birds, how much more will our loving Father care for his own children.

12:25-26: These verses seem to say: worry may be natural, but it really does not get us anywhere. Worrying is more likely to shorten our lives than lengthen them! Again, Jesus is not trying to shame or condemn those who struggle with worry. He is giving us resources and strategies for learning to trust instead.

12:27-28: Jesus used ravens as examples of creatures God feeds. Now he uses lilies as examples of God's generous provision of "clothing." These illustrations need to be examined with care. They are certainly not designed to teach that humans need not do anything at all and God will simply give us our food and our clothing.

Jesus lists numerous things ravens do not do – sow, reap, store (12:24) – but they still have to go find food. Lilies do nothing at all, and yet God cares for them (12:27a, 28). How do these illustrations teach humans not to worry? They remind us that all creatures (ravens, lilies, humans) do what God has equipped and designed for us to do, and that ultimately God cares for all our needs.

Ravens do not sow or reap or store grain. Does that mean humans should not do these things? Not at all. Ravens are hunters and gatherers. That is how their needs are met. Lilies are not hunters and gatherers. They do not wander around the field looking for better soil or sufficient water. They stand there and God supplies what they need. If birds tried that, they would starve.

Humans can do more than both lilies and ravens. We do not merely stand there like lilies. Nor do we only hunt and gather like ravens. If we mimicked the activities of the ravens, we would starve; if we mimicked the non-activity of the lilies, we would be without clothing. We plant, we reap, we store, we labor, we spin – and we should. Yet only God can ultimately make crops grow and provide the raw materials from which we make clothing. We do what we can and trust God to do what we cannot control.

While learning this lesson, let's make sure we do not forget the previous text (12:13-21). There is also a limit to how much we should store: when God gives us more than we need, it is for sharing!

I wonder if everyone would agree with Jesus that lilies are more beautifully dressed than Solomon was (12:27b). I suppose it depends on our value systems. Those who think extravagant fashion statements measure one's worth would no doubt scoff at Jesus's suggestion. Jesus's proposal that lilies are more beautiful challenges us to adopt kingdom perspectives.

12:29-31 are really the heart of this passage.

> *"And do not set your heart on what you will eat or drink; do not worry about it. For the pagan world runs after all such things, and your Father knows that you need them. But seek his kingdom, and these things will be given to you as well." (12:29-31)*

Jesus is contrasting the priorities that so often characterize this world's value systems with those that should characterize his followers. Seeking God's kingdom does not mean ignoring physical needs and focusing only on spiritual needs (as if these could be so neatly separated!). Rather, by pursuing God's priorities – contentment, trust, generosity – we not only help care for other people's needs for physical sustenance, but we learn to trust God to use other people (and sometimes even surprising divine interventions) to help meet ours.

> *"Do not be afraid, little flock, for your Father has been pleased to give you the kingdom. Sell your possessions and give to the poor. Provide purses for yourselves that will not wear out, a treasure in heaven that will never fail, where no thief comes near and no moth destroys. For where your treasure is, there your heart will be also." (12:32-34)*

The mixture of metaphors in 12:32 is quite characteristic of Jesus's teaching. We are God's flock, God's family, God's kingdom citizens. So God is for us a Shepherd, a Father, a King. As shepherds ensure their flocks' needs are met (see Psalm 23:1), so also does our God. As fathers care for their children (see 11:11-13), so also does our God. As kings assure the safety and welfare of their subjects (well, at least a godly king would!), so also does our God. An appropriate response is to trust God and prioritize those things that belong to God's flock/family/kingdom.

When we do, we will be investing our resources in ways that lay up treasure in heaven, where it is eternally secure. And when we do that, our hearts will be in the right place.

Watchfulness and Service (12:35-48)

Just as the previous passage mixed its metaphors (God is Shepherd, Father and King; see 12:32), so also does this passage. Jesus draws portraits of the Son of Man (see 12:40) that range from a master returning from a banquet (12:36), to a house owner guarding against robbery (12:39), to the thief himself coming at an unexpected time (12:40). Each image serves to teach its own lessons.

12:35-38: As servants await the return of a master who has just attended a wedding, they are dressed for service and keep their lamps burning. The point is that at all points of day or night, they are ready to serve their master. Yet surprisingly, when the master arrives, they do not serve him; *he serves them* (12:37). And so once again, Jesus, and Luke after him, insert hints that in God's kingdom, things are not like they are in the so-called "real world." We live faithfully by serving God, serving others, waiting in readiness for the master to return. And then we find the master becomes the servant, and we are motivated again to serve all the more faithfully.

12:39: The point of this verse is that no one can know the arrival time of a thief in advance. Those whose service to the house owner helps keep the house secure – those who watch or guard – must be faithfully at their posts *all the time*. The point is not to figure out when the thief will come but to serve without interruption.

12:40: Here the perspective shifts again. Now the Son of Man is compared, not to the one who owns the house, but to the thief who arrives at an unknown time. The Son of Man's arrival will be just as unannounced as the arrival of a thief. The lesson is that by serving the house owner at all times (12:39), we are ready for the final accounting at the end of the age (12:40).

The reference to the unpredictable arrival of the Son of Man clearly speaks of the final return of Jesus at the end of the age. That event might be sooner than we think. Or it might be delayed longer than we expect. It is not our task to try to figure out which is more likely. We are to be ready at every moment, and this passage teaches that readiness means watching and serving.

The rest of the passage does not narrowly focus only on the moment of the Son of Man's *final return*. Times of accounting recur in our service for Jesus. Our Master may show up at any moment (and often does!) to guide our service for him, and to serve us as well. And there are many thieves eager to break in whenever we are not vigilant.

12:41-46: Peter's question introduces a new issue, that of "servant leadership." The parable (or parables) Jesus has just told apply to everyone. But they have a special application to Jesus's own disciples, whom he is training to be leaders. So Jesus now distinguishes between ordinary servants and managers. Both groups work for the master, but the managers have special responsibilities to care for and facilitate the services of the others. That is how leadership in God's kingdom works.

The danger, of course, is that managers may take advantage of their leadership positions, either by abusing their power or by pursuing selfish desires. Jesus warns against both of these. Jesus also points toward diverse possible outcomes. Those who serve faithfully will be promoted to greater authority: they will be given even greater opportunities to serve. Those who abuse their positions will be "chopped in pieces." What an ominous image! Jesus is a master of metaphors. He can use the Jerusalem garbage dump (see 12:5) or the slaughterhouse (see 12:46) with equal effect. The point is that there will be significant consequences, for good and for ill, depending on how faithfully we lead and serve. And once more, Jesus makes clear that the time of the final accounting is completely unknowable, and therefore we are called to unbroken faithfulness.

12:47-48: This long passage ends by making this point: with

greater opportunity comes greater responsibility – and therefore also greater consequences if one is unfaithful. The disciples have been called into positions of responsibility. To prepare them for it, Jesus has given them extra instruction: now they will be held accountable for faithful service and leadership. So will we.

Not Peace but Division (12:49-53)

We read that Jesus will undergo the "baptism" of a violent death. He is prepared to give his life for the world he came to save; in fact, this is a major priority of his mission. It is the "constraint" he is under. But why is his death necessary? Luke's Gospel does not present detailed theological analyses of how Jesus's death on the cross accomplishes what theologians call "the atonement."

What is clear in this passage is that there must be a "baptism" before there can be "fire on the earth." That means Jesus's death will bring in the time of salvation, and only after that will come the judgment. In this context, the image of fire must refer to divine judgment. Yet we should not immediately think only of the "fires of hell." Fire is also a purifying agent, and God's judgment is ultimately God "making things right." So while there are real consequences for rejecting Jesus, the focus is regularly on God's intent to restore what has gone wrong with creation because of sin and its consequences.

It will be through death that death will be defeated, for Jesus has already predicted that after he is killed, he will be raised (9:22). Paradoxically, through that which is so wrong (the rejection and execution of an innocent man), God will make things right.

Jesus came to bring peace (see 1:79; 2:14). Yet this text acknowledges that where people reject the way of peace, there will be division. Division is not God's goal but the inevitable result of the free choice God gives people to accept or reject offers of grace. Jesus uses the example of family division. Jesus is clear the call to follow him supersedes any other call; that loyalty to him supersedes any other loyalty.

Interpreting the Times (12:54-59)

12:54-56: When Jesus first spoke these words, he likely referred primarily to the contemporary political situation. Israel was a conquered people ruled by the oppressive machinery of Rome's taxation system and military might. Jesus's contemporaries were frustrated by the injustice and they longed for the "liberation" they believed God had promised them. Violent clashes flared and were harshly subdued by Rome's might.

While some call for violent revolt, Jesus calls his hearers to love their enemies (6:35). In this text, he warns them they are a lot better at predicting weather changes than at understanding "this present time" – the time of political tension and the disasters to which it will inevitably lead if Israel will not learn "the way of peace" (see 19:42).

Luke, who almost certainly writes after Jesus's predictions of Jerusalem's destruction by the Romans had come true, sees in this text a further reference to the ultimate judgment God will send on those who do not recognize or accept God's offers of peace.

Does that mean Luke either misinterpreted or misrepresented Jesus? Not at all! Jesus himself always saw in the judgments of history images for, and at times, the first stages of God's final judgments. That is clearly the case with the predicted destruction of the temple and the holy city (see 21:6, 21-28). Jesus interpreted these as God's hand of judgment on those who had rejected their Messiah. If they do not bring in the final judgment, they at least point toward it and teach lessons that apply to it. Luke draws out these lessons.

12:57-59: The same can be said for these verses: Jesus's primary reference is to reconciling differences in interpersonal disputes, settling "out of court," choosing the restorative justice that characterizes God's kingdom rather than the retributive justice of this world's legal systems. At the same time, however, this text calls us to choose the way of peace before it is too late, before "the judge" imposes ultimate justice.

Peacemaking and ultimate justice (to make things right) are

what Jesus's ministry is all about – in interpersonal relationships, in Israel's existence within the Roman Empire, in terms of the whole world and all its peoples within the larger plan of God, the righteous judge, to restore creation.

Repent or Perish (13:1-9)

13:1-5: These verses address the difficult theological issue of God's justice (often called theodicy). This is a topic theologians wrestle with, but so do ordinary believers. Truth is, biblical writers wrestled with it as well. The Bible gives perspectives on it, but not clear ultimate answers.

In this world, there certainly appears to be an unfair distribution of suffering and evil. Disasters happen; perhaps in a fallen world, they are inevitable. But there does not seem to be anything "fair" about them. Are those who suffer most always those who have deserved it most, as some claim? Jesus responds to that proposal with an emphatic "No!" (13:3, 5). At the same time, he calls for repentance, as if that were a way to avoid perishing! So are disasters punishment for sin or not?

It all seems paradoxical, but if we remember the themes developed above and the geopolitical situation into which Jesus spoke, it makes good sense as well. No, it is not possible to guarantee immunity from calamity – whether natural disasters, accidents or human atrocities – by repenting or by being "less guilty" than others. But in the final judgment, those who have repented and received God's grace will be secure! We remember Jesus's words in 12:4: "Do not be afraid of those who kill the body and after that can do no more." Those who are right with God are ultimately secure, even if tyrants strike or towers fall.

But two more things must be said. First, this does not mean we should be lax about building codes, construction inspections, earthquake preparedness, political and religious conflict and terrorism, and everything else that goes into minimizing the risk of "towers falling." And it does not mean that tyrants should be given free rein to "mix the blood of their subjects with sacrifices." We work for justice. We work for safety. We work for *shalom*. And we recognize that until Jesus comes to restore creation, our efforts will never bring about a perfect world. When disasters still happen, we neither blame God nor claim that those who suffer somehow deserved it more than others.

Second, the two incidents cited here – mixing blood with sacrifices (making martyrs out of worshippers) and towers falling – indicate Jesus has at least one eye on the political tensions of the day, when Rome martyred the faithful and the demolition of Israel and its temple was on the horizon. The lessons go beyond that situation, especially for Luke who writes after these things happen. But just as the preceding verses see ultimate realities reflected in local political situations, so do these.

Jesus is calling Israel to repent of its headlong rush toward rebellion and its mistaken dreams of national liberation. If they do not turn away from that wrong path, "they will all perish" – the innocent with the guilty – when many new martyrs suffer and towers fall on the unsuspecting.

The fact that Jesus's warnings were, for the most part, not heeded, and that his prophecies of future destruction came true in AD 67-70 highlights the urgency of the warnings, in Jesus's day, in Luke's day and in ours. We too are called to repent, to work for peace and to rest secure in our ultimate destiny with God, until that day when atrocities and disasters are no more.

13:6-9: Like much of the preceding material, this parable speaks to the immediate situation Jesus and his hearers face, but also to all people everywhere, until the final accounting when God comes to judge and save.

A vineyard owner is eager to maximize his profits and does not want to waste effort and soil on an unproductive tree. But the caretaker of the land and its trees appeals for more time. He is eager to give it more attention, and he hopes to turn things around. Yet he acknowledges that a day of judgment is coming.

This is a word of warning for those who have not yet responded to the call of Jesus – time is running out; a judgment day is coming. And it is a word of warning to the nation that has been called repeatedly to abandon its foolhardy rush toward war with Rome. The time will come when they will be swiftly cut down!

We should certainly see in the vineyard worker an image of Jesus, working tirelessly and patiently to turn things around. But we should be cautious about assuming the vineyard owner is somehow an exact picture of God. Luke does not paint a picture of a patient, gracious Jesus trying to change the mind of an impatient, vengeful God. Reading this parable as if it says that is reading too much into the imagery.

In fact, while it is appropriate to see glimpses of God in the "lead characters" of many parables (the landowners, kings, bridegrooms, judges, shepherds, etc.), we should never think of these as exact replicas. They invite us to reflect on the ways in which God is like or unlike these characters.

No, God is not eager to root out trees that fail to produce; rather, God is eager to tend to unproductive trees, work with them and lead them to productivity. But yes, God knows that one cannot sit on the fence forever. There is a time of accounting ahead. Those who respond to the initiatives of Jesus will ultimately abide and bear fruit; those who do not will ultimately perish. That is true for Israel as a nation in its relationships with Rome. It is also true for each of us in relation to God.

Implications of the Text for Today

The "Unforgiveable Sin"

Luke 12:10 refers to blasphemy against the Holy Spirit as a sin that cannot be forgiven. I suggested above that this sin is really the sin of rejecting Jesus. Choosing against Jesus is a sin against the Holy Spirit because one of the Spirit's primary roles is to lead people to accept Jesus's offer of forgiveness. I. Howard Marshall defines this sin as "the conscious and wicked rejection of the saving power and grace of God towards man" (*Commentary on Luke*, 517).

In other words, you cannot be forgiven for rejecting the means of forgiveness!

At any rate, the oft-repeated pastoral advice is probably valid. If anyone worries they might have committed the unforgiveable sin, that is in itself sufficient proof they have not. It demonstrates that the Holy Spirit is still at work within them.

Not Peace but Division

Jesus lived in a hierarchical and patriarchal world. Men made religious choices for their entire extended families. Jesus, however, calls individuals, male and female, to make personal choices for or against his offer of grace and his call to discipleship. That may well result in divided families, as some accept Jesus and others reject him.

In comparison to others in Jesus's time and place, he was radically individualistic. He called people to make personal decisions. That might even mean choosing against "father and mother, wife and children, brothers and sisters" (see 14:26). It might mean leaving "home or wife or brothers or sisters or parents or children for the sake of the kingdom of God" (18:29). It might mean being "betrayed by parents, brothers and sisters, relatives and friends" (21:16). The call of Jesus takes precedence over family ties.

Yet Jesus would never have endorsed the runaway individualism of our modern and post-modern Western cultures. For Jesus, leaving one's family did not mean being alone, unattached, a singular individual. It meant joining a vastly more secure, loving and all-encompassing family, where all who follow Jesus are brothers and sisters, where Jesus claims as mother and brothers all who "hear God's word and put it into practice" (8:21).

How blessed are those whose natural families join them in their participation in the family of God. And what a challenge it is for us as Christian churches to truly be family for those who do not have supportive families or whose families oppose their participation in the family of Jesus.

Theodicy

Alongside arguments *for* the existence of God throughout history, there is one argument often formulated *against* God's existence: the problem of evil (often called the theodicy argument).

The argument goes like this: People claim God is all-knowing, all-powerful and good. But if such a God existed, there would be no evil, since an all-knowing God would *know how* to prevent evil, an all-powerful God would *be able* to prevent evil and a good God would *want to* do so. Therefore, the undeniable fact of evil proves no such God exists.

Some responses to this argument deny the existence of evil; some claim evil is a necessary condition for there to be good; some claim that after creating beings with a free will, even an all-powerful God is unable to prevent the possibility of evil. The Scriptures do not give any comprehensive logical responses to the problem of evil. Even though various texts in Scripture have been enlisted to support each of three above attempts at dealing with the problem, Scripture does not clearly refute the argument by any of those means. It does something else.

Scripture gives glimpses of how evil entered God's good creation. It presents evil as an intruder Jesus defeated through his death and resurrection, an intruder Jesus will eliminate through the restoration of God's creation when he comes again.

So Scripture does something more important and more satisfying than wrestle with the logical problems of the existence of evil. It gives reasons for confidence that evil will not have the last word. That is the Christian hope. In fact, God goes even further: promising that even though evil and suffering may not be distributed "fairly" or equally in this life, life with God in eternity will more than make up for anything people have unjustly suffered in this life.

Holding on to these great promises accomplishes more to sustain Christian confidence and endurance than any philosophical discussion could. God is good and always does what is right; one day, God's goodness will be fully revealed.

Judgments within History and Judgments at the End of History

Frequently, Old Testament prophets declared political and military defeats and what we call natural disasters were actually the hand of God coming in judgment. And Jesus is clear that the destruction of Jerusalem and its temple, which he foretells, would be more than Rome's revenge; it would be God's response to power brokers in Israel who rejected their Messiah and the way of peace he proclaimed, and who led the nation down the wrong path as a result.

Yet, we today should be very cautious about claiming to know how the hand of God is related to political, military and natural disasters in our world. How quickly people claim to know what moral or religious failures have called down God's judgment when tsunamis or terrorists, earthquakes or hurricanes strike. These pronouncements often sound more like propaganda for some moral, political or military campaign than the results of careful discernment.

Of course, there is a sense in which we often reap what we sow. When our political, economic or military policies alienate and oppress, and when those who know no other means of self-defense strike back with violence, an element of "judgment" is at play. That does not ever justify acts of terrorism, but it should call us to examine our own contributions to the world's peace – or to its violence.

If, in fact, hurricanes and floods become much more frequent as a result of humans polluting the air and depleting the ozone layer, then the added suffering such "natural disasters" bring is a form of judgment, or at least, a consequence of wrong choices. Sometimes we too need to repent to make sure we do not all perish (see 13:3, 5).

Insurance companies sometimes call natural disasters "acts of God." Without the prophetic authority of the writers of Scripture, we should not quickly assign blame, neither to God nor to the victims of disaster. Along with Jesus, we should deny that those directly affected were "more guilty than all the others" (12:3, 5). We should work for peace and justice, we should be there to support victims of disaster, whether "natural" or of human making, and we should live in such a way that bears witness to the promised future restoration of all things.

Personal Reflection Questions

- Where have you experienced, either in your own life or in the lives of others in your Christian community, the family divisions that sometimes happens when individuals choose to follow Jesus's call to discipleship and mission? How has the Christian community supported you or others where that has occurred?
- The primary meaning of judgment in the Bible is "making things right." Though life often seems unfair, God will one day judge justly. Where have you experienced life as unfair? How does the promise of Scripture that God will one day reveal his justice and abolish evil encourage you? What questions do you still have about "the problem of evil"?
- How do you understand the relationships between natural disasters, the natural consequences of human choices and "acts of God" as a form of judgment? Do you believe God is directly involved in disasters that cause suffering? Why or why not?

Who is in the Kingdom?

The Text: Luke 13:10 - 15:32 NIV

The Flow and Form of the Text

Luke rarely develops only one theme at a time. When we supply titles for sections that span several chapters, we are attempting to capture at least one of the main themes present in those chapters, recognizing that other themes will be present as well.

For this section, "Who is in the Kingdom?" seems most apt. We dare not make final judgments about who will finally be accepted into God's kingdom and who will not. Jesus's ministry is one of gathering people, often the outcast, into his family and into the kingdom he is announcing and bringing. Some will be excluded, and this section warns people of that danger. Yet the dominant emphasis is that Jesus welcomes all; indeed, he urges all to come and join the celebrations that anticipate God's final kingdom banquet.

Luke addresses these themes in many ways. There are references to who really counts as a "daughter of Abraham" (13:16) and to those who will join Abraham, Isaac and Jacob at God's kingdom feast (13:28-30). There are warnings and encouragements: don't presume you are "in" if you do not count the cost (13:24-27); don't assume people are "out" just because they are not from your group (13:29).

Jesus indicates that while initial responses to God's kingdom may be minimal, this kingdom will one day encompass the world (13:18-21). And we listen in as Jesus sorrows over those he diligently seeks and urgently calls who will resist the kingdom message and suffer for it (13:34-35).

Much of chapters 14 and 15 focuses on Jesus's concern for the outcast, the marginalized, the "poor." They are the specially invited! And they are contrasted with the self-righteous, those who ignore marginalized people and believe themselves to be the privileged insiders. Various images are used to contrast these two groups: the "rich neighbors" (14:12) versus "the poor, the crippled, the lame and the blind" (14:13); the "Pharisees" (15:2) versus the "sinners" (15:1); the 99 safe sheep versus the one lost (15:4); the nine coins versus the one that went missing (15:8); the self-righteous, hard-working, older brother (15:29) versus the so-called "prodigal" (15:13).

In the middle of all this is an important section on "The Cost of Discipleship" (14:25-35). Here the paradox is clear: salvation is indeed a gift of pure grace, yet it costs everything. God offers us the "terms of peace" (14:32) – to give up everything we have, relativize all competing loyalties and follow whole-heartedly the one who took up his own cross and calls us to do the same (14:26, 27, 33).

Outline:

Jesus Heals on the Sabbath (13:10-17)
The Parables of the Mustard Seed and the Yeast (13:18-21)
The Narrow Door and the Many Gates (13:22-30)
Jesus and Jerusalem (13:31-35)
Jesus Heals a Man with "Dropsy" (14:1-6)
Ironic Advice for Honor-Seekers (14:7-11)
Hospitality that is Rewarded (14:12-14)
The Parable of the Converted Host (14:15-24)

The Cost of Discipleship (14:25-35)
Parables about Lost and Found (15:1-32)
The Setting and the Occasion (15:1-2)
The Shepherd and the Lost Sheep (15:3-7)
The Woman and the Lost Coin (15:8-10)
The Father and the Lost Sons (15:11-32)

The Text Explained

Jesus Heals on the Sabbath (13:10-17)

> *Should not this woman, a daughter of Abraham, whom Satan has kept bound for eighteen long years, be set free on the Sabbath day from what bound her?" (13:16)*

Although this is a healing and deliverance narrative, the most prominent emphasis in the text is that it happens *on the Sabbath.* That is how the text opens: "On the Sabbath..." (13:10). That is at the heart of the synagogue ruler's complaint: "Indignant because Jesus had healed on the Sabbath, the synagogue leader said to the people, 'There are six days for work. So come and be healed on those days, not on the Sabbath'" (13:14). And that is what Jesus emphasizes in his response: "You hypocrites! Doesn't each of you on the Sabbath untie your ox or donkey from the stall and lead it out to give it water? Then should not this woman...be set free on the Sabbath day?" (13:15-16).

Yet there are other issues of importance here as well. Luke, who sometimes carefully distinguishes between healings and acts of deliverance, here clearly combines them. On one level, this woman is healed from a crooked back. But Jesus clearly discerns that the problem cannot be reduced to physical elements. She had been crippled "by a spirit" (13:11); Jesus "sets her free" (13:12); he says, "Satan had kept her bound" (13:16).

These two themes (Sabbath and delivering from Satan's bondage) come together when Jesus argues that it is entirely appropriate to "work" on the Sabbath because Satan does! In other words, the power of evil never rests. It relentlessly fights to hold its victim's captive. So also Jesus comes to undo Satan's work, to overthrow Satan's kingdom, to bring health and freedom to those who are suffering and in bondage – regardless of the weekly cycle of work and rest!

This does not mean people should no longer keep Sabbath, that we should no longer pause to rest and be refreshed, that now we should work seven days a week. Rather, it means Jesus lives the true meaning of Sabbath precisely by overthrowing Satan's power. Sabbath symbolizes God's finished creation (Genesis 2:3) and looks forward to its restoration. This "daughter of Abraham" experiences this day a deliverance and healing that point toward that restoration. What more appropriate day than the Sabbath for that to happen!

The final verse ominously signals that Jesus's popularity is at the expense of his opponents'. It is not Jesus's goal to humiliate, but those who oppose the healing and the restoration Jesus brings will find themselves on the losing side of the battle Jesus wages against the destructive power of evil.

The Parables of the Mustard Seed and the Yeast (13:18-21)

> *Then Jesus asked, "What is the kingdom of God like? What shall I compare it to? It is like a mustard seed, which a man took and planted in his garden. It grew and became a tree, and the birds perched in its branches."*
>
> *Again he asked, "What shall I compare the kingdom of God to? It is like yeast that a woman took and mixed into about sixty pounds of flour until it worked all through the dough." (13:18-21)*

The main point of the "mustard seed" parable is that God's kingdom will have a magnificent final destiny, even though its beginnings are small. Jesus's earthly ministry, including his death and resurrection, occurred over a very brief period of time in a tiny corner of the world. But it was the seed that has grown into a tree large enough to provide a nesting place for birds (possibly a symbol of the nations of the world).

So also a tiny amount of yeast can permeate and transform a very large batch of dough. God's kingdom, once introduced into this fallen creation, exerts its influence, slowly (perhaps) but surely – until all the dough is leavened.

These two parables, one about a man, one about a woman, take ordinary, everyday objects of garden and kitchen, and use them to provide glimpses of the world-encompassing kingdom Jesus came to establish and that he will come again to consummate.

The Narrow Door and the Many Gates (13:22-30)

An unnamed person in the crowd asks, "Lord, are only a few people going to be saved?" (13:23). Jesus does not answer that question. The first part of his response sounds like he might be saying, "Yes, only a few. It takes a lot of effort. Some try and fail!" But the second part of his response sounds like he is saying, "No, there will be many, very many. They will come pouring in from every direction" (13:29).

The point of Jesus's paradoxical response seems to be "It is none of your business to figure out whether there will be few or many. Just make sure you are one of them!"

We should not read 13:24 as saying some genuine seekers, by no fault of their own, will be excluded – as if God predetermines who will get in and who will not. We learn a few verses later why they were excluded. They thought that being with Jesus was all that was required (13:26). Jesus knows that they were in fact "evildoers" (13:27). They were people who rejected Jesus's message of the kingdom. The warning of this text is that those who persistently reject Jesus will one day discover they have made a tragic mistake, but then it will be too late. To "enter the narrow door" is to side with Jesus. It is not enough to "eat and drink with him while he teaches in our streets" (13:26). We must truly accept Jesus and his message of the kingdom and order our lives accordingly.

The passage closes on very positive note. After references to the wailing (grief) and gnashing (rage) of those on the outside, we have a picture of people streaming into the kingdom from east and west, north and south. These are the ones who will sit in the very places the "evildoers" failed to reach. In Jesus's ministry, these would be the tax collectors and sinners, the prostitutes and outcasts, the ones who accepted Jesus, while many in the religious establishment did not. In Luke's context, these would include Gentiles who were streaming into the kingdom feast, while those Jews who rejected Jesus were forfeiting their right to be there.

Will there be many or few? We cannot answer that question! God will do what is right. Those who respond to Jesus's invitation, to the gospel invitation, will be welcomed from every direction. Those who think they have a guaranteed seat at the table need to examine whether they really have said yes to Jesus or not. "There are those who are last who will be first, and first who will be last" (13:30).

Jesus and Jerusalem (13:31-35)

Herod has already executed John the Baptist (9:9). We learn from other Gospels that this was not a savvy political move, but the consequence of a foolish oath (Mark 6:17-28). Now another popular preacher is creating a stir in Herod's territory. Herod does not want another unpopular execution on his hands, yet he cannot sit idly by as Jesus gathers support for "another kingdom." To make the problem go away, he recruits the help of Pharisees to get Jesus to move elsewhere. That seems a more likely explanation of 13:31 than that the Pharisees are genuinely concerned about Jesus's safety.

Jesus's uncomplimentary reference to Herod ("that fox") shows how little deference he pays to corrupt earthly rulers and their regimes. By the way, we should not associate "sly" with fox here (as we do in our culture) – in Jesus's world, foxes were associated rather with "dirty" or "worthless."

So Jesus now appears to be on collision course with the powerful religious rulers of Israel and the powerful Gentile representatives of the Roman Empire. He continues his healing and deliverance ministries, trusting God to keep him alive long enough to reach the goal of his journey – Jerusalem, the center of religious and political life among his people. There he will complete his mission by giving his life to redeem the nation and the world.

Jesus's references here to "three days" (see both 13:32 and 13:33) represent an idiom that simply means "a short while." Jesus knows his time is limited. He also knows powerful people are resisting his message of peace. And he knows that rejecting his message will have disastrous consequences for Jerusalem and everything for which that city stands. Jerusalem (the very name means "city of peace") and its "house" (temple) will fail to find the peace God intends for them (see 2:14 and 19:42). Instead the city and its house will be laid waste.

All this has rich meaning on more than one level. On one level, Jesus is urging his people to abandon their nationalistic aspirations, their headlong rush to confront the Roman Empire. They mistakenly believe God will be on their side if they rebel against the imperial power. Jesus knows any violent revolt will result in disaster for his people, for their city, for the temple. And Jesus knows this not only because political and military calculations all point in this direction, but because God's way of peace is not the way of military confrontation but of learning to love even the enemy (6:27).

On another level, Jesus is also referencing the final judgment of God. Those who respond to Jesus and his message will be secure, while those who resist Jesus's invitations (like a hen calling her chicks under her wings; 13:34) will face the consequences at the final judgment.

So Jesus laments the inevitable. But note well that he is not lamenting his own coming death; he is lamenting the inevitable consequences for others who persist in rejecting his message. Here is where the metaphor Jesus uses is so apt.

> *"Jerusalem, Jerusalem, you who kill the prophets and stone those sent to you, how often I have longed to gather your children*

> *together, as a hen gathers her chicks under her wings, and you were not willing. Look, your house is left to you desolate. I tell you, you will not see me again until you say, 'Blessed is he who comes in the name of the Lord.'" (13:34-35)*

Where a brush fire rages, hens gather their chicks under their wings, so that as the flames pass by, the hen gives her life, but the chicks under the wings are preserved. Jesus knows his own death will be for the salvation of others. He is wooing his people to gather under his wings. He laments that so many will resist the invitation.

In the final verse of this section, we again encounter double meaning. Some of Jesus's hearers (perhaps the Pharisees who delivered Herod's warning; see 13:31) will not see Jesus again until he arrives in Jerusalem to complete his mission (see 19:28, 38). Others who now reject Jesus and his message will meet him once more when he comes at the end of the age. The warning, of course, is that they must choose Jesus before then, for then it will be too late to change their minds (see the previous passage, especially 13:25-28).

Jesus Heals a Man with "Dropsy" (14:1-6)

By now, the Pharisees and other religious groups are closely watching Jesus. His popularity is a threat to their own influence. His teaching challenges theirs. The goal of their "careful watching" (14:1) is to discredit him before others and find evidence they can use against him. In fact, they may have set up this Sabbath meal as a trap to catch Jesus. If so, it certainly backfired!

The issue again is Sabbath healing (see 13:10-17). But this time other issues become prominent. The man Jesus heals had "abnormal swelling," something that translations have typically called "dropsy." It was a condition that made a person crave more and more fluids, yet their thirst was never satisfied. Bloating was the result. Of great relevance to the rest of this chapter, "dropsy" had become a symbol for other cravings that could not be satisfied like loving money (accumulating it with a passion but never having enough) and – the most relevant meaning for what follows – loving honor (working feverishly to increase it, yet always craving more).

Ironic Advice for Honor-Seekers (14:7-11)

Here Jesus directly addresses the theme of honor-seeking. He observes people jockeying for the honored seats at this banquet. So Jesus tells an ironic parable – ironic because Jesus absolutely rejects the entire enterprise of honor-seeking and would surely not seriously want to help them figure out how to milk that system. He is actually mocking their status-seeking, making clear that true honor is never craved and fought for but freely given by the only one whose assessment of us should really matter!

The final verse of Jesus's "advice for guests" is doubly ironic. As a conclusion to Jesus's parable, it sums up the real issue: people who fight for their status and compete for honor really have no true honor at all; it is all just ascribed through the manipulation of the system.

The ultimate irony is that, even though Jesus is not seriously trying to help selfish dinner guests scramble more successfully for earthly honor, he really is trying to help us followers understand how they can be *truly* honored. We can achieve the kind of honor that really matters only by receiving it as God's gift to us. Fighting to raise our own status means downfall in God's kingdom. Humbling ourselves in God's sight means receiving God's grace and all that comes with it.

What contemporary readers may not realize is that this text (and the two that follow) assume some background knowledge about first century feasts. In Jesus's world, feasts had to do with more than food and fellowship. They were occasions for measuring and enhancing status and honor in the eyes of others. People watched very closely to see who was invited to whose dinner, to see who associated with which fellow guests, which seats of honor (or dishonor) the hosts assigned. All these served to test and compare who was considered more honorable. That theme is crucial for understanding not only the present passage about seating places, but the two sections to follow as well.

Hospitality that is Rewarded (14:12-14)

Having embarrassed the guests, Jesus now turns to (or perhaps we should say turns *against*) the host. "You, sir, you invited all the wrong people to your dinner!"

This host had, as usual, invited important people, people who would honor him with their presence, who would be expected to repay the favor at a later time. Jesus directly challenges the entire system. He counsels inviting precisely those who cannot ever repay – the outcasts, those marginalized by society, those with no means to repay and no honor to bestow. Jesus calls for radical conversion to the values of God's kingdom, where all are treated equally and God rewards all for doing so.

In this text, as in many others in Luke, "poor" is not a measure only of financial status. Those who are "poor" are those who are without earthly standing, without society's credentials. Even a "rich" tax collector can be "poor," if he is despised by his society. Jesus calls "hosts" to share hospitality freely with one and all, in order to symbolize and enact the equal status of all who participate in God's kingdom.

And Jesus promises that for every sacrifice made in earthly terms, there will be more than adequate compensation and reward at the final resurrection.

The Parable of the Converted Host (14:15-24)

Jesus has just referred to God's repayment at the end of the age (14:14) and now mentions "the feast in the kingdom of God" (14:15). Many interpreters read the parable that follows as if it were a description of that final repayment at the heavenly banquet (the one Jesus referred to already in 13:29). Read that way, it represents a warning that if we do not respond positively to the kingdom invitation, we will be excluded from the banquet in the end.

But there are significant reasons to doubt this is Jesus's main point. Let's not forget that Jesus is sitting at a dinner where guests are competing for honor (14:7-11), hosted by a man who wants to enhance his own status by associating with all the "right people" (14:12-14). Let's not forget that Jesus has just counseled his hearers to join the upside-down kingdom that operates by a completely different set of values.

The story Jesus tells is actually one about an *earthly* host (not God as the *heavenly* host). The host in Jesus's parable acts just as typical first-century hosts did; he invited his rich neighbors to his banquet. He did precisely what Jesus has just critiqued (14:12). In Jesus's story, the host experiences a "conversion." Before the story ends, he has done exactly what Jesus just counseled: he has invited the "poor, the crippled, the blind and the lame" (compare 14:21 with 14:13). This is a story about someone who learns the values of the kingdom. He certainly cannot expect to gain earthly rewards for doing that. But Jesus assures him God will richly reward him at the end of the age, when God pours out abundant blessings on all who have sacrificed in this life for the sake of God's kingdom.

In Jesus's story, what was it that led to the conversion of the host? He discovered that the "status game" can backfire. In typical parabolic style, Jesus tells an exaggerated story about invited guests coming up with ridiculous and implausible excuses for backing out of the banquet at the last minute. It is clearly a conspiracy to shame the one who hoped they would come to honor him. And it is enough to persuade this host it is time to give up this earthly pursuit of honor and to adopt the values of God's kingdom.

Sometimes it really does take more than Jesus's warnings and invitations to persuade people to say "yes" to Jesus and the way of the kingdom. Sometimes it takes earthly disaster, personal crisis or society's rejection. Whatever it takes, *God* invites us to adopt the values of the kingdom before it is too late (see again 13:24-28).

Though this parable has often been interpreted as God inviting people into the kingdom, the context suggests an alternative: those who invite to their dinners the undeserving will be rewarded at the resurrection. This parable describes such a person. He is snubbed by his peers and realizes the precarious nature of the earthly game of tit for tat. He converts to the way of Jesus and practices what

Jesus just called people to do (14:12-15). It is the host in Jesus's story, not the Pharisee who invited him that day, who will one day "eat at the feast in the kingdom of God" (14:15).

One final suggestion: readers who find this alternative attractive, but are not quite ready to give up the traditional reading of this text might consider a third option. Perhaps we can have it both ways! Maybe Jesus told his story just ambiguously enough that it can challenge us to practice hospitality according to the values of the kingdom and, at the same time, give us glimpses of the heavenly banquet that will one day repay us for doing so. It would not be the first time in Luke's Gospel, nor even in this section of it, that a text effectively speaks on more than one level!

The Cost of Discipleship (14:25-35)

> *Large crowds were traveling with Jesus, and turning to them he said: "If anyone comes to me and does not hate father and mother, wife and children, brothers and sisters—yes, even their own life—such a person cannot be my disciple. And whoever does not carry their cross and follow me cannot be my disciple." (14:25-27)*

The two parables in this text illustrate important truths about discipleship: we need to "count the cost"; we need to consider the alternatives; we need to invest everything we've got! Yet it is not quite self-evident how the two parables make these points and which one makes which points.

Most people interpret the parable of the tower builder as a challenge to invest everything *so that we will be able to get the job done* (build the tower).

Others fear that this sounds like so-called "works righteousness" and propose an alternative. It goes something like this: we are to consider carefully whether we really have the resources to build the tower, *realize that we do not* and then not even start down that road. Salvation is not found in giving it our best shot; salvation is given as a gift. So don't try to build the tower! Let God do it for you.

Many contemporary Christians, I think, are far more concerned about what they call "works righteousness" than either Jesus or Luke seemed to be. This is a text about discipleship. It is a text about "giving up everything" (14:33). That sounds to me like it really is about giving up everything *else*, so that we can "build the tower" (be a disciple). It does not sound like we are supposed to give up building the tower! So I go with the traditional interpretation on this one.

As to the warring king, again there are two options. One idea is that our smaller army can only defeat the bigger enemy if we truly "give it our best shot" (or perhaps trust God for the victory, as Gideon's small army was called to do). In other words, true disciples really can defeat the more powerful king!

The alternative is to see the more powerful king coming against us, not as an enemy, but as God! If we with our meager human resources think we can stand against God and God's far more powerful kingdom, we had better think again! Rather than rush to inevitable destruction, we should ask for terms of peace. God offers them. What are they? Unconditional surrender to God's kingdom – or, to use the language of this text, "Give up everything you have" (14:33). Again, there are two ways of reading it. This time, I think the second approach coheres best with this whole passage.

To summarize, if we are considering saying "yes" to the call of Jesus, we had better think carefully about whether we are willing to pay the price: it will cost everything. But if we are considering saying "no" to the call of Jesus, we had better think carefully about whether we are willing to pay the price of that: opposing God will also, in the end, cost everything! Or perhaps we can put it this way: if we decide *against* investing our lives in faithful discipleship, we will find ourselves headed for disaster. The only way to avert it is to invest our lives in faithful discipleship.

Four more important points: first, 14:28 might seem to suggest that some people just do not have what it takes. It is not their fault;

they just do not have enough! But 14:33 makes very clear what it truly costs to build the tower – it costs everything we have. How many people have that much? We all do.

Second, the call to "hate" family members is, in my view, a very unfortunate way of translating the original. It is true that the underlying Greek word can literally be translated "hate." But it is an idiom. To produce literal translations of idioms is usually a bad idea. In English, "hate" means hate. In the idiom Jesus uses, it means "relegating to second priority," in other words: putting *Jesus* first. There is no such English idiom for "hate." When we put Jesus first and our family second, we do not hate them. In fact, putting Jesus first should not make our family suffer; it should benefit them!

Third, 14:27 speaks of carrying our cross. "Cross" does not mean "suffering" per se, nor "martyrdom" per se. It stands for unconditional surrender. Roman criminals were forced to surrender to the power of Rome. We voluntarily surrender to the will of God. When Jesus surrendered unconditionally to God's will, it led to a literal cross. Ours will likely be a figurative one. It will be whatever God brings our way when we say along with Jesus, "Not my will, but yours, be done" (see 22:42).

Fourth, the final verses of this section call for "hearing ears" and "salty lives" – metaphors for careful attention to the teaching of Jesus and faithful obedient responses. Only in this way can we be the kind of disciples this section has been calling us to be, people fully dedicated to Jesus and the kingdom of God.

Parables about Lost and Found (15:1-32)

The Setting and the Occasion (15:1-2)

A whole book could be written on this well-known chapter. In fact, many have been! Three I heartily recommend are *The Return of the Prodigal Son: A Story of Homecoming* (Henri Nouwen, Doubleday, 1994), *The Cross and the Prodigal: Luke 15 through the Eyes of Middle Eastern Peasants* (Kenneth Bailey, InterVarsity, 2005), and

Prodigal God: Recovering the Heart of the Christian Faith (Timothy Keller, Penguin, 2008). All of them will add important dimensions to the brief comments included here. (See also my book *Double Take*, pages 125-134.)

The introduction to this chapter is crucial for understanding its main concern:

> *Now the tax collectors and sinners were all gathering around to hear Jesus. But the Pharisees and the teachers of the law muttered, "This man welcomes sinners and eats with them." (15:1-2)*

In each of the three parables to follow, there is a character that corresponds to Jesus (the shepherd, the woman, the father). In each, there is a character corresponding to the "tax collectors and sinners," that is, those who were lost (a sheep, a coin, the younger brother). And in each, there are characters corresponding to the Pharisees and teachers of the law (the 99, the 9, the older brother).

It is particularly interesting to note how Jesus characterizes his critics. They are like the sheep who are safe and sound (so they think, anyway!); they are like the coins that never got lost (so they think, anyway!); they are like the older brother, faithfully serving their father (so they think, anyway!). But in the end, Jesus springs the trap. Actually they are not "faithfully serving," they are slaving away, complaining, disowning their brother, rebuking their father.

The theme of meal fellowship is also prominent. Jesus is eating with all the "wrong" people. But then, why not? They have been found. It is time to celebrate. We can almost imagine the shepherd killing a fatted calf to celebrate finding his one lost sheep or the woman spending nine coins to celebrate finding the one that had been lost. What a waste! But that is just what God is like.

The Shepherd and the Lost Sheep (15:3-7)

In Matthew's Gospel, a similar parable illustrates the erring person who wanders away from the Christian fellowship. Luke's version has a different function. The sheep here stands for those lost, presumably injured (notice how the shepherd needs to carry it back), totally dependent on the loving concern of a caring shepherd for its very survival.

We should not imagine a small lamb nestled in the arms of the shepherd. This is a sheep, a heavy burden to carry. But the concerned shepherd dearly loves this vulnerable sheep, and at great cost will find it and carry it home.

Some have wondered whether the shepherd did not jeopardize the security of the other 99 by leaving them alone in the wilderness while he sought the lost one. Actually (as Bailey points out), all the others find their deepest security in the fact that each individual sheep is important enough to the shepherd that he will give up everything to restore it. If the shepherd sacrificed the one lost sheep for the sake of the majority, all would be insecure.

The final rejoicing is a portrait of what Jesus himself is doing, eating with tax collectors and sinners and celebrating their salvation. It is a picture of what is happening in heaven.

The Woman and the Lost Coin (15:8-10)

As so often in Luke, a narrative about a man is matched by a narrative about a woman. Luke does not hesitate to use female imagery to portray what God is like and how Jesus represents God on earth. He has done that twice already in just this section of Luke (see 13:21, 34).

Notice how the numbers are changing. *Ninety-nine* sheep still in the fold are down to *nine* coins still in the purse. In the next parable, the number will be down to *one*, and the one will not be nearly as "safe and secure" as Jesus's critics imagine they are.

Again, Jesus cites heavenly rejoicing over finding the lost to justify his own rejoicing that tax collectors and sinners have been found.

The Father and the Lost Sons (15:11-32)

Instead of calling this parable "the prodigal son" (or something similar that characterizes only the younger brother), I have chosen to name it for all three characters. Both sons are portrayed in detail, and the main character is actually the father.

The younger son squanders more than his money. He squanders family relationships. He abandons his village and clan. He throws in his lot with the Gentiles. He substitutes all that is meaningful in life for fleeting pleasure. And he finds himself penniless, hopeless and starving. His plan to return home is not, at first, genuine repentance. It is a desperate plot to try to win back favor in his family and his village.

Only when he sees his father running to meet him, only when he is welcomed with open arms, no strings attached, does he throw to the wind his desperate plan to rehabilitate himself. He accepts his father's offer of grace and rejoins the family and the village he foolishly forfeited.

The father's running to meet him is one of the most stunning expressions of grace in the entire Bible. Old men in that culture did not run; for that they would have to pick up their robes. They would make themselves laughingstocks! This loving father risks everything, throws caution to the wind, joins his son as an object of scorn, to share his own honor with his undeserving son.

The older brother actually disdains family relationships as much as the younger, only in a different way. He stays at home but thinks of himself as a slave. He disowns his brother and rejects his father's loving invitation to join the party.

The parable ends without closure. It ends with the father still trying to woo his older son. And we never find out what the son chooses to do. That is quite deliberate, for Jesus is inviting the Pharisees and teachers of the law to change their stance toward him and those with whom he fellowships. And Luke is inviting his readers to adopt the heart of Jesus, to adopt the stance of the good shepherd, the diligent woman, the generous father.

Implications of the Text for Today

Are only a few people going to be saved?

It is very important to note that Jesus does not answer the question posed to him in 13:23. The correct answer is surely no. The number saved will be hundreds, thousands, millions, billions. But it is important to guard against imagining either that we are the final judges or that we can predict with any kind of accuracy what the final judge will do. While there are many warnings in Scripture about missing out, there are far more invitations to "come on in!" We should not presume God is less compassionate than we are; God is infinitely more compassionate.

We should also guard against understanding "saved" too narrowly. While our final destiny will either be in God's presence or somehow banished from it (as this section of Luke makes very clear), the word "save" applies not only to final destinies. The word can mean protect, rescue, heal, forgive, restore and much more. To be saved, according to the Gospels, is pretty much the same as to experience *shalom*, that all-encompassing well-being that characterizes those living under God's goodness.

We "enter through the narrow door" (13:24) by joining Jesus. When we do, we learn from him to be open-hearted and generous. We anticipate taking our places "at the feast in the kingdom of God" and seeing people pouring in from east and west, from north and south (13:29). And in the meantime, we share our own table fellowship with "the poor, the crippled, the lame and the blind" (14:13), celebrating the lost who are found.

Texts with Multiple Meanings

Several times in this section, I have suggested that texts can speak on more than one level. There are multiple reasons why this is the case. Sometimes we can and should distinguish between what *Jesus* was aiming to say and what *Luke* was aiming to say. In the historical context in which Jesus first spoke, his teaching had specific meaning and application. In the later context to which Luke addressed his Gospel, some of the issues had changed and Luke presented the words and actions of Jesus in ways that enable them to address new realities.

Sometimes other things are going on. Jesus often saw in events around him glimpses of something greater yet to come. He saw in the mundane experiences of life (planting seeds, making bread) pictures of kingdom realities. He saw in the desires of people around him the longings of all humanity. He saw in the political miscalculations of his fellow Israelites the disastrous choices people make in light of eternity. He looked at those seated around him at the table and pointed out how it foreshadowed the feast in God's kingdom. Jesus himself was seeing things on multiple levels. And Luke was able to see things on those various levels as well.

And then there is the "Holy Spirit" factor! The texts we are studying represent not only historical records of what Jesus said and did. They represent not only the creative genius of the writer Luke. This is Scripture, inspired by God's Spirit, discerned by the church to be authoritative for all time. Sometimes God's Spirit takes those ancient texts and speaks their message into contemporary hearts, into contemporary communities, and makes them come alive all over again in new ways.

The texts are rich and deep. We will never exhaust their full potential. The safest place to start is to ask, what was Luke trying to communicate to the reader? But if we find ourselves unable to claim with confidence that we have figured out the text's meaning once and for all, that is usually a good thing. This is Scripture. It deserves our careful study, our openness to new possibilities, our never-ending search for a fresh word from God.

Texts about Honor and Shame

The contemporary culture of most Western countries focuses on guilt more than shame. Yet all people experience both of these and we not only misunderstand our own experiences but also ancient texts if we do not consider carefully how deep-seated the human need to experience honor and avoid shame really is. The ancient world and many traditional cultures today are far more focused on that than we are.

This section of Luke has multiple texts where these factors loom large. Luke 14:1-24 (all four parts of it) can be understood adequately only if we take this into account. That is also true for the parable of the father and his two sons. But it goes beyond that. From our cultural perspective, we easily overlook lines like "all his opponents were humiliated" (13:17) and "if you...are not able to finish it, everyone who sees it will ridicule you" (14:29). At the beginning of the next section we will encounter, "I am ashamed to beg" (16:3). A very powerful motivator in life is to gain honor and avoid shame.

Taking this into account helps us understand ancient texts. This in turn helps us learn how to avoid the misguided striving for honor that Jesus here condemns. Jesus calls his followers to do exactly the opposite of what many in his world were doing. He said quit competing for honor; quit withholding honor from the outcast; recognize that even God will sacrifice honor to join returning prodigals in their shame. In God's kingdom, we do not fight for honor; sometimes we willingly embrace shame. We do it because God freely bestows honor on all who join Jesus, and God calls us to freely bestow honor on others.

Who is the Prodigal?

Jesus's parables are often fictional narratives, creatively composed by Jesus to make crucial points. But sometimes we wonder whether there were real people who "sat for the portrait." Did Jesus know a family in which similar things happened? Or was Jacob from the Old Testament the model? (Kenneth Bailey wrote a whole book exploring the parallels.) Or is this a retelling of the story of Israel's exile and the restoration they still longed for? (N.T. Wright proposes this option.) Do the characters actually explore aspects of ourselves, so that each of us can be each of the characters in turn? (This is the view of Henri Nouwen.)

Or is this the story of Everyman, of Everywoman? Each of us finds ourselves somewhere between the extremes of older and younger brother. The challenge is to recognize the ways in which we run from or hold at a distance our loving heavenly Father. The challenge is to open ourselves to God's undeserved grace, and pass it on to every lost sheep, lost coin and lost son whom God diligently seeks.

Personal Reflection Questions

- What are the advantages and disadvantages, the safeguards and dangers of treating Bible texts as if they have only one right meaning? What are the advantages and disadvantages of exploring multiple layers of meaning and multiple alternative interpretations?
- How has this section of Luke provided new insights into the ways God's kingdom is counter-cultural, both in Jesus's day and in ours? You can consider the concepts of honor and shame, the paradoxes of free grace and costly discipleship, the way of peace Jesus calls for, etc.
- How has the parable traditionally called "the prodigal son" impacted you in the past? Are there interpretations you are aware of that were not cited in this section? Have you experienced expressions of it in art or music that have spoken to you?

Responding to the Kingdom

The Text: Luke 16:1 - 19:48 NIV

The Flow and Form of the Text

Back in 9:51, Luke reported: "As the time approached for him to be taken up to heaven, Jesus resolutely set out for Jerusalem." Jesus has been on the way to Jerusalem since then. This section of Luke is the final leg of that journey.

The closer Jesus gets to his goal, the more "journey markers" Luke includes in the text:

- 17:11 Now on his way to Jerusalem
- 18:31 "We are going up to Jerusalem"
- 18:35 As Jesus approached Jericho
- 19:1 Jesus entered Jericho and was passing through
- 19:11 He was near Jerusalem
- 19:28 He went on ahead, going up to Jerusalem
- 19:29 As he approached Bethphage and Bethany
- 19:37 When he came near the place where the road goes down the Mount of Olives

- 19:41 As he approached Jerusalem and saw the city

The journey framework is an effective device, not only as a way of showing how Jesus got to Jerusalem, but as a graphic way for Jesus to call disciples (and for Luke to call readers) to faithful discipleship. They and we are called to follow Jesus on a journey to Jerusalem and all that it entails.

Jerusalem will be the place where Jesus will "be taken up to heaven" (see 9:51). But it will first be the place where he is rejected and killed. To follow Jesus is to respond to his message, to take up our crosses, to identify with Jesus's life, death and resurrection and to discover that this is not only the way Jesus went, but the way he calls us to go. This is the way of the kingdom that Jesus proclaimed, embodied and inaugurated.

This long and quite diverse section of Luke provides numerous insights into what it means to respond to Jesus and his kingdom message. Jesus is compared to a king in various places: he is a rejected king, a misunderstood king, a king whose kingdom is the very opposite of earthly kingdoms. And this section shows us what it means to respond to Jesus and his unique brand of kingship.

One of the primary ways we respond appropriately is by being faithful with worldly possessions, investing them in ways that match the values of God's kingdom. That, Jesus insists, is nothing new. Moses and the prophets had already called God's people to precisely that (as the parable of the rich man and Lazarus makes very clear).

We also respond to the kingdom by receiving God's forgiveness and forgiving others in return, by receiving God's grace and returning gratitude and worship, by adopting the upside-down values of the kingdom, by placing high value on children and "outcasts," by practicing justice and generosity.

Luke's Gospel speaks often of the future reward Jesus offers those who live for God's kingdom in this life, and of the judgment to fall on those who do not. This section addresses those issues both directly (see 16:23; 18:8, 22, 30) and indirectly (see 17:22-24, 27-

29, 33-34; 19:15, 27). Jesus's disciples and Luke's readers are urgently called to respond to the kingdom call – eternal destinies are at stake.

Jesus ends his journey to Jerusalem with a grand, but highly paradoxical, "donkey ride" into Jerusalem, a dramatic action thoroughly misunderstood by the crowds who cheer their coming king. Unfortunately, it is also usually misunderstood by contemporary Christians who celebrate the triumphal entry for all the wrong reasons!

We include in this section Luke's brief report on what is usually called Jesus's temple cleansing and two brief notices: 1) Jesus was teaching regularly in the temple; 2) the official rulers of Israel rejected Jesus. These are the two themes that will feature prominently in the next section of Luke's Gospel.

Outline:

Living Faithfully with Possessions (16:1-15)
The Law and the Prophets (16:16-18)
The Rich Man and Lazarus (16:19-31)
Sin, Faith, Duty (17:1-10)
The Grateful Samaritan (17:11-19)
The Coming of the Kingdom of God (17:20-37)
The Bothersome Widow and the Unjust Judge (18:1-8)
The Pharisee and the Tax Collector (18:9-14)
Jesus Receives Little Children (18:15-17)
The Rich and the Kingdom of God (18:18-30)
Jesus Again Predicts His Death and Resurrection (18:31-34)
A Blind Beggar Receives his Sight (18:35-43)
Zacchaeus, the Tax Collector (19:1-10)
The Parable of the Ten Minas (19:11-27)
The Donkey-Riding King (19:28-44)
Jesus at the Temple (19:45-48)

The Text Explained

Living Faithfully with Possessions (16:1-15)

The parable of the shrewd manager (16:1-8) has often been called the most difficult of all Jesus's parables. Why would Jesus use an unscrupulous, dishonest cheat as a model for his followers? A common response is that Jesus (through the words of this man's worldly master) commends him for one thing only, his shrewdness. Nothing else in the parable should be seen as exemplary. Thus the message of the parable is reduced to merely this: "Be clever!" But that surely reduces the parable way too much. Jesus did not need an elaborate story to make that point.

Others have attempted to explain the man's "unscrupulous" behavior in more noble terms: by reducing the debts, he was foregoing his own commission, or deleting the (illegal) interest his master was charging or creating the impression that his master was a generous and caring person. In other words, he was not only clever; he was a model of generosity, or law-keeping or bringing glory to the master. Each option has some plausibility.

In my view, our best clues are found in 16:9-15. Jesus may well have used and reused parables in various forms for various purposes. We are usually on safest ground if we avoid speculation about what Jesus's parables must originally have meant and focus on how the Gospel writers present them. The verses following the parable seem to be Luke's commentary on what readers are to learn from the parable. If that is the case, then I propose at least the following lessons:

- Followers of Jesus do not live for worldly resources, but rather to honor and serve God (see 16:13);
- The resources we often consider our own actually belong to our master; we are only stewards of them (see 16:12);
- How we manage those resources will have significant consequences both in this life and in the age to come (see 16:9);

- "Managing" worldly resources actually means giving them away, using them to alleviate human need in service to God (see 16:9);
- If "worldly people" find the means to make "worldly ways" turn out to their advantage, how much more should "kingdom people" realize the eternal consequences of "kingdom ways" (see 16:8).

Not to be overlooked is the fact that "eliminating debt" is one of the primary metaphors used in Luke to speak of "forgiveness" and "deliverance," two of Jesus's own ministry priorities. It turns out that Jesus's parable serves admirably to illustrate and inspire Jesus's followers (and Luke's readers) to be faithful with "worldly resources" for the sake of God's kingdom.

Two more points. The call to love one and hate the other (16:13) is to be taken seriously, but not literally – as are all idioms. Jesus does not call us to (literally) hate our family and our own life (see 14:26), nor does he call us to (literally) hate earthly masters. Rather, Jesus calls us to make him and our participation in God's kingdom our highest priority – over the demands of family, over personal ambition, over earthly careers, over worldly possessions. We do not live to serve money; we invest it in ways that serve God.

Finally, Jesus uses money-loving and self-justifying Pharisees as counter-examples (16:14-15). They may look good on the outside, but their hearts are not in the right place. Jesus calls his followers (and Luke, his readers) to have transformed hearts that lead us to adopt kingdom values, especially in the way we invest our resources – God's resources, actually – for kingdom purposes.

The Law and the Prophets (16:16-18)

This short section emphasizes three things:

- When John completed his ministry and Jesus began to proclaim God's kingdom, something changed: God's kingdom became real and present through the ministry of Jesus. That means it is time for decisive action in response.

- What did not change is the status of the Law and the Prophets – they remain valid. This is a strong theme in Luke (see especially the last verse of this chapter). How the church fleshes that out is one of the main concerns of Luke's second volume, the Book of Acts (especially chapter 15), but the main points Jesus and Luke make here are that the Law and the Prophets prepare for the new things Jesus is doing, they bear witness to Jesus, they guide Jesus's ministry and (when we properly interpret and apply them) they guide our lives as Jesus's followers.
- Divorce and subsequent remarriage is outside God's plan for marriage. We must, of course, recognize nuances within Scripture as we apply this ideal to specific situations; other texts and emphases in Scripture also come to bear in cases where marriages are in trouble. But God's basic intention is clearly stated here. If 16:18 seems out of place in this context, it serves at least as one example of the continuing validity of the Law and the Prophets.

The Rich Man and Lazarus (16:19-31)

This is the only parable of Jesus in which an individual character is ever named (with the exception of biblical characters like "Abraham" and "Moses"). Interestingly, it is not the wealthy man, but the beggar he never notices, who is named – and his name means "the Lord helps."

This is a parable about God turning the tables on a man who has everything going for him in this life and faces torment in the next, and on the poor, suffering beggar, who finds himself feasting in the presence of Abraham in the life hereafter.

Still, we should not read this parable as if it predicts a terrible fate for everyone who has been rich in this life – remember that Abraham was also rich! Rather it is a strong call to take seriously

"Moses and the Prophets" (see 16:31), and especially their call to invest worldly resources in alleviating human suffering. That is how we live out the values of God's kingdom.

The parable itself is carefully structured. The first half describes the two men's situations in life (16:19-21), their deaths (16:22), then their situations in the afterlife (16:23). In the second half, we listen in on a dialog between the rich man and Abraham. It contains two requests:

- send Lazarus to alleviate my suffering (16:24-26);
- send Lazarus to warn my brothers (16:27-31).

Each time, Abraham refuses the request, and each time, he gives two reasons – denying both the necessity and the possibility of carrying out the rich man's wishes. The overall effect is to say, "It is now too late; you and your brothers had your chance!"

Some obvious effects of the parable are to warn of the dangers of wealth, especially when it is hoarded; to insist that justice will be done in the end; to declare that one day it will be too late and we will experience the consequences of how we have lived. Perhaps less obvious are these lessons: even a resurrection will not persuade those who have hardened their hearts to the teaching of the Scriptures (16:31); and (an important corollary for preachers) our calling is not to produce mighty miracles; it is to faithfully teach "Moses and the Prophets."

Yet none of these lessons should crowd out the obvious main point: pay attention – concretely attend to – the needy person at your gate. Jesus's parable dramatically challenges his hearers to share his priorities – ministering to the poor, the prisoners, the blind, the lepers (see 4:18, 27), giving priority to "the poor, the crippled, the lame and the blind" (see 14:13), giving away worldly wealth so that we will be "welcomed into eternal dwellings" (see 16:9). If we speculate too much about the exact nature of the afterlife but miss the obvious call to care for those around us, we have missed the point entirely.

I grew up hearing that parables are "earthly stories with heavenly meanings." This story is more like a "heavenly (or hellish) story, with an earthly meaning!"

Sin, Faith, Duty (17:1-10)

Often Jesus addresses one group even though other groups are also present. For example in 16:1, Jesus addresses his disciples, but we learn in 16:14 that the Pharisees were listening in, and Jesus then turns to address them and their issues (16:19-31).

In 17:1 Jesus again turns to his disciples, but the Pharisees are still listening in. And that helps explain how the first ten verses, containing diverse topics, actually fit together. Jesus is warning his disciples against the typical faults of the Pharisees. By implication, he is also inviting the Pharisees to change their ways.

From that perspective, this passage can be read like this:

17:1-2: Pharisees were not known for honoring "little ones." Jesus may be referring here to children, but just as likely he means vulnerable ones, those the Pharisees labeled "sinners," those society pushed to the margins, the outcast with whom Jesus gladly associated. Jesus here calls his disciples to be careful not to cause the "little ones" to stumble (17:2). Pay attention to them and their needs!

17:3-4: Pharisees typically scolded and despised sinners. Jesus calls his followers to lovingly confront and graciously forgive.

17:5-6: Pharisees majored on legal obedience and religious rituals. Jesus calls his followers to a life characterized by faith and faithfulness (the Greek word means both of these). A genuine faith will result in miracles happening – especially the miracles of "protecting the vulnerable" and "forgiving one another."

17:7-10: Pharisees typically worked hard to carry out religious duties, but then they expected their share of praise and reward for doing so (see especially Matthew 6:2, 5, 16). Jesus calls his followers to faithful service, simply because they owe this to their master, not for the sake of personal benefits. Even worldly servants do that for earthly masters. How much more should service be our attitude in God's kingdom! And how astonished and grateful we should be when our master does exactly what earthly masters do not do – he serves us! (see 12:37).

The Grateful Samaritan (17:11-19)

> *One of them, when he saw he was healed, came back, praising God in a loud voice. He threw himself at Jesus' feet and thanked him—and he was a Samaritan.*
>
> *Jesus asked, "Were not all ten cleansed? Where are the other nine? Has no one returned to give praise to God except this foreigner?" Then he said to him, "Rise and go; your faith has made you well." (17:15-19)*

Jesus has already used a Samaritan as a hero (10:33-37). Here again, a Samaritan is a positive model, and not just because he remembered to say "thank you."

In 4:27, Jesus reminded his hearers God has always crossed barriers to serve the outcast, and that includes curing them of leprosy. Now Jesus does the same. Yet it is not only Jesus who crosses barriers in this narrative; so does the grateful Samaritan. Samaritans despised Jews as much as Jews despised Samaritans. Yet this man appeals to a Jew for healing, falls gratefully at his feet when it happens and worships God exactly where it is appropriate to do so – at the feet of Jesus!

One thing about this story intrigues me and makes me wonder. Leprosy had drawn together this mixed group of outcasts. They were already shunned by their villages; they might as well throw aside their own ethnic and religious biases and share their common fate. But when Jesus sends them to show themselves to their priests (17:14 – notice "priests" [plural!]), he obviously expected the Jews to go to their Jewish priest and the Samaritans to their Samaritan priest. On the way, they are healed. So now they can go back to life as usual. Life as usual, however, would mean Samaritans going back to their Samaritan villages and avoiding Jews, and Jews going back to their Jewish villages and avoiding Samaritans. Or had this encounter with a common problem and a common healer done more for them than remove external leprosy? Had it also transformed their hearts? The evidence of the text is that, at least for the healed Samaritan, racial and religious prejudices were now gone. He was gratefully worshiping "the enemy," for in him, he saw the face of God.

One more thing. The text says, "As they went, they were cleansed" (17:14). Sometimes our healing happens in response to our obedience. When Jesus affirms the Samaritan's faith (17:19), he is referring to a faith that dares to obey without any proof the obedience will make a difference.

The Coming of the Kingdom of God (17:20-37)

> *Once, on being asked by the Pharisees when the kingdom of God would come, Jesus replied, "The coming of the kingdom of God is not something that can be observed, nor will people say, 'Here it is,' or 'There it is,' because the kingdom of God is in your midst." (17:20-21)*

Appropriate responses to the kingdom message of Jesus involve receiving it by faith, recognizing its upside-down values, responding to it in obedience, accepting its blessings. But what exactly is this kingdom? From Luke's perspective, it is the reign of God, exercised through Jesus and taking root in the present, even though its full manifestation, its final victory over all that opposes it, is still future.

In Jesus's day, people had all sorts of expectations about what would happen when God came down (or sent his Messiah) to establish the kingdom of God. Some expectations centered on religious renewal, some on political reform, some on military victory, some on world-transforming interventions from heaven. Everyone was sure when God's kingdom was established, Israel would be strong and free again. All agreed that when the kingdom arrived, you would know it!

Jesus disagreed with precisely those points on which others agreed. His kingdom announcement did not imply Rome would be defeated and Israel would be free and powerful once more. And he dared to announce that God's kingdom was already present and among them, even though most people were completely oblivious to this fact. They needed hearts of faith and divinely opened eyes to recognize that God really was establishing his kingdom through Jesus's life and message.

In this text, Jesus first corrects the Pharisees' assumption that God's kingdom would arrive in obvious and visible ways. "That is not the sort of kingdom it is!" Jesus says. And yet it truly is present "in your midst" – present in the person of Jesus and in the reigning of God Jesus was bringing about (17:20-21a).

The last words of 17:21 have sometimes been translated "within you," as though the kingdom of God is a purely internal spiritual experience. But for multiple reasons, this cannot be correct. Jesus did not proclaim a merely internal kingdom: almost all of his kingdom parables point in a different direction. Moreover, if we translate the words as "within you," we would have to understand that to mean *within the Pharisees*. English uses the expression "within you" to mean "within a person (in general)," but Greek does not.

The NIV translators got it right when they translated the words as "in your midst." God's kingdom was right among them, in the person and work of Jesus; the problem was they were looking for a different kind of kingdom and did not recognize it.

17:22-25 predict hard times ahead for Jesus's disciples. They will long for the "good old days" (when Jesus was with them); they will long for special interventions of God (like Jesus's transfiguration, his resurrection, his ascension); they will long for promised future interventions, like the second coming of Jesus. But their longings should not make them gullible, so that they run after anyone promising God's presence. Rather they should keep two things in mind:

- Before there is final victory, there will be tough times ahead for Jesus and for them. So be patient and endure!
- When the returning Son of Man accomplishes the final victory of God, it will not be a secret arrival (as it was at Jesus's first coming), but a phenomenon that nobody could possibly miss. So do not be deceived by people claiming special insight into the signs of its arrival.

17:26-32 use two analogies (the flood and God's judgment on Sodom) to make the point that people need be ready ahead of time for God's coming in judgment and salvation. If they just go on with normal life, they will be caught unawares. When judgment falls, there will be no time for final preparations.

"I tell you, on that night two people will be in one bed; one will be taken and the other left. Two women will be grinding grain together; one will be taken and the other left." (17:34-35)

These verses are often interpreted as if they predict a "rapture" that "takes away" those who are on their way to heaven. But the context requires a very different interpretation. Being "taken" does not mean being taken safely to heaven, but rather the opposite. Like those "taken" by the flood, the unprepared will face disaster when judgment falls – they will be *taken*. Only the prepared will be "left" (that is, saved).

But what is Jesus talking about? There is lots of evidence from Luke's writings that texts like this refer first and foremost to the coming disaster Jesus saw on the horizon for a nation that continued its headlong rush toward confrontation with Rome. It would result in the destruction of both the temple and the nation. If Israel assumed God was in support of her nationalistic aspirations, she was heading for a disaster comparable to the flood or the destruction of Sodom! That is, of course, exactly what happened about forty years after Jesus foretold it. Israel went to war with Rome, and Rome destroyed the temple, the city of Jerusalem and the nation of Israel.

Jesus says it is because they "did not know the things that make for peace" (19:42), because they "did not recognize the time of God's coming" (19:44). Peace comes, says Jesus, by learning to love the enemy. It comes by trusting God to make things right in the end.

So is this text not about the second coming of Jesus? Yes, it is that as well. When God intervenes dramatically in judgment and salvation, it always points toward that final day of ultimate judgment and eternal salvation. We do not know in advance which divine intervention will be the last one, the one that determines once and for all who was ready and who was not. That is why the burden of this whole passage is almost the opposite of what many Christians assume.

Many read a text like this as if it were designed to help us predict when and where and how "the rapture" will happen. But its point is that the kingdom is now arriving in a form that prevents all such calculations. And when its final arrival occurs, no advance warnings will give us one last opportunity to get ready. So from now on, there is no "life as usual" – those who listen to Jesus invest their whole lives living for a kingdom that is coming secretly today, but will catch the unsuspecting unawares when it finally comes in its fullness.

Verse 37 is puzzling, but its main idea is that the presence of vultures makes dead bodies easy to locate. Similarly, when the Son of Man returns in final judgment and salvation, it will be a public event, completely unmistakable (reiterating Jesus's point in 17:24).

The Bothersome Widow and the Unjust Judge (18:1-8)

This parable is often interpreted as a call to "persistent prayer." We should learn from this widow how to come to God in prayer – be persistent! But there are good reasons to doubt that Jesus (or Luke) intended this parable to teach that.

This widow is not only persistent: she is also bothersome and threatening. How does that model prayer for us? Granted, we can hardly blame her: look at what kind of judge she is dealing with! Since God is so very different than this judge (the exact opposite, actually), why should our prayers mimic this widow's behavior?

There are actually lots of reasons to challenge the traditional interpretation of this parable:

- God is not like the judge; why should we behave like the widow?
- Jesus explicitly says God will *not* keep putting us off; God will respond *quickly* (18:8a).
- The final sentence does not call for persistence but faith.

Moreover, the arguments usually used to insist this parable calls for persistence do not stand up:

- 18:1 does not say we should "pray and not give up *praying*." It rather calls for prayer as the *alternative* to "giving up" (becoming discouraged)! It says, when you need God's justice, do not give up; pray instead.
- The reference to crying "day and night" is not really a reference to how *long* we pray. A reference to how long we pray would have used the accusative case in Greek. Instead the genitive is used, so it means something more like this: God will hear "a prayer of the day" and just as much a "prayer of the night." So call anytime and expect God to respond quickly!

It seems to me that the main lesson in this parable is this: in this worldly system of grabbing what one can and trying to wring justice out of reluctant people in power, there is no alternative but to fight for one's rights. But since God has promised generous justice, we can maintain courage and hope ("not give up"). We can live as people of faith, assured that one day the Son of Man really will return and make all things right. This last point is indicated not only in this parable (18:8) but by the whole context of Luke's Gospel.

The Pharisee and the Tax Collector (18:9-14)

Some of Jesus's parables are puzzling, but this one is pretty straightforward. The opening and closing lines tell us exactly what point Jesus is making. Jesus is challenging self-righteous people who look down on others (18:9), warning them they will be the ones who lose out in the end. And he is encouraging the humble (18:14); they are the ones God will exalt.

His examples are striking. Pharisees were admired for their strenuous efforts to keep the law. But they were often filled with pride, and they scorned those less "righteous." Tax collectors were despised for being dirty cheats, collaborating with the enemy power.

In Jesus's parable, the Pharisee's self-righteous prayer of praise (praise about himself!) never makes it above the temple walls. The tax collector's prayer of repentance and his cry for mercy reach the loving, forgiving heart of God.

What a powerful encouragement to those who know they can never live up to people's expectations, let alone the righteous demands of God. And what a powerful indictment of those who think they are so much better than others. There is surely something in this parable for each of us!

Jesus Receives Little Children (18:15-17)

> *People were also bringing babies to Jesus for him to place his hands on them. When the disciples saw this, they rebuked them. But Jesus called the children to him and said, "Let the little children come to me, and do not hinder them, for the kingdom of God belongs to such as these. Truly I tell you, anyone who will not receive the kingdom of God like a little child will never enter it." (18:15-17)*

This text refers both to "babies" (note that the parents are *bringing them*; 18:15) and to "little children" (who could come on their own; 18:16). Jesus welcomes them, blesses them and uses them as an object lesson. Those *like children* will inherit the kingdom (meaning they will receive it now and inherit its fullness one day).

But what is it about children that makes them models for receiving God's kingdom? It can hardly be their age or their cuteness. Nor (contrary to popular claims) are children necessarily innocent or humble. Perhaps it is children's ability to embrace without reservation, without feeling they have to earn or pay back. This would fit well with the preceding parable. The humble tax collector knew he could never earn God's favor, nor did he need to. Children often model precisely that receptiveness.

The Rich and the Kingdom of God (18:18-30)

A man we often call the rich young ruler comes to Jesus with a question. But before Jesus answers it, he critiques the man for his opening address to Jesus – "good teacher." "Why do you call me good?... No one is good – except God alone" (18:19). These words have puzzled a lot of people. Is Jesus denying his own goodness? Is he saying, "Who, me? Good? Oh, no. That applies only to God!"

Actually something more profound and subtle is going on here. Of course Jesus is good. But by responding as he does, he is putting a choice before this man: "Either stop calling me good, or start calling me God!" You can't have it both ways. This text challenges the man to recognize Jesus as God!

And it challenges this man's ideas of both "God" and "good." The young man actually thinks he is pretty good himself. He claims to have kept all God's commandments all his life (18:21). Jesus knows better. He may have done pretty well with the second half of the Ten Commandments, but what about the very first one: "You shall have no other gods before me" (Exodus 20:3). The text shows clearly that this man gives his own wealth higher allegiance than the call of God (the call of Jesus!) on his life. He is not willing to give up his false god (wealth) and follow the true God (Jesus). So he walks away sad, without the eternal life he came asking about.

Jesus uses the occasion to make a series of important points about salvation and discipleship:

- It is especially hard for rich people to set aside false gods (like their own wealth) in order to follow Jesus (18:24-25);
- Salvation is a gift we receive, never something we can earn, neither by obeying laws nor by giving to the poor (18:26-27);
- Those who do respond to Jesus's demand and invitation to leave all and follow him experience that, even in this age, the rewards are astronomical;
- These are the ones to whom Jesus guarantees eternal life in the age to come.

You may have heard preachers refer to the tiny gate in Jerusalem called the Needle's Eye through which a camel could pass only with great difficulty, and only after unloading its pack and getting down on its knees. Unfortunately, there is not a shred of evidence in literature or archeology that there ever was such a gate. Yet the lessons often attached to this completely imaginary gate are quite consistent with the main concern of this text. Only by unloading our own pack (whether that be our wealth, other false gods or self-righteous obedience to laws), and only by getting on our knees (repenting and receiving forgiveness and salvation as God's gift), can we be assured of the eternal life this young man sought.

Jesus Again Predicts His Death and Resurrection (18:31-34)

Jesus again foretells in detail the passion and resurrection he anticipates in Jerusalem. The point of these predictions is to show that Jesus is fully aware of what will happen to him there. He knows it is part of his mission; he knows it will fulfill Scripture.

The fact that the disciples just cannot grasp this should not be chalked up to "divine hardening." (Some interpreters claim God was blinding their eyes.) Rather, they are still struggling to understand what kind of Messiah Jesus came to be and what sort of kingdom he is establishing. They cannot imagine how death at the hands of those in power in Jerusalem makes any sense, nor how there could be a resurrection for Jesus if that were to happen. Perhaps they think all this talk about death and resurrection is just one more parable.

But let's give them some credit. Despite all their struggles to understand, they do stick with Jesus! And that is why they will be in a position to understand all this later, when the resurrected Jesus opens the Scriptures, when the Holy Spirit opens their spiritual eyes and when they themselves pore over the Scriptures, trying to grasp the texts that were so unclear until they saw how Jesus fulfilled them.

A Blind Beggar Receives His Sight (18:35-43)

This text is Luke's version of the healing of blind Bartimaeus (Mark 10:46-52), only Luke does not tell us his name. Luke emphasizes first his persistence (18:35-39): he will not let the rebuking crowds prevent him from getting Jesus's attention. Then Luke emphasizes his faith (18:40-43): He humbly brings his request before the Lord, and when Jesus heals him, he responds in faithful discipleship (he followed Jesus) and worship (he praised God).

Luke ends this text by referring to the crowds praising God as well. This is a common refrain in Luke. Our praise should rise to God not only when we experience God's goodness, but also when we see God pour it out on those around us who so desperately need it.

Zacchaeus, the Tax Collector (19:1-10)

> *"Today salvation has come to this house, because this man, too, is a son of Abraham. For the Son of Man came to seek and to save the lost." (19:9-10)*

Jesus apparently loves to shock people. (So did Luke.) They keep lifting out unlikely heroes and using them as models. In this section, we have already seen him highlight a grateful Samaritan at the expense of ungrateful Jews (17:11-19), a humble tax collector at the expense of a self-righteous Pharisee (18:9-14), little children at the expense of rebuking disciples (18:15-17) and a persistent beggar at the expense of the silencing crowd (18:35-43).

Just when we think we have Jesus figured out – he pours out grace on the foreigners, the sinners, the helpless, the poor – he shocks us again. The hero of this text is rich!

But he is also an outcast, a chief tax collector and a cheat. We are not sure why he wanted to see Jesus that day, but he goes to great lengths (or rather great heights!) to make it happen. His problem is that he has a hard time holding his head high. That is my attempt to pass on the ambiguity of a text that says he was "short of stature." Perhaps he was physically short, or perhaps he was just a social outsider; maybe he was both. The text reads something like this: "In terms of his stature, he came up short!"

He throws caution (and his dignity) to the wind and climbs a tree. Grown men in that world did not do that, if for no other reason than because they wore skirts!

And yet, for all his efforts to see Jesus, this narrative is about Jesus seeing him. Notice how often the words "see" or "look" are used in the text! Actually, the Greek original text has one more that the NIV translators omit. The passage begins with a challenge to the reader: "Behold!" So this text invites us to reflect. What does Zacchaeus want to see? What does Jesus see? What does the crowd see? What do we see?

The crowd sees Jesus compromising his integrity. Jesus sees in a cheating tax collector an opportunity to pursue his mission (seeking the lost), and he sees in a converted tax collector a true son of Abraham. Zacchaeus sees an opportunity to begin a whole new life. This is his "day of salvation" (19:9), the day he welcomes Jesus into his home and into his life. This is the day he adopts the priorities of Jesus, the day he joins Jesus and Luke in demonstrating that being a true son of Abraham is not about ethnicity but about a transformed heart (see 3:8).

The Parable of the Ten Minas (19:11-27)

One of the functions of this long parable is to address the question "Will the kingdom appear at once or will it not?" (19:11). Apparently, the crowds hope Jesus's arrival in Jerusalem will signal the arrival of the "great and dreadful day of the Lord" (see Malachi 4:1-5 – great for Israel; dreadful for their enemies!). They clearly misunderstand the paradoxical already/not yet kingdom Jesus is inaugurating, right in the middle of the present evil age.

Jesus's parable addresses the crowd's question by speaking of a king (19:12) who takes up his full and final kingly role only when he comes back again (19:27). In the context of Luke, this clearly teaches that, after Jesus's first coming, there will be a period of time when his servants must be faithful stewards while they wait for the time of accounting at Jesus's second coming.

Yet we should not equate Jesus with the king in the parable. The characters in Jesus's parables are usually not exact replicas of those they represent. This king bears similarities to Jesus, but he also looks a lot like the historical figure Archelaus, who experienced exactly what the parable narrates (delegations trying to prevent him from becoming king; see 19:14) and who responded as the parable character did (with harsh vengeance on those who opposed his kingship; see 19:27). So we should catch the points of similarity between Jesus and this king without assuming they are more alike than they are.

The main points of similarity are:

- Jesus's first coming will not yet lead to the ultimate day of the Lord, when final judgment and salvation occur. That answers the question the crowds were asking in 19:11: no, Jesus's arrival in Jerusalem will not represent the final establishment of God's kingdom. Readers of Luke, of course,

know it will be a significant event in the inauguration of a kingdom now coming secretly!
- Jesus entrusts his followers with resources he expects them to invest for their master until his return. That is the main challenge of this parable.
- How we invest those resources will have consequences when Jesus finally returns to reward those who have been faithful and judge those who have not.

Luke 19:22-23 has often raised questions. Does Jesus really present himself as "a hard man, taking out what I did not put in, and reaping what I did not sow"? Not really. That is pushing the comparison between Jesus and this king too far. Actually, even the king in the parable is not admitting he is that. He is simply saying, "So that is what you think I am like? Well if you do, your actions should at least have been consistent with that. That would have been better than doing nothing." There is more irony here than literal description.

The challenge of the parable is to serve faithfully the one who has given us so much. Then, when he returns, he will invite us to join him and reign with him forever.

The Donkey-Riding King (19:28-44)

This text (along with parallels in the other Gospels) has inspired the church worldwide to celebrate "the triumphal entry" on "Palm Sunday," one week before Easter. It is a day of celebration, though we all know Good Friday is still coming before the even greater celebration of the resurrection can begin.

But we should be careful how and why we celebrate Jesus's so-called triumphal entry into Jerusalem. The crowds did not understand! They were cheering precisely because they thought that with Jesus's arrival in Jerusalem, the long-awaited kingdom would "appear at once" (see 19:11). Jesus just addressed this misunderstanding.

This text ends with Jesus weeping, not only at the condition of Jerusalem, now that he has finally arrived and can see for himself what is going on (19:41); he is weeping because so many in Israel do not understand what would bring peace (19:42). They expect peace to come when God's Messiah helps them defeat the hated Romans. Jesus knows that true peace is possible only for those who learn to love their enemies. True peace is found in joining Jesus on the road through suffering and death to resurrection and glory on the other side. True peace is God's gift and will be full and final only when Jesus comes again to make all things new.

Jesus knows if Israel continues its misguided rush toward confrontation with Rome, it can expect nothing but disaster ahead. And if Jerusalem rejects its "donkey-riding king," the coming disaster will represent not only Rome's revenge, but also God's hand of judgment.

So Jesus stages a protest against the ways of the world. That is what the script for this dramatic action is all about (see Zechariah 9:9-10). He chooses a donkey. Jesus knows true peacemakers are not those who mount warhorses (or tanks). Jesus's mission was to "take away the chariots from Ephraim and the warhorses from Jerusalem" (Zechariah 9:10). He came to break the battle bow and proclaim peace to the nations. That is the way to extend God's rule from sea to sea.

It is completely appropriate to cheer this triumphant king. If we do not, the rocks will! (19:40). But let's be careful not to cheer along with the crowds who misunderstood. Let's rejoice along with Jesus: "For the joy set before him he endured the cross" (Hebrews 12:2). Meanwhile, we also weep with Jesus, knowing that in this world there are still so many who do not "recognize the time of God's coming" (19:44).

Jesus at the Temple (19:45-48)

When Jesus entered the temple courts, he began to drive out those who were selling. "It is written," he said to them, "'My house

will be a house of prayer'; but you have made it 'a den of robbers.'"
Every day he was teaching at the temple. But the chief priests, the teachers of the law and the leaders among the people were trying to kill him. Yet they could not find any way to do it, because all the people hung on his words. (19:45-48)

This long section ends with a very short description of what we usually call "the cleansing of the temple" and then a reference to Jesus's ministry of teaching there.

Jesus protests the misuse of the temple. It is intended for prayer, but has become a place of commerce. As Jeremiah had done long before, he refers to it as a "den or robbers" (Jeremiah 7:11). The temple merchants were probably cheating pilgrims coming to exchange coins and purchase animals for sacrifice. But it means something else as well. A "robbers' den" is not normally a place where robberies occur. It is rather the robbers' hideout, the place they hide their spoils, the place they are able to ward off capture. The temple officials think their allegiance to the temple is their safeguard. They can live as they please, but as long as they stick to the temple and its ceremonies, they are secure. Jesus knows better. Precisely their misplaced allegiance to the temple system, their inability to recognize "the time of God's coming" (19:44), and their rejection of the true peace Jesus proclaims will lead to disaster for them, their temple, their city and their nation.

So this "cleansing" is really a protest action, not unlike Jesus's ride into Jerusalem (19:28-40) and his prophecy of its destruction (19:41-44). But it performs another function as well – it cleanses (at least symbolically) the place where Jesus will now take the podium and teach the people.

We should not imagine Israel as a whole rejected Jesus. Israel was divided. On one side were "the chief priests, the teachers of the law and the leaders among the people" who were trying to kill Jesus (19:47). On the other were Jesus and the community of his followers. Many in the crowd were still undecided, and Jesus will give them multiple opportunities to be persuaded by his message and accept his offer of salvation.

In the end, it is not true that Israel rejected Jesus. Those Jews who accepted Jesus became the nucleus of the renewed people of God, commissioned by Jesus to bring the message of salvation to the ends of the earth. Nowhere in the New Testament is the church characterized as a Gentile church that takes the place of Israel. The New Testament view is that the true church is "faithful Israel" incorporating into itself all who turn to Jesus.

For now, sympathetic crowds prevent Israel's leaders from doing away with Jesus. That will all change as we move closer and closer to the cross.

Implications of the Text for Today

The Faults of the Pharisees

I suggested above that we find the unity of 17:1-10 in the fact that Jesus is addressing the typical faults of the Pharisees. But we are sometimes too hard on the Pharisees. While there are major differences between Jesus and the Pharisees, they also have much in common, maybe more than Jesus has in common with other religious groups of his day (Sadducees, Essenes, Zealots, etc.). But that is perhaps also why the Gospel writers highlight the ways the Pharisees fall short. Their point is that followers of Jesus should study the Scriptures as carefully as the Pharisees do, pray as diligently, follow God's law as thoroughly, evangelize as passionately, but not fall into the traps that are so enticing when we practice faith with a passion: hypocrisy, legalism, looking down on others.

When we recognize that we as a Christian church have often fallen into those same traps, we let the Gospel texts about the faults of the Pharisees challenge and instruct us, rather than lead us to look down our noses at the Pharisees.

As Gordon Fee points out in his comments on Jesus's parable of the Pharisee and the tax collector (18:9-14), the Pharisee's attitude was all wrong when he thanked God he was not like the tax collector; ours will be just as wrong if we thank God we are not like the Pharisee.

"Increase our Faith"

When Jesus calls on his disciples to forgive without limit, their appropriate request is "Increase our faith!" (17:4-5). Jesus responds by saying that faith does not need to be large – a mustard seed-sized faith will do! So should our faith increase or get smaller? It sounds paradoxical, doesn't it?

Our problem is that we often think of faith as a skill at which we can get better and better, or a commodity of which we can gain more and more. Jesus challenges that idea of faith. Faith is measured by its genuineness, not its size. We put sincere faith in a trustworthy God. We should also note that the New Testament word for "faith" is also the word for "faithfulness." In fact, these really are not two things at all, but two sides of one coin.

When Jesus commands unlimited forgiveness (17:4), he is calling us to be a community of unlimited faith/faithfulness – trusting each other enough to challenge each other, confess to each other and forgive each other; trusting God to make us more loving, more humble and more helpful as we walk the faith journey together. In that sort of faithful and faith-filled community, miracles happen.

Celebrating Palm Sunday

If the crowds who cheered Jesus as he rode a donkey into Jerusalem misunderstood the whole point of Jesus's dramatic action, we shouldn't really join them in their (misguided) praises, should we? If the events of the triumphal entry made Jesus weep, why do we celebrate these events? Truth is the paradox of Palm Sunday is a lot like the paradox of the whole Easter season.

Israel wanted to experience deliverance from her enemies, so they celebrated the one they hoped would bring in the sort of kingdom for which they longed. Then they crucified him when he disappointed their expectations. Yet paradoxically the true enemies of Israel and of all humanity really were defeated through Jesus's death and resurrection. The principalities and powers, the devil and the demons, sin and death – all were ultimately defeated because

Jesus, the perfect one, was faithful through death and because his resurrection inaugurated in power the victorious kingdom of God.

Jesus knew all this was coming as he rode into Jerusalem that day. He knew it really was a victory march, even though victory came in ways so different from what people expected. He wept not for his own coming fate, but for those who did not understand and who refused the kingdom he was bringing. He knew that through their evil deeds, God's will would be accomplished. He knew also that Rome's wrath and God's judgment would come upon those who rejected him and the kingdom he proclaimed. And Jesus wept.

Nevertheless, we really should celebrate Palm Sunday, not as the misunderstanding crowds did, but as people of faith, confident that this Jesus who disappointed false expectations will one day fulfill all God's purposes.

When Jesus came the first time, he turned the world upside down by siding with the weak, by offering grace to the sinner, by loving his enemies, by prioritizing people over rules. When he comes again, it really will be a triumphal entry into our world to make all things new.

So we celebrate, even though we also weep. We walk the discipleship road with Jesus, carrying our own crosses. We follow Jesus through death to new life on the other side. And we join his donkey-riding protest as messengers of peace.

Personal Reflection Questions

- Jesus came announcing that God's kingdom was arriving. Yet it seems most people, including the disciples, misunderstood what kind of kingdom Jesus was proclaiming. The church throughout history has also held very diverse views on the nature of God's kingdom, sometimes identifying it with heaven, sometimes with the inner life of the Spirit, sometimes with a future kingdom of peace on earth, sometimes with the visible church, sometimes with what they called "Christian" nations. How has Luke's portrait of Jesus and his ministry helped you catch glimpses of the kind of kingdom Jesus taught and demonstrated in his ministry? What questions do you still have about the meaning of "kingdom of God" in Jesus's teaching and in Luke's Gospel?
- How has this section of Luke's Gospel challenged you in your commitment to discipleship? Are there topics on which the ethics Jesus taught and lived seem impossible or impractical in our world?
- What are your own personal reflections on the event we call the triumphal entry? How do you think we should celebrate an event Jesus responded to with tears?

Jesus and the Temple

The Text: Luke 20:1 - 21:38 NIV

The Flow and Form of the Text

Apart from some editorial comments about who is in dialog with Jesus and what they ask or claim, these two chapters represent almost exclusively the spoken words of Jesus himself. Sometimes he teaches the crowds or the disciples; sometimes he debates with or condemns the ruling authorities.

The theme of conflict is pervasive. Jesus has arrived in Jerusalem, the place where he foretold he would be rejected and killed (18:31-33). The previous section gave notice that, as soon as Jesus arrived in Jerusalem, "the chief priests, the teachers of the law and the leaders among the people were trying to kill him" (19:47). But they face a significant problem: Jesus is popular with the people. Any swift move to do away with Jesus would cost them their own popularity. Moreover, any move that might incite the rebellion of the crowds would be quickly quelled by the ruling Roman authorities.

The strategy of Jesus's enemies is to try to trap Jesus into words and actions that will either cost him his popularity among the people or get him in trouble with the Roman authorities, or both. One might expect that Jesus would speak and act cautiously under these circumstances. Sometimes he exercises caution, refusing to answer questions (20:8) or using veiled speech to make his points (20:18). But mostly he seems to go out of his way to antagonize the authorities, embarrassing them in public, outsmarting them in debate or pronouncing God's judgment on them, both in parabolic speech (20:16) and in plain speech (20:47).

As central as the theme of conflict is here, Jesus also makes other important theological and ethical points. Significant christological claims (questions of "Who is Jesus?") appear in 20:9-16 and 20:41-44. Important teaching on loyalty to Jesus instead of the state is embedded within 20:20-26. Insights into the nature of God's kingdom are revealed in 20:27-38 and 21:1-4. Warnings of impending persecution, glimpses of coming judgment and promises of future salvation are central themes in 21:5-38.

Not to be overlooked is the temple theme. The temple is the location for all of Jesus's teaching from 20:1 onward until at least 21:4. And the destruction of the temple is a major theme in all the rest of chapter 21. The authorities in Jerusalem are regularly associated with the temple. In subtle ways, Jesus presents himself as the new temple, the new place where heaven and earth meet, where sins are forgiven, where worship rises to the one true God.

Outline:

By What Authority are You Doing These Things? (20:1-8)
The Parable of the Tenants (20:9-19)
Paying Taxes to Caesar (20:20-26)
Marriage and the Resurrection (20:27-40)
David's Son or David's Lord? (20:41-44)
Warning Against the Teachers of the Law (20:45-47)
The Widow's Offering (21:1-4)
The Destruction of the Temple (21:5-24)
Being Ready for the Return of the Son of Man (21:25-38)

The Text Explained

By What Authority are You Doing These Things? (20:1-8)

Though Jesus often confronts, his primary goal is really to convert. Even here in Jerusalem, where Jesus will be in sharp conflict with powerful religious leaders, he sets out, first and foremost, to "proclaim the good news" (20:1). Yet that which is good news for those ready to receive it represents condemnation for those who oppose it.

Jesus has just enacted a dramatic protest against what is going on in the temple (19:45-46), and this provokes a strong reaction from those invested in the temple system and in maintaining their authority within it. So they confront Jesus, asking what authority he claims for himself. Is he claiming to be a rabbi? A prophet, maybe? Perhaps even the promised Messiah?

Truth is, Jesus is all of these and more. The parable he will soon tell makes clear that he claims to be the very Son of God! Yet he offers none of these responses to those confronting him. Rather, he uses the occasion to expose their hypocrisy. Jesus is popular with the crowds (see 19:48). But so also was Jesus's forerunner, John the Baptist. So Jesus turns the tables on the religious leaders, asking the same question about John that they asked about him: "In whose authority did John carry out his ministry?"

The trap is brilliant! The crowds are convinced John was a prophet, sent by God (20:6). If the religious leaders now claim otherwise, they risk being stoned by the people. But if they agree with the crowds, they reveal their own disobedience to God, for John called them to believe in Jesus and they are doing the opposite. In fact, John did more than call people to turn to Jesus. He also challenged the ethnocentricity and nationalism of the entire system over which these religious leaders presided. He called Israel to be reconstituted as God's people by personal repentance and by re-entering (through baptism) a community held together, not by Jewishness per se, but by covenant faithfulness to God.

"We do not know!" is the religious leaders' cowardly attempt to walk out of the trap. But it backfires. For Jesus has succeeded in getting the religious leaders to admit their ignorance of God's ways, and thus also disqualified them from assessing the rightness or wrongness of what the crowds believe. Since they have refused a forthright answer to Jesus's question, he refuses to respond to their question. At least, he refuses to give a direct answer! An indirect but ultimately just as powerful and condemning answer to the question comes next in the parable Jesus tells the crowds in the hearing of the religious leaders.

The Parable of the Tenants (20:9-19)

To understand the impact of this parable, we need to hear it against the backdrop of Isaiah's famous vineyard parable (Isaiah 5:1-7). That parable condemned Israel for being unfaithful, for bearing only bad fruit, and it prophesied the destruction of the vineyard.

Jesus's vineyard parable sounds like it will retell Isaiah's story, but then it veers off in a new direction. The vineyard in Jesus's parable also provides no useful crop for the owner. But this time the problem is not an unfruitful vineyard; the problem is unfaithful *tenants* trying to steal the crop for themselves. Jesus is placing the blame for all that has gone wrong, not on Israel as a whole, but on their religious leaders. And Luke makes unmistakably clear that the religious leaders understood this very well. They knew Jesus was comparing them to the unfaithful tenants (20:19); they knew Jesus was prophesying their own destruction at the hands of the vineyard owner (that is, as an act of divine punishment; 20:16).

Unfortunately, many interpreters claim that with this parable Jesus predicts the transfer of "the elect people of God" from "unfaithful Israel" to "the Gentile church." Not only does this interpretation easily lead to anti-Semitism, but it thoroughly misreads what Jesus said and what Luke wrote. Jesus does not contemplate replacing the vineyard (God's elect people). Rather the owner (God) assigns new tenants (new leaders) for it.

Jesus is referring to his own followers, the apostles, whom he already commissioned to lead faithful Israel (that is, those who believe in Jesus). Jesus, his apostles and the church that will emerge after Jesus's earthly ministry will be "faithful Israel" and will carry out the mission God always intended for Israel – to be a blessing to the nations and to draw people from all corners of the world, from all tribes and nations, into a covenant relationship with God (see especially 6:12-16; 13:29; 24:46-48). See additional discussion of this important issue under "Implications of the Text" below.

In 20:17, Jesus quotes Psalm 118:22, shifting his imagery (from son to stone), but not his message. Just as the son in Jesus's parable was rejected, so also the stone in Jesus's scriptural quotation. But God will vindicate the "stone," raising it up to be the capstone, the most important stone in the building (a symbolic reference to Jesus's resurrection and exaltation). Those who reject that stone ("fall on it") will be crushed by it (20:18). With these ominous words, Jesus predicts God's hand of judgment falling on Israel's leaders. They think they will be able to secure their own position and power by doing away with Jesus; in fact, that very act will be their undoing.

By publicly predicting the demise of Israel's present leaders, Jesus is calling the crowds to distance themselves from them, lest the people share their leaders' fate. Unfortunately, he already knows many will not heed the warning (see 19:41-44).

One last point: in Jesus's parable, the owner of the vineyard deliberately puts his beloved son at risk (20:13). The father is willing to risk everything, even his own son, to gain the fruit of the vineyard. While one might question the wisdom of this in terms of earthly farming practice, we must remember this is a parable. And it provides a beautiful image of what atonement with God through the death of Jesus involves. It involves God giving the Son and the Son giving himself for the sake of the vineyard.

Within the parable, the plan backfires: the father gambles that the wicked tenants would at least respect the son, and he loses that beloved son. But as the parable ends, Jesus makes clear to his hearers it is actually the wicked tenants' gamble that backfires (20:16).

So much in the gospel depends on deferring judgment about winners and losers until the end of the story!

Paying Taxes to Caesar (20:20-26)

The Jewish leaders need to overcome at least one of two problems before they can do away with Jesus (see 19:47-48). Either they must decrease his popularity with the crowds (so they can hand him over to the Romans without fearing an uprising), or they must get him in trouble with the Romans themselves (in which case, the opinion of the crowds no longer matters).

In this text, the leaders aim to accomplish either one or the other of these two goals. If he opposes the tax, he is in trouble with Rome; if he supports the tax, he loses popularity with the people. Jesus, however, springs the trap back on his questioners, just as he has done throughout this chapter. Again he avoids a direct answer to their question (as he did in 20:8). Again he tricks them into condemning themselves.

> *"Show me a denarius. Whose image and inscription are on it?" "Caesar's," they replied. He said to them, "Then give back to Caesar what is Caesar's, and to God what is God's." (20:24-25)*

The tax they needed to pay was a specific coin stamped with Caesar's blasphemous claim to be "The Son of God." Even handling such coins was an abomination to the Jews, let alone being forced to use them for a tax to support the costs of running the temple. Yet apparently Jesus's questioners have a coin ready at hand, right there in the temple itself. Jesus's reference to the image on the coin (Caesar's) gets at the real issue. They themselves are the image of God! But they are much more concerned with coins and taxes, and especially with eliminating Jesus, than they are with the high calling of giving themselves to God, the one whose image they bear.

This text is about priorities. Our duties to God always and in every way supersede any responsibilities we have to earthly authorities. This text does not say, "Some things we owe God; other things we owe the empire." Rather, it says, "All we are and have belongs to God; earthly demands are duties only when they are consistent with God's values." This means that we sometimes obey earthly authorities and sometimes disobey them. Depending on the circumstances, sometimes one choice and sometimes the other represents full loyalty to God.

Marriage and the Resurrection (20:27-40)

This is the only reference to Sadducees in the Gospel of Luke. Sadducees were a group of ruling officials who based their beliefs on the five books of Moses and resisted some of the beliefs based more directly on later Old Testament texts. In particular, unlike the Pharisees, they did not believe in a general resurrection of believers at the end of the present age (at the beginning of "the age to come"; see 20:35).

Here the Sadducees try to embarrass Jesus (as they often tried to embarrass the Pharisees) by posing dilemmas, hypothetical situations in which there would be no logical way for the "resurrection life" to be ordered. Their goal was to show that the law did not anticipate any future resurrection.

The dilemma here involves determining which of seven brothers would have a seven-times-widowed woman as his wife in the age to come. Jesus, the Sadducees and everyone listening would have known that the "Levirate marriage law" was in the background (see Deuteronomy 25:5, 6). The law required a childless widow to marry a brother of her deceased husband, so that their first child would count as the heir of the first husband. This would allow his family line to continue and the inheritance of his land to be regulated.

The Sadducees' strategy here is to show that the idea of a resurrection poses a dilemma for remarried widows. The Sadducees themselves were convinced that the law of Levirate marriage was the divinely ordained means by which people "live again" after their death. They live on in their descendants and thus in future generations of God's people.

Jesus's response should be read as an answer to the question: will Levirate marriages still be relevant in the age to come? Jesus's answer is that they will not. There will be no more death, no more need to produce offspring for others, no more need to regulate inheritances. *In that respect*, the resurrected "are like the angels" (20:36). The text does not make any claims about whether the relationships we enjoy in this life will continue or discontinue in the next, nor even whether or not there will be gender or intimate relationships in the age to come.

Having responded to the Sadducees' dilemma, Jesus gives a positive argument for a future resurrection based on the Scriptures the Sadducees accept (the books of Moses). Hundreds of years after the first patriarchs died, God identifies himself in Exodus 3:6 as "the God of Abraham, Isaac and Jacob." This, Jesus claims, demonstrates that even the books of Moses contemplate a resurrection.

We certainly should not read the text as a claim that these three patriarchs must have been resurrected in the meantime in order for God to still be their God centuries later. The biblical view is that their resurrection is still future. Nor should we think that "life after death" is what resurrection means. As N.T. Wright often says, resurrection actually means "life after life after death."

The Bible teaches a resurrection that is still future for those who, as Jesus worded it, "are considered worthy of taking part in the age to come and in the resurrection from the dead" (20:35). So how does Exodus 3:6 prove such a resurrection? Perhaps Jesus meant something like this: "Since God made great promises to the patriarchs but did not fulfill all of them in their earthly life, we can be certain they will one day be raised from the dead." That is the only way God can truly be their God – faithful to all that God promised them.

David's Son or David's Lord? (20:41-44)

The Old Testament prophesied the coming of an "anointed one." ("Messiah" is the Hebrew word for "anointed.") It also prophesied a descendant of David would one day rule forever on David's throne (1 Chronicles 22:10). The implication is "When the Messiah arrives, he will be a son of David."

Jesus came to fulfill the prophecies. Among many other titles, he was called both Messiah and Son of David. Yet, most of his contemporaries misunderstood his intentions, believing he had come to set up an earthly kingdom and rule over a restored Israel. Though Jesus accepted the title Son of David, he called his followers to a new understanding. Yes, Jesus was indeed destined to rule as king, but not only over Israel. Jesus would reign as king over all the earth.

In this text, Jesus challenges the adequacy of the title Son of David. Yes, properly understood, it does apply to him, to the Messiah. But Jesus knows he is much more than David's son; he is also David's Lord! So he quotes Psalm 110:1. There David, the presumed Psalmist, calls the one destined to rule the nations "my Lord." David says "the Lord" (Yahweh, the God of Israel) declares David's "Lord" (the Messiah) as the world's universal ruler. If we translate that into the later language of the church, Psalm 110:1 is saying, "The Lord (God the Father) said to my Lord (God the Son): 'Sit here at my right hand until I give you all the nations of the earth as your inheritance.'" Jesus's point is made. Yes, he is David's son, but he is far more than that!

The final question, "How then can he be his son?" is a rhetorical question, meaning "He must then be more than merely his son, right?" But perhaps we can also read it as a genuine question. How exactly does it come about that the one who is in fact David's son is also David's Lord? The rest of the New Testament supplies an answer: "By the fact that he was raised from the dead!" See especially Acts 2:32-36.

Warning Against the Teachers of the Law (20:45-47)

Jesus has already challenged his disciples not to assume their future role as leaders among God's people will bring fame and fortune or a comfortable life. They are only "unworthy servants" (17:7-9). Now Jesus makes the same point, but this time by using the current rulers as negative models. They flaunt fancy robes. They demand respect from the people. They enjoy the benefits of their high offices. And they make sure they retain all that with shows of piety, lengthy public prayers. Yet Jesus knows they are neither sincere nor just. In fact, they use their power and influence to rob the most vulnerable, the widows. By prophesying their coming punishment, Jesus is warning his disciples to practice a completely different kind of leadership. He is also warning the crowds, who are listening in, to distance themselves from those whose doom he has predicted.

The Widow's Offering (21:1-4)

> *As Jesus looked up, he saw the rich putting their gifts into the temple treasury. He also saw a poor widow put in two very small copper coins. "Truly I tell you," he said, "this poor widow has put in more than all the others. All these people gave their gifts out of their wealth; but she out of her poverty put in all she had to live on." (21:1-4)*

The chapter break after 20:47 is unfortunate. (Luke did not put any chapter or verse breaks into his text.) We should see in this poor widow an example of someone whose livelihood was stolen by the unscrupulous legal experts Jesus just condemned. Therefore we should see this text both as an expression of praise for her generosity and as a lament for the corrupt system that was impoverishing the most vulnerable.

Moreover, the gift she gives is ultimately a waste, for it goes to the corrupt temple system Jesus is about to declare bankrupt and doomed to destruction. Lamentable indeed! In fact, this woman, whose house was devoured (see 20:47) is a fitting symbol for the whole system, whose house (the temple) will also be "devoured" (destroyed; 21:6). We are reminded of the most famous of all biblical laments: "How deserted lies the city.... How like a widow is she" (Lamentations 1:1).

Yet there is also praise here. This woman's heart is in the right place. Our translations say she put into the offering "all she had to live on." Translating it literally, the text says she put in "the whole life that she had." That makes her a symbol also of the one who is about to give "the whole life that he has" for the salvation of the whole world.

Giving "all she had" is doubly impressive when we take into account that she gave her last two coins. If she had had only one, she would also have had only two options – give it or keep it. With two coins there was a third option – one to give, one to keep. She gave all. A fitting symbol of Jesus indeed! And so also a fitting expression of discipleship (see 14:33).

The Destruction of the Temple (21:5-24)

Some of his disciples were remarking about how the temple was adorned with beautiful stones and with gifts dedicated to God. But Jesus said, "As for what you see here, the time will come when not one stone will be left on another; every one of them will be thrown down."

"Teacher," they asked, "when will these things happen? And what will be the sign that they are about to take place?"

He replied: "Watch out that you are not deceived. For many will come in my name, claiming, 'I am he,' and, 'The time is near.' Do not follow them. When you hear of wars and uprisings, do not be frightened. These things must happen first, but the end will not come right away." (21:5-9)

Two prophecies: Connected and Disconnected

Two main topics are addressed in this long discourse by Jesus:

- Verse 6 introduces the first topic: the destruction of the Jerusalem temple.
- Verse 9 refers to the second topic: "the end," later identi-

fied with the return of the Son of Man at the end of this present age (see 21:27, 31, 36, etc.). Jesus makes clear that "the end will not come right away."

Paying attention to how these two events are related to and disconnected from each other is important for understanding this passage.

Most interpreters of Luke believe Mark's Gospel was one of the written sources Luke references in the first verses of his Gospel. It is likely Mark wrote before the temple was destroyed. Jesus predicted the temple's destruction and the Son of Man coming in glory, but did not make explicit how connected or disconnected these events would be. Nobody could know until the first prophecy was fulfilled whether or not it would lead directly to the fulfillment of the second. Jesus himself declares neither he nor anyone else knows the timing of the end (see Mark 13:32).

However, when the temple in Jerusalem was destroyed in AD 70 and the Son of Man did not arrive at that time (at least not in the full and final sense), everything changed. Now everyone who had heard Jesus speak or read Mark's account would know they were living in the waiting period between the first fulfilled prophecy and the second. It is likely in this time period that Luke writes his Gospel.

In Luke's account, we can detect a separation between the events associated with war in Judea leading to the destruction of the temple and events associated with Jesus's return as the victorious Son of Man to judge and to save. Luke's version *chronologically* disconnects these two sets of events from each other.

However, that does not mean they are not *theologically* connected. Jesus's resurrection vindicated his claim to be the promised Messiah and incarnate Son of God. Yet it did that only for those who believed Jesus rose. When Jesus foretold the temple would be destroyed and that this event would be God's judgment on those who rejected him as Messiah and Lord, he set up a public proof of his claims. If that prophecy were to go unfulfilled, Jesus's claims would be left unsupported. But if they should come true, those willing to go where the evidence leads ought to change their minds about Jesus. As we know, Jesus's prophecy about the temple, uttered in about AD 30, came true in AD 70. Jesus predicted it would be within the present generation (21:32), and forty years is exactly what most Jews would have understood that to mean.

Jesus is thus vindicated, not only as a prophet, but as the Messiah and the Lord he claimed to be. The fall of the temple becomes the outward evidence that Jesus really is Lord of all, destined to return as the victorious Son of Man to judge and to save. So the two topics of this discourse are theologically connected, even if chronologically separated.

We should also note that some of the events predicted in this discourse (such as persecution for believers) occur during both of the time periods in question, so that it is not possible to make a strict separation between the events associated with the first and those associated with the second prophesied period. Yet it seems appropriate to divide Jesus's discourse into two parts. Luke 21:5-24 is primarily about the Jewish war with Rome that resulted in the destruction of Jerusalem and its temple. Luke 21:25-38 is primarily about events leading up to and accompanying the final return of Jesus.

Throughout his ministry, Jesus took a critical stance against the temple and the events and people associated with it. It seems rather inappropriate, in the light of this, for the disciples to be awestruck by the splendors of the temple (as impressive as they were; 21:5). Jesus no doubt shocks them with his prediction of the temple's coming demise (21:6).

It is understandable that the disciples might want to know when this unimaginably great destruction would take place, but to ask for signs to help them predict its nearness is to set themselves up for deception. That is often the case in Scripture. Whereas modern Christians often comb through the Scriptures to detect "signs of things to come," the Scriptures warn against that attitude. Jesus here certainly does. Do not watch for signs, or you will likely be deceived!

Sign seekers often read 21:8-9 as if they predict the first three signs: deceivers, wars and uprisings. Exactly the opposite is the case. Deceivers are not signs – they are the ones who capitalize on the misguided desire for signs. Wars and uprisings are not signs – they are recurring events that Jesus says do not signal the soon arrival of anything. The point of these two verses is to warn against seeking signs. If sign seeking is our preoccupation, we will be easily deceived and we will wrongly interpret what is going on in the world.

Verses 10-11 name things that happen over and over throughout history. We can expect that they will happen both before and after the destruction of the temple. Jesus says they will happen before the end (compare 21:11 and 21:25). They are "signs of what happens over and over"; they are not "signs" of the type the disciples desired. Precisely because these things keep on happening, they cannot help predict the nearness of anything.

The text now backtracks to talk about what will happen before the events associated with the end. Verse 12 is the crucial verse that separates the rest of this section (21:12-24 which talks about the temple's destruction) from the next section, where the "signs from heaven" signal the end of the age (21:25).

Jesus warns his disciples of coming persecution and promises divine help when they face it (21:12-15). He warns that the coming events will put them at odds even with family members and friends (presumably those who do not follow Jesus; 21:16-17). Verses 18-19 give the ultimate assurance – even if persecution costs them their lives, they lose nothing, for even in death, they gain the life that lasts forever.

Verses 20-24 predict the hardships people in Jerusalem and in the surrounding countryside will face when the war is raging. Jesus counsels the opposite of conventional wisdom. Normally people rush into walled cities to be secure in times of war. Jesus warns them to flee, for he knows the city will be destroyed.

In the present context, we should read 21:24 as a reference to the length of the war itself. "The times of the Gentiles" means the God-ordained time for the Roman troops to be instruments of God's judgment on those who have rejected their Messiah. This is the implication of the crucially important 21:22: "This is the time of punishment in fulfillment of all that has been written." Jesus makes very clear that, whatever else the Jewish-Roman war is (a political rebellion, a power play by a new emperor, an attempt to re-establish Roman rule on the Eastern frontier), it is, first and foremost, God's act of judgment on those who rejected their promised deliverer.

They wanted someone to deliver them from Rome; he came to deliver them from sin and death and all the power of God's ultimate enemy. That was not good enough for them. Now they are facing the consequences of their rebellion against God.

Of course, we must be careful never to interpret this as though "the Jews" or "the nation" rejected Jesus. They were divided. Judgment fell on those who rejected Jesus. Salvation came for those who accepted him.

Being Ready for the Return of the Son of Man (21:25-38)

> *"There will be signs in the sun, moon and stars. On the earth, nations will be in anguish and perplexity at the roaring and tossing of the sea. People will faint from terror, apprehensive of what is coming on the world, for the heavenly bodies will be shaken. At that time they will see the Son of Man coming in a cloud with power and great glory. When these things begin to take place, stand up and lift up your heads, because your redemption is drawing near." (21:25-28)*

The second half of Jesus's discourse shifts the focus from Jerusalem's destruction to the final coming of the Son of Man at the end of the present age. When Jesus returns, it will not be for Israel alone, but for the whole world (see 21:35).

And it will not happen to the generation of those standing around Jesus. It will happen to the final generation on earth before God visits this earth once more. This is signaled even by the change in pronouns: 21:20 says, "When *you* see"; 21:27 says, "*They* will see." Whichever generation is alive at the end of ordinary history will experience the final convulsions of heaven and earth as the Son of Man makes his grand entry to judge and to save. For believers, it is the time of redemption, the time to "lift up our heads" (21:28). For those who reject Jesus, it will be a judgment even more final than the one in Jerusalem Jesus just predicted for his contemporaries.

We should not think of the "signs" in 21:25-26 as events designed to help people predict that the end is coming soon. They are rather part of Jesus's description of the end itself. When the Son of Man comes in judgment and salvation, it will be too late to start getting ready, as Jesus already warned his disciples in 17:24-30.

Verses 29-33 assure Jesus's disciples of a series of things. First, we can track the passing of the seasons by observing the regularities of nature (21:29); in the same way, we can see how God is working out divine purposes by observing how the things Jesus foretold keep coming to pass (21:31). Second, the crucial events that must precede the end will all happen within one generation of Jesus's own prophecy (21:32). That implies that after the temple falls, no one can any longer be sure of a necessary delay for the final return of the Son of Man. After that, it could happen at any time. The fact that it has not yet happened does not invalidate that. It still could happen at any time! And third, Jesus's prophetic words will be fulfilled. They stand as secure and certain as heaven and earth.

When Jesus says, "Heaven and earth will pass away" (21:33), he does not mean God will demolish the created universe and start all over again. Rather these words mean one or the other (or both) of the following:

- Even if heaven and earth could pass away, my words never would. That would be an idiom for "count on it"!
- Heaven and earth *in their present form* will one day pass away (so that they will be renewed and reconnected); my words, however, need no revision or correction. They stand

firm and will be fulfilled as I have spoken them.

Luke 21:34-38 calls for an appropriate response to all Jesus has just prophesied. Be ready! There are dangers all around. Loose living (carousing and drunkenness), lack of faith (being weighed down with anxieties), lack of vigilance (that day closing in like a trap) – all these can dull our anticipation of the Son of Man's return. Be ready! Everyone will be called to account in God's great act of final judgment and salvation.

Implications of the Text for Today

Israel and the Gentiles

Because so many interpreters read Jesus's parable of the vineyard (and other texts in the New Testament) as predictions that God will turn away from the Jews and create a covenant people out of the Gentiles *instead*, we need to address this issue.

Charles Talbert helpfully points out that Jesus's parable does not signal a shift from Jews to Gentiles but rather is "an attack on the religious bureaucracy (vs. 19) and says that because of their rejection of Jesus, their position as caretakers of God's people is cancelled and in their place others are appointed (in the Lukan context, the apostles, 22:28-30; Acts 1:15-26)" (Talbert, 189). Luke's position, Talbert says, is that "Christianity is completed Judaism;...one becomes a part of God's people by individual decision for Jesus" (182).

Even in the Old Testament, Israel as a nation-race was never *synonymous with* the people of God. The people of God were the faithful minority that existed within the nation-race. Into this covenant people, Gentiles were invited (see Numbers 15:15); from it, disobedient Israelites were excluded. "The people of God" was ultimately defined, even in the Old Testament, more by faith and obedience than by ethnicity and race. And that is of course all the more so after the coming of Jesus, for now through Jesus, all tribes and peoples are invited into the covenant people of God, no matter what nation-race they may represent.

Yet, as Talbert makes clear, Jesus's parable of the vineyard is not about that topic. It is about the disqualification of evil tenants – the religious rulers, who control Jerusalem and reject Jesus. And it is about the authorization of those Jesus is recruiting – the disciple-apostles, whom he is training for future leadership for the people of God.

Loyalties to God and to the State

Jesus's demand that we give Caesar what belongs to Caesar and God what belongs to God raises the question of ultimate loyalties. We all have multiple loyalties – to friends and family, to employers, to our nation. This text and other passages in Scripture (for example, Acts 4:19; 5:29) make very clear that all other loyalties are subordinate to our loyalty to Jesus. The demands of Jesus justify our disobedience of any authority whose demands are inconsistent with our highest loyalty.

This became a real issue for me when I was summoned for jury selection.

Dozens of people were sent home because they had knowledge of, or experiences with, or prejudices about, the subject of the case. Among the questions the judge posed to prospective jurors, one seemed purely routine, and never resulted in anyone's disqualification: "Will you agree that you will obey all of my instructions, even if you disagree with them?" Everybody agreed, until the judge came to me.

I chose not to offer the judge my promise of unconditional obedience. The judge seemed stunned. He politely asked me to explain myself.

"Your honor," I said, "I have high respect for the judiciary and the role of the judge. I also have high respect for you as a person. But you have asked me to agree in advance that I will do whatever you ask me to do, no matter what that is. I cannot promise you that. I cannot promise that to any judge, or to any employer, president or emperor. I do not anticipate that you will ask me to do anything I cannot do, but a promise that, if you would, I would do it anyway is something I cannot give."

The next morning, I found myself sitting in jury seat number two. I could serve with a good conscience, knowing I had preserved clarity about the main thing: Jesus is Lord.

What Will it be Like in the Age to Come?

Jesus's response to the Sadducees in 20:34-36 has led some to make detailed conclusions about the nature of the resurrection life – conclusions about gender and sexuality and family relationships. We need to be cautious about proposing details, not only because the text is unclear about this, but also because the pastorally appropriate answer for one person is not the pastorally appropriate answer for another person.

When a grieving widower longs for his own death, so he can be united with his recently departed wife, we dare not raise questions about whether the relationships of this life really will resume in the next. But when a remarried widow or widower (like myself) ponders these questions, suddenly everything looks very different. My wife does not take great delight in imagining my reunion with my first wife!

Perhaps Jesus deliberately avoided clear answers on the nature of the resurrection life precisely because our limited earthly perspectives would leave us wondering, along with the Sadducees, "How is God going to solve that puzzle?"

End Time Speculation

People often refer to "signs of the end times" and then assume Scripture calls us to watch for them and recognize them, so that the final return of the Son of Man does not catch us unawares. What they mean is that we will be able to figure out in advance, based on the signs, when the "end" is about to arrive. But that seems to be the opposite of what Jesus teaches.

Jesus actually teaches his return will, *and is intended to*, catch people *unawares* (that is, they will be unable to predict when it will be). Jesus wants us to make sure it does not catch us *unprepared*! If we are faithfully following and carrying out our calling, then when the Son of Man returns (unexpectedly!), we will be ready. That seems to be the obvious teaching of texts like 12:35-40.

Signs in Scripture are not intended to facilitate speculation about when the Son of Man will return. They have two other functions. One is to call for discernment, urging us to recognize how God is at work, fulfilling ancient promises. The other is to call for insight into the *significance* of the events we are experiencing. That is what the Greek word for sign (*sēmeion*) actually means.

In Luke 21, the disciples want "signs" (advance indications), that will help them predict when Jesus's prophecies will be fulfilled. Instead of giving them that, Jesus provides "signs" (evidence) that God is at work in history and "signs" (interpretations) of what it all means.

When the End comes, we will be caught by surprise. Let us not be caught unprepared. In the meantime, we live with joy and confidence that the one who has always been faithful will carry us, our communities of faith and our world through whatever challenges lie ahead, until the Son of Man comes to judge and to save.

Personal Reflection Questions

- Where have you experienced conflicting loyalties, and in particular, demands from "earthly authorities," that stand in tension with the call of Jesus and the values of God's kingdom? In such situations, how have you responded to the pressure of those authorities?
- Do you have fixed opinions about the nature of the afterlife (what happens immediately after death)? Do you have fixed opinions about the nature of the resurrection life that begins with the future return of the Son of Man, when "the dead in Christ rise" and when "those still alive are transformed"? (see 1 Corinthians 15:52). When have those opinions created dilemmas for you as you try to respond pastorally to those around you?
- What motivates people to scan the heavens (or the newspapers) for "signs of the end times"? What surprised you about the claims made in this section by Jesus, by Luke and by the author of this commentary? Do you have a different interpretation of end time prophecy than was offered here?

The Suffering and Death of Jesus

The Text: Luke 22:1 - 23:56 NIV

The Flow and Form of the Text

Luke 22 and 23 record the events surrounding Jesus's death. At some point during this so-called Passion Week, Judas agrees to betray Jesus (22:1-6). On Thursday of that week, Jesus's disciples prepare for the Passover meal. All the rest of the events in these chapters, with the exception of the last half verse, take place within a 24-hour period between sundown Thursday and sundown Friday.

Luke's account of these events closely parallels what we find in the other three Gospels (Matthew 26:14 - 27:61; Mark 14:10 - 15:47; John 13:1-38, 18:1 - 19:42). If our only interest were in the historical details, we might want to draw on all four biblical accounts to reconstruct the whole story.

But if we did that, we would be abandoning the goal of each of the Gospel writers. None of them wrote simply so that historical facts could be known. All four evangelists recorded these momentous events in order to interpret them for their readers as God acting through Jesus for the salvation of the world. Yes, all these things happened in "ordinary" history at a particular time and place. Drawing on all four accounts helps reconstruct what happened. But these things also happened in "salvation" history; they represent the pivotal events in which the powers of evil aim to defeat God's plans, and through which God paradoxically triumphs over those evil powers. Each Gospel writer emphasizes particular aspects of this all-encompassing plan of God to redeem the world. Each Gospel writer highlights particular ways in which that larger story encourages, challenges and transforms the reader.

We will focus on Luke's account of these events. Along the way, we will watch for clues in the way Luke narrates the details, clues that reveal the deeper significance of what is going on and that teach readers how to respond.

This section will end with the burial of Jesus on what has come to be called Good Friday and with a brief reference to what we sometimes call Holy Saturday (for the participants back then, the Sabbath). That will leave only Luke 24, the grand announcement of Jesus's resurrection and all that it entails.

Outline:

- Judas Betrays Jesus (22:1-6)
- The Last Supper (22:7-38)
    - Preparing for the Passover (22:7-13)
    - The Bread and the Cup (22:14-23)
    - True Greatness (22:24-30)
    - Predictions of Disloyalty and Violence (22:31-38)
- Jesus Prays on the Mount of Olives (22:39-46)
- Jesus Arrested (22:47-53)
- Peter Denies Jesus (22:54-65)
- Jesus on Trial (22:66 - 23:25)
    - Trial Before the Jewish Council (22:66-71)
    - First Trial Before Pilate (23:1-7)
    - Trial Before Herod (23:8-12)
    - Second Trial Before Pilate (23:13-25)
- The Crucifixion of Jesus (23:26-43)

The Death of Jesus (23:44-49)
The Burial of Jesus (23:50-56)

The Text Explained

Judas Betrays Jesus (22:1-6)

Luke reminds the reader the religious leaders have been unable to arrest Jesus because of his popularity with the people. This text solves their problem. Judas, one of Jesus's own disciples, turns traitor and makes a deal to hand over Jesus to them. Judas knows Jesus's whereabouts and his habits, so he will be able to accomplish the betrayal when no crowds are present (22:6; see 22:47).

What motivated Judas? We cannot be sure, though that has not stopped people from speculating. Was it greed for money? Was it disillusionment with what Jesus had been saying and doing? Was it a misguided belief that his act would force Jesus to finally do what Judas (and many others) wanted Jesus to do – intervene to bring about an earthly kingdom? Some have argued that human motivations are not relevant: Satan made him do it! (see 22:3). But things are more complex than that. Judas's deed was also in the plan of God (see 22:22a), was prophesied in Scripture (Psalm 41:9) and foretold by Jesus (Mark 9:31). Yet none of these external factors forced Judas to act. Jesus is clear that Judas is fully accountable for his own actions. The fact that human evil is sometimes part of the means by which God's plans are accomplished does not make the deeds any less evil, nor the evildoers any less accountable (see 22:22b).

The Last Supper (22:7-38)

The events directly linked to the final meal Jesus ate with his disciples are narrated in the next long section (22:7-38). They include careful preparations, the meal itself (with attention to two cups and the bread), and various conversations about greatness, leadership and failure, future persecution and "the need for swords." (Note the quotation marks around this last point: if we do not examine that part of the text carefully, we can easily reach conclusions quite the opposite of what Jesus really meant!)

In a Jewish context, meal fellowship focused on hospitality and solidarity. Jesus critiqued those who used meals as occasions to enhance their own honor (see 14:7-24). Jesus himself used meal fellowship in just the opposite way, welcoming the outcast and creating family out of diverse people. In a Gentile (especially Greek) context, meal fellowship also took on the character of a "symposium" where topics were debated. Luke's narrative of Jesus's last meal with his disciples seems to combine Jewish and Greek emphases.

This story bears resemblance to many "farewell discourses" in biblical literature where a leader – sometimes a father – bids farewell to his people before his death. Such a farewell discourse normally involves the gathering of family and friends, a reference to the approaching death, a review of the departing person's life and priorities, and often, a transfer of leadership responsibilities to those gathered. Farewell discourses also include promises, encouragements, predictions, warnings, prayers, etc. The final element was usually a parting blessing. Interestingly, all of these elements are present here except for the blessing. That will come in the last four verses of Luke's Gospel. It is as though Jesus knew this would be a farewell, but not a final farewell. He would be regathering them once more for a final blessing before passing the baton to them and to those who would follow.

Of course, we should not overlook the important fact that this meal is a Passover celebration (see 22:7, 8). That means there is a strong focus on such things as:

- liberation of the marginalized (in ancient times, Israelite slaves in Egypt; in Jesus's day, those excluded as outcast);
- sacrifice (the Passover lamb was a substitute and the means of Israel's ransom);
- covenant (God delivered Israel from Egypt to enter a new covenant with God);

- promise (Israel looked forward to final deliverance).

Despite the fact that this is obviously a Passover meal, there is no reference here (nor in any other New Testament account of this meal) to the lamb or to most of the other unique features of the Passover meal (bitter herbs, spices, etc.). Rather Jesus provides a new interpretation of the elements that were common to all festive meals (the wine and the bread). It is as if every fellowship meal from now on can be an occasion for remembering Jesus's presence and the salvation he brings.

Preparing for the Passover (22:7-13)

This text narrates the sending of two disciples, dialog about their assignment, prearranged signals or perhaps foreknowledge (we cannot be sure) and detailed preparations for Jesus's next act. All these elements are closely parallel to what we observed in 19:28-36, before Jesus rode into Jerusalem on a donkey. It is as though Luke wants to highlight the parallels between these two events. Yes, Jesus comes in triumph, but it is the paradoxical triumph of a martyr, faithful even to death. Yes, Jesus will be killed by his enemies, but in that very event he fulfills his role as "the king who comes in the name of the Lord" (see 19:38).

The Bread and the Cup (22:14-23)

Footnotes in many Bibles indicate that the oldest manuscripts of Luke do not all say exactly the same things here (see 22:20). But I will interpret the text as printed in the New International Version (2011), which I think is closest to Luke's original wording.

Those who regularly celebrate communion services and hear readings that refer to the bread and the cup may be surprised that in Luke's version there are two cups. Actually the Passover meal included four cups. Perhaps Jesus reinterpreted for his disciples all four cups and many other features of the Passover celebration.

Verses 14-18 are Jesus's way of signaling that his departure is very near, but that his mission is not yet complete. Still unfinished are, of course, this meal and the accompanying teaching. But these verses indicate Jesus has another mission to fulfill beyond this evening, the ultimate outcome of his entire life, death and resurrection: the final establishment of God's kingdom. Jesus had been eagerly awaiting this meal; how much more the great feast in God's kingdom to which this meal points (see 14:15).

> *And he took bread, gave thanks and broke it, and gave it to them, saying, "This is my body given for you; do this in remembrance of me."*
>
> *In the same way, after the supper he took the cup, saying, "This cup is the new covenant in my blood, which is poured out for you. But the hand of him who is going to betray me is with mine on the table. The Son of Man will go as it has been decreed. But woe to that man who betrays him!" They began to question among themselves which of them it might be who would do this. (22:19-23)*

Verses 19-20 explain the bread and the cup: they stand for Jesus's body and his blood, sacrifices on our behalf, sealing a new covenant that brings us into fellowship with God through Jesus. As we eat the bread and drink the cup, we re-enact Jesus's last meal with his disciples, just as the Israelites at every Passover were re-enacting the last meal before the original exodus from Egypt. We are thus joined to the whole people of God, as we live in covenant with God and with each other.

Notice that Jesus shares the cup and the wine even with Judas, who (as he well knows) is about to betray him. This should caution us against viewing this recurring celebration as a place to draw clear lines about who is "truly committed" and who is not.

Verses 21-23 again highlight the coming betrayal by Judas, the fact that it contributes to the fulfillment of God's purposes, but that Judas is fully responsible for his evil deed. Notice that the other disciples are unsure to whom Jesus is referring. This suggests two things:

- Judas's participation in the group had been indistinguish-

able from that of the others; and (therefore)
- Any of them, and any of us, could potentially also turn against Jesus, so we must be on our guard.

True Greatness (22:24-30)

Luke's Gospel presents Jesus as the one who fulfills Isaiah's texts that speak of a faithful, suffering servant of God (see especially 4:18-21). One of Jesus's parables indicates that in God's kingdom even the master plays the role of the servant (see 12:37). Now Jesus says it clearly, "I am among you as one who serves" (22:27).

How inappropriate for his own disciples to argue about who is greatest! The greatest is the one who serves and who pays no attention to any reputation for greatness. That sets Jesus and his kingdom apart from the normal worldly status-seeking ways of leadership and greatness. In God's kingdom, there is only one benefactor, only one who makes every act of sacrifice and service worth it. And that is God, who repays not in terms of earthly prestige and power, but in the final unveiling of God's upside-down kingdom.

Jesus declares that his Father has bestowed on him this kingdom and he in turn bestows it on his followers. We are privileged to join with Jesus's first disciples in our anticipation of that great kingdom feast, when we will sit at the table with our servant-master, Jesus, and eat and drink in fellowship with him.

Yet our participation alongside Jesus's first twelve disciples does not imply that we exactly share their roles. Their role was unique: to symbolize and bring to reality the new faithful minority of Israel – the new "twelve tribes." Through this renewed Israel, the mission of God's people reaches its goal: to be a blessing to all nations. So faithful Israel comes to fruition in the church as it carries that gospel to the ends of the earth.

Verse 30 speaks of "judging the twelve tribes." The word implies "ruling." (Remember that in ancient Israel, the judges were actually rulers.) So Jesus's disciples are rulers who serve, and servants who rule. What a paradoxical kingdom! What a counter-cultural kingdom!

Predictions of Disloyalty and Violence (22:31-38)

This text puts Simon Peter at the center of the community. Despite the overconfidence he displays (22:33), despite the fact that he will explicitly deny his allegiance to Jesus (22:34), Simon is singled out for a special role: strengthening the others (22:32).

This text again gives us glimpses of the cosmic battle being waged. Satan aims to "sift" (lead astray); Jesus prays for our faithfulness. Neither of these influences, however, absolves us of the need to make personal decisions: will we, or will we not, take our stand with Jesus and his kingdom?

> *Then Jesus asked them, "When I sent you without purse, bag or sandals, did you lack anything?"*
> *"Nothing," they answered.*
> *He said to them, "But now if you have a purse, take it, and also a bag; and if you don't have a sword, sell your cloak and buy one. It is written: 'And he was numbered with the transgressors'; and I tell you that this must be fulfilled in me. Yes, what is written about me is reaching its fulfillment."*
> *The disciples said, "See, Lord, here are two swords."*
> *"That's enough!" he replied. (22:35-38)*

And now we come to those verses that can easily be misunderstood. Verse 35 makes reference to the previous missionary journeys and the instructions Jesus gave the missionaries (see 9:3; 10:4). Now Jesus gives new instructions. We always trust God to meet our needs. But sometimes God chooses to meet them through those with whom we come in contact (that seems to be implied in Luke 9 and 10). Sometimes God does so through careful preparations (the point here). Sometimes the mission will obviously be successful (as it was in chapters 9 and 10); at other times, it will invite persecution more than favorable responses (the expectation here). Jesus will be the one "numbered with the transgressors" (22:37), but his disciples will also face hard times.

That sets the stage for the "two swords" text. Some interpreters read these verses as though Jesus is giving his followers permission (or even instruction) to practice self-defense, to take out the enemy that comes to attack. However, what the text actually says, especially when read together with its sequel in 22:49-51, points in the opposite direction. Defending themselves or their master with their two swords was precisely what the disciples were not supposed to do. Jesus rebukes them for that misunderstanding.

The fact that Jesus's disciples had two swords in their possession should not seem surprising. After all, there might well be a wild animal to guard against (including dogs, most of which in the first century were not pets!). Jesus does not rebuke his disciples for having swords; he will rebuke them for thinking they should use them against human enemies.

A great deal in this text is not meant to be taken literally. The cloak, for example, was considered a person's most essential possession; one would sell everything else first before parting with the cloak (which doubled as a blanket at night). An English equivalent expression might be "You'll need a sword more than anything in the world." It is like my friend Ray's favorite slogan: "If you can't afford this book, sell your bed to buy it." None of these expressions are intended literally. They all mean "This is a very serious matter." So Jesus is actually saying, "There will be hard times ahead!"

So "cloak" was used metaphorically in their world; but so also was "sword." It often simply meant "division" (compare 12:51 with Matthew 10:34).

The disciples seem to miss the real point and pull out literal swords. And that provokes the response of Jesus that has led to such diverse interpretations. Jesus's words could be translated either as "That's enough!" or "Enough of that!" Several contemporary translations go with the second option (CEB, CEV, HCSB, ISV; see also The Message: "Enough of that; no more sword talk"). Taken this way, Jesus is responding in frustration that his disciples could possibly think he wants them to fight with literal swords.

If we stick to the way the NIV translates these words, "That's enough," what could Jesus then mean? Two possibilities fit the context. Jesus might be saying, "Two swords should be about the right number to take out the combined forces of Jewish and Roman opposition, including temple guards and the Roman military power." How literally are we supposed to take that? Or else Jesus might be saying, "Any number of swords would be enough to fulfill the prophecy just quoted, that Jesus will be among transgressors [i.e. among disciples resorting to violence]." Either way, the idea that he is authorizing his disciples to use those swords to defend themselves or him is ruled out.

Why would Jesus speak words that can easily be misunderstood to mean the opposite? We cannot know, partly because we cannot know what else Jesus said to make the meaning clear. But we can observe what Luke does in presenting the material. He leaves it somewhat ambiguous here, but then makes clear later in the chapter that those disciples who thought Jesus intended for them to strike out at others in self-defense had completely misunderstood him.

So we leave the issue for now and pick it up again at 22:49-51.

Jesus Prays on the Mount of Olives (22:39-46)

Luke's version of Jesus's prayer on the Mount of Olives emphasizes four things:

- Jesus models appropriate prayer: we lay our requests before God, but do not presume to know how God will respond. Ultimately God's will, not our own, should be our highest concern (22:42).
- When we struggle to accept the will of God, God will strengthen us to accept it (22:43). Here an angel comes to Jesus's aid; elsewhere God promises the Spirit's help (see Romans 8:26).
- Submitting to God's will can be agonizing; even Jesus found it so (22:44).
- Those who do not pray are in danger of falling into temp-

tation (22:40, 46).

As we will see in the next passage, the disciples who slept instead of praying did indeed fall into temptation, and in Luke's account, we see this in their use of the two swords already discussed above.

Jesus Arrested (22:47-53)

Apparently Judas knew where Jesus was likely to go after celebrating the Passover. That is why he was able to lead Jesus's enemies to him away from sympathetic crowds (see 22:6). This is not a sympathetic crowd! It is identified in 22:52 as composed of chief priests, officers of the temple guard and elders. They represent the corrupt leaders of Israel and an armed guard who will carry out their wishes.

And now we find clear evidence that the disciples had completely missed the meaning of Jesus's earlier counsel to "acquire swords." As soon as the disciples see danger, they imagine Jesus wants them to fight for him. They ask Jesus if they should, but then (perhaps acting on impulse) they jump into the fray without even waiting for a go-ahead from Jesus. How do we know that was the wrong thing for them to do? Because Jesus clearly rebukes them and immediately undoes the damage they have already done. 22:49-51 refutes any notion that 22:36-38 provides Jesus's endorsement of violent action in defense of self or one's companions.

Jesus said earlier that he would be "numbered with the transgressors" (22:37), fulfilling Isaiah's prophecy about the suffering servant who gives his life to redeem sinners (Isaiah 53:12). Jesus will indeed soon hang between two "lawbreakers"; that will fulfill the prophecy. Jesus has spent a lot of time with "transgressors" (outcasts and sinners) throughout his ministry, and that also fulfills the prophecy. Yet here on the Mount of Olives, the prophecy is also fulfilled: Jesus is found among "lawless" ones, his own sword-wielding disciples. Somehow they have forgotten Jesus's call to love enemies and to give up their own lives, rather than take the lives of others (see 6:27-36).

Christians disagree on what the Scriptures teach about violence, and whether it may ever be used legitimately by followers of Jesus in defense of self or others. This very important question should be addressed with careful attention to what texts actually say and what following Jesus ultimately implies. But Luke's "two swords" text should not be used to defend acquiring and using weaponry. If anything, it argues for the opposite conclusion. Bible interpreters broadly share this viewpoint, whether or not they themselves come from peace church traditions (e.g. Howard Marshall, pages 823-837; Joel Green, *Commentary*, pages 774-775.)

In 22:53, Jesus declares the powers of darkness have won – for now! That will all change when resurrection day dawns and God bathes this dark world with a whole new light!

Peter Denies Jesus (22:54-65)

"Peter followed (that is good!) at a distance (that is not so good!)" (22:54). Impetuous and sometimes foolhardy Peter dares to follow along as Jesus's enemies take him away. He already displayed his overconfidence (22:33). Now he will fail just as Jesus predicted he would (22:34).

By showing us how Jesus's prophetic word is fulfilled exactly, Luke assures his readers they can confidently await the fulfillment of all the other things Jesus promised. The irony is, in the next verses, Jesus is mocked as a (false) prophet by those who reject him (22:63-65).

> *Just as he was speaking, the rooster crowed. The Lord turned and looked straight at Peter. Then Peter remembered the word the Lord had spoken to him: "Before the rooster crows today, you will disown me three times." And he went outside and wept bitterly. (22:60-62)*

The crowing of the rooster (22:60) is Peter's wake-up call – that and the look from Jesus (22:61). The tears Peter sheds: are they tears of shame or repentance? We cannot be sure. Either way, we can be sure that Jesus's look was an invitation to turn back, for Jesus had already anticipated Peter's failure and given him an assignment beyond that failure. "When you have turned back, strengthen your brothers" (22:32).

Jesus on Trial (22:66 - 23:25)

There is irony throughout Luke's account of Jesus's trial and crucifixion. Those who genuinely believe Jesus to be a false prophet consider it their duty to do away with him. They think they are doing God's will. But since Jesus is God's appointed deliverer, his enemies are actually opposing God's will. Yet this very opposition results in Jesus's unjust death, the very means by which God fulfills the divine purpose after all. So God uses the misguided evil deeds of sinful people as part of God's plan to save the whole world.

Trial Before the Jewish Council (22:66-71)

Jesus is tried first by the Jewish Sanhedrin. The trial revolves around Jesus's claims about himself. Does he claim to be the Messiah? Does he claim to be God's Son? Jesus does not exactly say "yes" to either of the questions. His answers are designed to communicate something like this: "Well, not exactly in the way that you mean those terms." Jesus is indeed the Messiah, just not the kind that plans to rally troops and defeat the Romans. Jesus is indeed God's Son, though their conception of what that means falls far short of what Jesus actually claims for himself.

After not explicitly affirming the two titles his enemies use, Jesus alludes to two other roles he fulfills. Jesus is the "Son of Man" who will sit at God's right hand. From there, he will sit in judgment over those who are judging him now (22:69). And in 22:70, Jesus utters the words *ego eimi* (I AM), aligning himself completely with Israel's God who bears that name.

The Jewish leaders see in Jesus's responses evidence enough to charge him with blasphemy. The word is not used here, but clearly this is their intention.

First Trial Before Pilate (23:1-7)

The rulers of Israel know that Pilate, the Roman governor, will have no interest in the religious claims Jesus makes for himself. So they trump up a completely different charge. Jesus is a troublemaker, inciting people to rebel against the authority of Rome. The irony is that they had refused to accept him as their Messiah precisely because he did *not* do that!

Jesus, of course, did none of the things for which they now charge him. He did not oppose paying taxes to Caesar (see 20:20-26). He did not claim the sort of messiahship (earthly kingship) that would challenge the rule of the Roman governor. He did not stir up people in Galilee and Judea, though admittedly, those who oppose him sometimes did that around him.

The only words Jesus speaks this time are "You have said so" (23:3). Again, he is neither affirming nor denying the charge. Jesus does indeed claim to be Israel's king – the whole world's king, actually – but not in the way that Jesus's enemies use the word. The irony, of course, is that Jesus really is a threat to Rome's empire. Ultimately, his own self-sacrificing love will prove far stronger than Rome's armies.

When Pilate hears Jesus is a Galilean, he thinks he can sneak out of his responsibility to judge Jesus by sending Jesus to Herod.

Trial Before Herod (23:8-12)

Herod is intrigued by Jesus and uses the opportunity to make fun of him. Despite vehement accusations by the religious leaders and a raft of questions by Herod, Jesus stands there in silence. Again, there is irony in the text. Jesus is mocked as if he were a king. Yet that is precisely what he is. Indeed, it will be his reign, not Herod's, that will one day be established forever.

The final sentence of this text, reporting the newfound friendship between Pilate and Herod, could be understood simply as a confirmation of the well-known phenomenon that a common enemy often draws people together. But Luke may have wanted the reader to see more in it. Ultimately the cross of Christ is what brings down barriers and turns enemies into friends.

Second Trial Before Pilate (23:13-25)

The Jewish leaders obviously have not persuaded Pilate that Jesus is a rebel leader (23:14-15). So he really should let Jesus go. But Pilate's primary concern is not doing justice; it is keeping the peace. So he proposes a compromise: "I'll punish him, but not execute him" (see 23:16). That leads the crowds to propose their own compromise: "If you want to set a man free, give us Barabbas. We want to see Jesus crucified in his place" (23:18-21).

The theological imagery is fascinating here. Jesus, the innocent one, will die in place of Barabbas, the guilty. The one who loved his enemies will die in the place of the one who chose to kill them.

> *But with loud shouts they insistently demanded that he be crucified, and their shouts prevailed. So Pilate decided to grant their demand. He released the man who had been thrown into prison for insurrection and murder, the one they asked for, and surrendered Jesus to their will. (23:23-25)*

Pilate does not change his mind about Jesus's innocence. But the incessant cries of the crowd finally convince him to take the easy way out. Let the crowds get what they want. That way "peace" can be restored.

We should not imagine that everyone in Jerusalem was on Jesus's side a few days ago and all these same people have now turned against him. While some people may have changed their minds about Jesus, these chapters reveal that Jerusalem is a divided city, that the Jews are a divided people. Some reject Jesus as a false prophet and imposter; some accept Jesus as their Messiah and Lord. Which side of this great division faithfully carries forward the mission of God, the call of Abraham, the mandate to reach the whole world with the good news? On that issue, each side was absolutely convinced "Our side is right; the other side is wrong."

The first nine chapters of Acts show a bitter rivalry between the two sides. Those against Jesus and his followers use the weapons of this world to try to stamp out the Christians – court trials, imprisonment, persecution and execution. Those on Jesus's side use the far more powerful weapons of God's kingdom to win over the others – self-sacrifice, courageous witness, prayer, love of enemy, preaching the gospel. They learned it from Jesus, as exhibited all through the trial and crucifixion scenes.

The Crucifixion of Jesus (23:26-43)

Just as Barabbas symbolizes all the guilty whose place Jesus takes, so Simon symbolizes all those who take up their cross and follow Jesus. The two sides of Jesus's crucifixion (he did it in our place; he did it as a model for us to follow) cannot be separated (see especially 1 Peter 2:21).

The fact that many mourn Jesus's execution verifies that not all Israel rejected Jesus. Yet Jesus, selfless as ever, counsels them to weep for the tragedy they themselves will soon face. Jesus previously predicted the tragedy that would come on Jerusalem and its inhabitants (13:34-35; 19:41-45; 21:20-24). Because their leaders have rejected God's Messiah, the beloved Son in Jesus's parable of the vineyard, God's hand of judgment will fall on them, their temple and their city.

Verses 29-30 are proverbial expressions meaning "Those will be terrible days!" The enigmatic 23:31 probably means "If the Romans do this to an innocent man (the green tree, Jesus), what will they do to those truly guilty of rebellion (the dry tree, Jewish leaders who have rebelled against God's Messiah and Jewish Zealots who will rebel against the Roman Empire)?"

Jesus spent his life among sinners; now he hangs between two of them (23:32-33). As Jesus hangs between heaven and earth, he draws them together. He prays forgiveness for his executioners (23:34). He promises a sinner a place with him in paradise (23:43).

Luke does not quote Psalm 22 (as does Mark), but Luke's narrative reveals how various verses within that Psalm are re-enacted here: others casting lots for Jesus's clothes (Psalm 22:18); bystanders mocking Jesus (Psalm 22:7); people challenging Jesus to call down a divine rescue (Psalm 22:8).

> *There was a written notice above him, which read: THIS IS THE KING OF THE JEWS.*
>
> *One of the criminals who hung there hurled insults at him: "Aren't you the Messiah? Save yourself and us!"*
>
> *But the other criminal rebuked him. "Don't you fear God," he said, "since you are under the same sentence? We are punished justly, for we are getting what our deeds deserve. But this man has done nothing wrong."*
>
> *Then he said, "Jesus, remember me when you come into your kingdom."*
>
> *Jesus answered him, "Truly I tell you, today you will be with me in paradise." (23:38-43)*

The sign above Jesus's cross is intended to be a form of mockery: Those in charge of executing Jesus do not believe he is Israel's king. Yet it proclaims the ironic truth: Jesus is the king; Jesus's enthronement is on a cross; Jesus's death and resurrection establish God's kingdom forever.

Verses 39-43 portray two criminals. The first is concerned only with salvation in this life, so he joins those mocking Jesus (23:39). The second is concerned with salvation in the life to come, so he joins those who trust in Jesus for life eternal (23:42). The first, we presume, died with a curse on his lips. The second, we are assured, joined Jesus in paradise before the day was over. He qualified for that honor by his fear of God (23:40), his humble admission of guilt (23:41a), his confidence in Jesus's innocence (23:41b) and his confession that Jesus is the world's true king (23:42).

The rest of the New Testament assures us that those who die in the Lord are ushered into Jesus's presence as they await the final resurrection from the dead. That is presumably what is meant by "paradise" in this text.

As Jesus hangs on the cross, he continues the roles he has fulfilled all through his ministry. He speaks the words of a concerned prophet (23:28-31), an interceding priest (23:34) and a pardoning king (23:43). Now we will see him fulfill his role as suffering Messiah and self-sacrificing servant, who gives his life to redeem others.

The Death of Jesus (23:44-49)

> *It was now about noon, and darkness came over the whole land until three in the afternoon, for the sun stopped shining. And the curtain of the temple was torn in two. Jesus called out with a loud voice, "Father, into your hands I commit my spirit." When he had said this, he breathed his last.*
>
> *The centurion, seeing what had happened, praised God and said, "Surely this was a righteous man." When all the people who had gathered to witness this sight saw what took place, they beat their breasts and went away. But all those who knew him, including the women who had followed him from Galilee, stood at a distance, watching these things. (23:44-49)*

Jesus already declared this was the time when darkness rules (see 22:53). Now even the sun forbears to shine (23:44-45a). The tearing of the temple curtain (23:45b) symbolizes many things: access into God's presence is now available because Jesus has offered the ultimate sacrifice; we should no longer imagine God confined behind a curtain, but rather "on the loose"; the physical temple no longer plays the central role in God's salvation plan; its destruction, already predicted, now symbolically begins.

Jesus's final words exhibit calmness and certainty: he knows his own future is secure in the hands of his Father. Much earlier, he resisted the temptation to take shortcuts (4:1-13). Throughout his ministry, he stayed the course (9:51). On the Mount of Olives, he declared God's will should prevail (22:42). Now he is ready to trust his Father to accomplish what he promised all along: death would not be the end. It would be the doorway to a whole new beginning!

The centurion's confession may sound less impressive than

what we read in other Gospels, where the centurion declares Jesus to be God's Son. Here he merely declares him righteous. But we should not exaggerate the difference. Jesus set things up so that the ultimate choice was to accept his claims for himself or reject them. He claimed divine sonship for himself, so either he was a blasphemer or he really was God's Son. His judges had opted for the former; now this executioner opts for the latter. Jesus left no room for a middle ground. He never intended to.

Verses 48 and 49 remind us that it is simply wrong to claim "all Israel" rejected Jesus. Many did not. Some were faithful all the way to the cross. Some will be there to meet the resurrected Jesus. Many will gather in an upper room to await the promised Holy Spirit. The Jesus movement, begun among his fellow Jews, will continue among his fellow Jews, until they learn that Gentiles too can enter on their own terms and be part of the people of God alongside them. So the Jewish people of God will grow into the Christian church, where people of all tribes and nations can become one family, one people, the people of God.

The Burial of Jesus (23:50-56)

It is amazing how often we find positive models where we least expect them: in a compassionate Samaritan (10:33-37) and a grateful one (17:16); in despised tax collectors (18:13, 14; 19:8-10) and disdained panhandlers (Luke 16:19-31; 18:35-43); in a condemned criminal (23:40-43) and a Roman executioner (23:47). And now we find one who belonged to the Jewish Sanhedrin! Joseph was an upright man, who had not joined the others in rejecting Jesus. His heart and his expectations were in the right place. And now he acts selflessly, identifying with a condemned criminal, so that Jesus can have a proper burial.

Luke's reference to the women who accompany Joseph (23:55) sets the stage for their visit to the tomb on the first day of the week. Verse 54 suggests that Joseph acted so as to preserve the sanctity of the Sabbath. Verse 56 portrays the women doing the same. And so

Luke reminds us all these events take place within a context where God's law was intended to guide God's people. That same law and all its deepest demands were fully met in this Jesus, who now lies buried. The truly righteous one has become the ultimate sacrifice on behalf of the unrighteous. It remains for the miracle of Easter to verify this, to spell the final defeat of the principalities and powers and to inaugurate the new creation made possible because Jesus was faithful – all the way to the grave.

Implications of the Text for Today

Communion: Practicing Table Fellowship as Jesus Did

Throughout history the Christian church has practiced Communion (the Lord's Supper, the eucharist, the mass) in many different ways. Sometimes the focus has been on repentance and forgiveness, sometimes on the mystical presence of Jesus, sometimes on hope and longing for renewed communion with Jesus in glory.

Luke's version of the Lord's Supper reports that Jesus eagerly desired *one last chance* to have meal fellowship with his disciples (see 22:15). This suggests the focus here is on the same values always central to those meals where Jesus was present – assumed equality, freely offered acceptance, demolished social and religious barriers, servants and masters on equal footing. We see this both in the example Jesus set (see 15:1-2) and in the instructions he gave others (see 14:7-14).

Luke's version of Jesus's last meal may seem like an "insider meal," a gathering of like-minded people who are all committed to Jesus. But that does not take into account that Jesus is eating with one he knows is a betrayer, with one he knows will deny him, with friends squabbling about greatness. Even this meal, perhaps *especially* this meal, is about breaking down barriers, accepting the outsider, creating family out of diverse individuals.

Communion means many things. We remember Passover; we remember above all Christ's self-sacrifice. We anticipate the final fulfillment of God's kingdom; we experience Jesus's presence in the meantime. We receive the gift of forgiveness offered through Jesus's death.

Sometimes, however, we overlook those emphases Luke has been highlighting. Communion is a context for the radical reordering of priorities the way Jesus modeled and taught – honoring the outcast, welcoming sinners, serving instead of being served. As I wrote in my commentary on Mark's Gospel:

> We not only look back and remember; we not only look forward and anticipate. We also look around. Jesus is indeed present at communion, but not simply in the elements or in the remembering. He is chiefly present, as he promised, in the *gathering* (Matt. 18:19-20). The church is not a collection of individuals mystically bound by common participation in a sacrament; instead, the church is a real, living, and interrelating family (Mark 3:34-35).
>
> This family experiences the presence of Jesus in every gathering, and especially so when we gather to relive and reenact our mutual participation in the "body" of Christ (the church) symbolized by the sharing of the one loaf and communion cup (cf. 1 Cor. 10:16-17). Thus communion requires no sacred food, no sacred place, no sacred officiating person, and no sacred occasion. Where believers gather in unity to celebrate their oneness in Christ, there communion is rightly experienced in the presence of Jesus who died and rose to make it all possible. There our covenant with Christ and with each other is regularly renewed." (*Mark*: 343-344)

Christ's Death: Substitute and Example

First Peter 2:21 says it most succinctly: "Christ suffered for you, leaving you an example." Jesus died to accomplish on our behalf what we could not have done on our own. He was our substitute. Jesus died to show us what his followers are called to do. He was our model.

Luke's Gospel symbolically portrays Barabbas as the one for whom Jesus became the substitute, and Simon as the one who took up the cross and followed. These two sides must always be kept together. Jesus, our Savior, is also the one we follow as our Lord.

It is essential that we understand the gospel as the good news of grace, God's unmerited favor, God in Christ providing what none of us could ever earn or achieve. It is equally essential that we understand this gospel as Jesus defined it, when he said: "Whoever wants to be my disciple must deny themselves and take up their cross daily and follow me" (9:23). God provides salvation freely as God's gift; we access it by turning all of life over to Jesus and following him.

Following implies relationship, it implies obedience, but it also implies doing what Jesus did. No, we cannot "die for sin" (ours or anyone else's); in that respect, what Jesus did was unique. Among other things that means we are called to treat our enemies as Jesus did, loving and forgiving them.

Personal Reflection Questions

- When Paul challenged the Corinthians to celebrate communion "in a worthy manner" (1 Corinthians 11:27), he did not mean that everyone participating needed to be "personally worthy." He meant rather that the meal should break down barriers between people. What would it mean for our congregations to celebrate communion "worthily" in a context where there is division – between rich and poor, between conservatives and liberals, between those holding diverse views on important ethical issues, between any two people who have a hard time getting along? How can our communion celebrations accomplish the goals of Jesus's own table fellowship?
- In the commentary above we addressed the issue of the "two swords." The context for that conversation was Jesus's revision of his earlier mission instructions. Previously the disciples were told simply to trust that God would meet all their needs. Now they were told to make careful preparations and expect opposition and rejection. How do we discern which of these instructions most appropriately applies to our own participation in God's mission? When is the right time for "simple trust"? When is the right time for careful preparation?
- When we do not keep the two sides of the cross in careful balance, our understanding of salvation and the Christian life can also get out of balance. What is likely to go wrong if we emphasize free grace strongly, but underemphasize the call to faithful discipleship? What is likely to go wrong if we emphasize discipleship strongly, but underemphasize that salvation is God's free gift?

The Resurrection and Beyond

The Text: Luke 24:1-53 NIV

The Flow and Form of the Text

Luke's narrative of Jesus's life, death and resurrection reaches its climax in this final chapter. The story, however, does not find its conclusion here! We are nearing the end of Luke's first volume. There is another that follows this (The Book of Acts). The truth is even that book will not bring the story to its conclusion.

Luke's Gospel ends with the disciples waiting for the next stage of this gripping drama. The Book of Acts will end with the mission of the church in full swing. It is Luke's way of passing the baton to his readers. They will take it on from there. The story itself will reach its climax at some unknown future date when the Son of Man returns to judge and to save, and ultimately, to make all things new.

Luke's final chapter has much material in common with the final chapters of Matthew, Mark and John. There is a resurrection announcement, there are resurrection appearances, there is an important meeting between Jesus and his disciples. Yet each Gospel's account of the resurrection and the events to which it leads is unique.

Luke's resurrection account is about Jesus's exaltation to the right hand of God. More clearly than most New Testament writers, Luke presents that exaltation as the final act in a series. First comes the resurrection, the victory over death Jesus accomplished because he was faithful to the plan of God. Then comes the ascension; that is, Jesus (in his resurrected human body!) is taken up into the heavenly realms. Finally, there is Jesus's exaltation to his new status as Lord and Christ. While Luke does not speak directly of this exaltation in the final chapter of his Gospel, he refers to it in his second volume, as he looks back on what the resurrection of Jesus was all about (see especially Acts 2:31-33; 5:30-31).

Another emphasis of Luke is the corporeality of the resurrected Jesus. Yes, his resurrection body is different from his body before his death, but it is the same person and it is still a body, certainly much more tangible than an angel or a ghost (according to Luke). We will explore how Luke emphasizes this and why it matters below.

This final chapter of Luke shows how Jesus both fulfills Scripture and interprets it. And it portrays Jesus fulfilling his own promises and making new ones for his disciples. In various ways, it guarantees and gives glimpses of what the final restoration of all things will be like.

This chapter, as we shall see, completes Jesus's farewell, as he passes on the baton to his followers. They will pick up the mission from here on, always following their resurrected Lord and doing it in the power of the promised Holy Spirit.

Outline:

Jesus has been Raised (24:1-12)
Two Travelers Meet Jesus (24:13-33a)
    Jesus Explains the Scriptures (24:13-27)
    Jesus Breaks the Bread (24:28-33a)
Meeting the Resurrected Jesus (24:33b-43)

Fulfilling the Scriptures (24:44-49)
Final Blessings (24:50-53)

The Text Explained

Jesus has been Raised (24:1-12)

The chapter divisions in our Bibles were added centuries after the original books were written. In the gap between what we call chapter 23 and what we call chapter 24 everything changes! At the end of chapter 23, Jesus lies buried in the grave. The chapter ends with the pause button pressed ("They [the women] rested on the Sabbath").

By the time chapter 24 opens, everything is different. The Sabbath of waiting is not forever. Death is not the end. Somewhere in the gap between chapters 23 and 24, Jesus wins, God wins, life wins! Chapter 24 opens and it gradually dawns on the reader, as it did on the participants: Jesus has conquered death and inaugurated a whole new creation.

> *On the first day of the week, very early in the morning, the women took the spices they had prepared and went to the tomb. They found the stone rolled away from the tomb, but when they entered, they did not find the body of the Lord Jesus. While they were wondering about this, suddenly two men in clothes that gleamed like lightning stood beside them. In their fright the women bowed down with their faces to the ground, but the men said to them, "Why do you look for the living among the dead? He is not here; he has risen! Remember how he told you, while he was still with you in Galilee: 'The Son of Man must be delivered over to the hands of sinners, be crucified and on the third day be raised again.'" Then they remembered his words. (24:1-8)*

First we read of the women who planned to embalm the body. They are surprised to see an open and empty tomb. They are startled by the sudden appearance of gleaming heavenly messengers. And then come the announcements: Jesus is alive again! He told you he would rise again! It has really happened!

Luke masterfully reveals the changing disposition of these women. They come early, well-prepared and dedicated. The discovery of the empty tomb leaves them wondering. The heavenly messengers leave them frightened. They bow in reverence, they remember, they return, they bear witness.

Luke now names these faithful women, these proclaimers of the good news. The men, to their shame, assume (as so many did in the ancient world) that women are simply unreliable witnesses. But let's give Peter credit. He may not have been convinced by the women's testimony, but at least their witness sets him on the road to discover for himself (24:12). Jesus had prophesied that, after Peter's failure, he would become a leader among the apostles (22:31-32). It starts here.

Peter does not receive a heavenly announcement, nor (at this point in the story) does Jesus appear to him. He just sees that something amazing has happened, and he wonders! Maybe he does not yet believe, but at least he is beginning to have doubts about his doubts!

Twenty-two verses later (in 24:34) the reader learns that at some point on that momentous Sunday, the resurrected Jesus appeared personally to Simon Peter. Notice the sequence: he heard the testimony of others, he wondered, he investigated, he was puzzled, eventually Jesus appeared to him and he was convinced. It will not happen the same way for everyone. The women heard the testimony of angels; Peter heard the testimony of women. No matter: the good news was proclaimed, it was heard and it bore fruit as the hearers investigated for themselves, experienced the resurrected Jesus and became part of the believing community.

But we are getting ahead of ourselves. Before Luke even hints that Peter's curiosity and his investigations will eventually lead to an encounter with the resurrected Jesus, he pens one of the most well-told narratives in the Bible. One more important point before we turn to that.

Was the resurrection of Jesus something that Jesus *accomplished*, or something that was done *to him*? Asked another way: Did Jesus *rise* or was Jesus *raised*?

In 24:6 and 24:7, the NIV translators actually get things backwards. According to the NIV, 24:6 reports, "He has risen" (as if Jesus got up all by himself!). Verse 7 then reports Jesus's earlier prophecy that he will "be raised" (as if that is something done to him). In Greek, it is the other way around. The messengers at the tomb say, "He was raised" (passive voice!). Earlier Jesus had predicted that he would "stand up" (active voice).

There is a proper order here. The resurrection of Jesus was first done *to him* before anything could be done *by him*. Yes, Jesus rises victorious over sin and death, but only because God first turned everything on its head. God raised Jesus from death, and then Jesus "got up"! The apostles will later confront Jesus's enemies with words like this: "The God of our ancestors raised Jesus from the dead – whom you killed by hanging him on a cross" (Acts 5:30; see also Acts 2:23-24; 3:15; 4:10-11; 10:39-40). This is of great importance.

Evil men pronounced Jesus guilty and killed him. God in heaven overturned the verdict and raised him back to life. Jesus is vindicated and granted resurrection life. Only after that is done *to Jesus*, is anything done *by Jesus*. He stands up, he walks out of the tomb, he appears to people, he interprets Scripture, he breaks bread, he blesses, he sends his Spirit – all because his Father in heaven raised him from death to life.

Two Travelers Meet Jesus (24:13-33a)

> *Now that same day two of them were going to a village called Emmaus, about seven miles from Jerusalem. They were talking with each other about everything that had happened. As they talked and discussed these things with each other, Jesus himself came up and walked along with them; but they were kept from recognizing him. (24:13-16)*

We know almost nothing about the two travelers who meet Jesus in this amazing narrative. One bears the name Cleopas. Perhaps the other was his friend; maybe it was his wife. The resurrected Jesus walks with them, opens the Scriptures to them, shares a meal with them and opens their eyes.

Our examination of this text is divided, as is Luke's narrative, into two movements. The first takes place on the road, where Jesus opens the Scriptures for them. The second takes place around table fellowship, where Jesus opens their eyes.

Jesus Explains the Scriptures (24:13-27)

The heavenly messengers announced to the women that Jesus is alive again. But what kind of body does that suggest he had? All we learn from the empty tomb is that somehow the old body is "used up" in the process of becoming the resurrected body. Now we discover that the resurrected body is in many ways similar to and in some ways different from the old body. It can walk along the road, converse with fellow travelers, eat with them. It looks and acts much like "normal" human bodies. In fact, the travelers think their companion is just some other visitor to Jerusalem. Yet their eyes are kept from recognizing Jesus. Something is different. Jesus can be recognized, or not, by his own choice!

The travelers are downcast. They were hoping Jesus would be the one to redeem Israel. And then his enemies killed him. All their hopes came crashing to the ground. They do not know what to think. The resurrected Jesus pretends he does not know all about them and their troubles: "What are you talking about? (24:17). "What things have been happening in Jerusalem?" (24:19).

That is what sets up the amazing irony. The travelers think Jesus must be the only one who does not know what has been going on (24:18). Actually he is the only one who really does understand all this (24:25-27).

As the travelers "inform" their companion of all these things, we learn of their hopes, their doubts, their questions. Jesus patiently waits for them to pour out their confused thoughts and feelings.

They had such high hopes. This Jesus had been powerful in word and deed. They were convinced he would be the redeemer of Israel. But he had been rejected by powerful people and killed by the Romans. And yet maybe, just maybe, the story is not over. Now there are rumors of an empty tomb and messengers from heaven. They do not know what to believe anymore.

That is when Jesus takes over the conversation. He does not identify himself. In fact, he speaks of himself in the third person, explaining what had to happen to "the Messiah." When this lesson ends, these travelers will understand the Messiah so much better, but they still will not realize that their companion is Jesus, talking about himself!

Jesus opens the Scriptures for them. We should not imagine Jesus accessing his mental concordance and quoting individual verses from all over the Old Testament, creating proofs from prophecy that all sorts of events had been predicted down to the tiniest detail. That is often the way we use the Bible, ripping verses out of context, making them refer to things they were never designed to address.

No, this was more like a profound retelling of the whole biblical narrative, tracking God's plans and purposes through "Moses and all the Prophets." God had never intended to send the promised Messiah so he could crush Israel's human enemies. Rather, the Messiah would die at their hands. Self-sacrifice, not swords, would be God's weapon. Faithfulness, not ferocity, would be the Messiah's way. Infinite love and mercy would lead to a cross. But then God would turn the tables and make all things new. The Messiah "had to suffer these things and then enter his glory" (24:26).

This, I think, must have been the gist of that amazing lesson in biblical theology that, for reasons unknown to us, was never transcribed and included in our New Testament. How astonished these travelers must have been to have this stranger present the biblical story in ways they had never heard it before.

Later, they will describe what Jesus does here as "opening the Scriptures" (see 24:32). The word Luke uses is *dianoigo*. It is a word this chapter uses on three separate occasions to tell us about three different things that the resurrected Jesus opens. Watch for them!

Jesus Breaks the Bread (24:28-33a)

The travelers reach their village and extend hospitality to the stranger. Given the customs of the day, they might well have offered a meal and lodging to any stranger. But they must have been intrigued and fascinated by this one who at first seemed to know nothing about what happened in Jerusalem (24:18) and then revealed a knowledge of the Scriptures and their meaning that surpassed anything they had ever heard before (24:27).

As they share a meal, this unusual stranger surprises them again. He takes over the role of the host. Taking bread, thanking God, breaking bread, sharing it – this sounds to us like another communion service. For them, however, it was the way every meal began. Something in the way this stranger does all this pulls the veil from their eyes. This is Jesus, the resurrected Jesus. He had walked with them, explained the Scriptures, burned the truth into their hearts (24:32), joined their family circle. And just as they recognize him, he disappears.

Now they know. Jesus really is alive again. The rumors have proved true. They abandon the meal they had prepared and hasten back along the same road they just traveled. Yes it is late, but they have a story to tell!

In 24:31-32, we encounter that important Greek word *dianoigo* twice. Along the road, Jesus "opened" the Scriptures; at the table, he "opened" their eyes. Soon this same word will appear one more time, as Jesus "opens" people's minds to understand what this all means (24:45).

Meeting the Resurrected Jesus (24:33b-43)

> *There they found the Eleven and those with them, assembled together and saying, "It is true! The Lord has risen and has appeared to Simon." Then the two told what had happened on*

> *the way, and how Jesus was recognized by them when he broke the bread. (24:33b-35)*

The Emmaus travelers race back seven miles, eager to share their good news. When they arrive, the place is already abuzz. Simon has also been granted an appearance of the resurrected Jesus. They share stories. No doubt the travelers talk about the Bible lesson Jesus gave them. And suddenly he is there. He is there in some form that leaves them wondering. Is it really the flesh and blood Jesus? Or is it just an apparition, a ghost (24:37, 39)?

The resurrected Jesus goes out of his way to demonstrate that his body, this resurrected body, is real and tangible and – well, really a body! It has hands and feet (and in Jesus's case, nail scars); it has flesh and bones. It can be touched. It can eat (24:39-43); in fact, Jesus proves it by doing so in their presence.

And so we learn more about the resurrection body of Jesus, and thus the resurrection body that we will one day receive when Jesus returns again. It will share many characteristics of our present physical bodies. Yet it will be different. Present human eyes do not necessarily recognize it (24:16). It can suddenly disappear (24:31) and appear (24:36 – perhaps through closed doors, as we read in other New Testament texts). Apparently, it is equally at home in the "physical world" as in the "spiritual realm," passing back and forth through the veil that currently separates them. Somehow it is perfectly suited for that great day when heaven and earth will be reunited forever.

Fulfilling the Scriptures (24:44-49)

Jesus always maintained that his mission on earth was to fulfill God's purposes, and that these divine purposes were most clearly seen in Scripture. Now Jesus again leads his eager students through Scripture, showing how those texts find their true fulfillment in him – in his life and especially in his death and resurrection. And once again, that word *dianoigo* appears in the text. This time Jesus "opens" their minds.

To understand God's ways, we need Scripture and we need to understand it. Luke 24 helps us recognize the various components of that. Opening the Scripture is often a matter of studying. Opening minds is often a matter of being receptive, of being teachable. Opening eyes is a gift of the divine Spirit. In combination, these three are life-transforming.

From 24:46 onward, we hear the "bottom line" of Jesus's walk through Scripture. The Scriptures, Jesus helps them see, speak of the suffering and death of the Messiah. They speak of his resurrection from the dead. They speak of the need for repentance and of God's offer to forgive. They speak of Israel's mission to the whole world. Yes, it begins in Jerusalem, but it was never intended to stay there. The Scriptures even speak of "being witnesses": God's evidence that all this is true and God's mouthpieces to share the good news to the ends of the earth.

Note well that Jesus is not referring to the New Testament, in which much of this is spelled out so clearly. He is speaking of the Old Testament, the only Scriptures available to him and his first followers. Not all of these things are spelled out in black and white, demonstrable with long lists of proof texts. But all of them are there in the story line of Scripture: in the call of Abraham both to be blessed and to become a blessing for all nations; in the mission of Israel to be a faithful people at all costs, bearing witness to the ways of God; in Isaiah's faithful suffering servant who would give his life as a ransom for many; in the Psalms' promises that God will never abandon those who faithfully serve him; in the hints of a coming resurrection that emerge in places like Psalm 73 and Daniel 12.

In a few months, it will no longer be Jesus explaining these things to his disciples; it will be the apostles themselves explaining these things to their fellow Jews and eventually to Gentiles as well. Yet something must happen first! The same Spirit of God that empowered Jesus for his ministry (see 3:22; 4:18) will soon be given to all who follow Jesus. Then their ministry will indeed be an extension of his, so that the good news can be preached "to all nations"

(24:47).

And with that, we move to the last short incident in this Gospel. We quickly recognize some things are brought to closure, while others are left open-ended. Jesus will now complete his "farewell discourse" and his earthly ministry. But the Gospel will end with the disciples waiting. They wait for that which Jesus calls "what my Father has promised" (that is, the Holy Spirit and the Spirit's empowerment for ministry). Until the Spirit comes, they cannot move on with their own mission, to carry the gospel to the ends of the earth.

Final Blessings (24:50-53)

> *When he had led them out to the vicinity of Bethany, he lifted up his hands and blessed them. While he was blessing them, he left them and was taken up into heaven. Then they worshiped him and returned to Jerusalem with great joy. And they stayed continually at the temple, praising God. (24:50-53)*

Luke's account of the Last Supper contained all the usual elements of a biblical farewell discourse (see comments before 22:7) – except a parting blessing. Jesus left out that part, confident that he would be raised from the dead not long after that farewell meal. He knew he would have a final opportunity to bless them before bidding them farewell. That final blessing is here!

We should note that the word "blessing" (*eulogeo*) is used three times in this text – twice for what Jesus does to his disciples, once for what they do to God. Jesus blesses (*eulogeo*) his disciples (24:50-51); they bless (*eulogeo*) God (24:53). As they so often do, Bible translators here use two different words. When God does something for us we say God *blesses* us; when we do the same thing for God we say we *praise* God. (See Ephesians 1:3 for another example.) By changing the word, we get the impression that the benefits are all ours and the affirmation all goes to God. But it is completely mutual. We are blessed, and we bless in return. God is blessed, and

God blesses in return. God and God's people – their words and their lives are mutually shared for each other's benefit!

Note also that, even though the text says the disciples praised/blessed God, it also says they worshipped Jesus (24:52). Worship is clearly reserved for God! So this text implies again what Luke's Gospel has implied throughout – Jesus is not just a human person; Jesus is God in the flesh! That was true of the human/divine Jesus who walked the roads of Galilee, of the human/divine Jesus who died and rose again, and now of the human/divine Jesus who passes through the curtain that separates earth from heaven and enters the presence of God. Jesus brought the presence of God with him when he became a human. And Jesus brings the presence of humanity back with him when he ascends to God.

Only Luke among the Gospel writers narrates the ascension, and he does it twice, once here and then again as his second volume opens (see Acts 1:9). As Acts 2:33 makes clear, the exaltation of Jesus to God's right hand makes possible the gift of the Holy Spirit to Jesus's followers. The ascension and Pentecost are therefore two sides of the same coin – Jesus is transferred into the heavenlies: the Holy Spirit is poured out on Jesus's followers. One might almost say, "There is still a veil separating heaven and earth – but it is starting to come apart. One of us has already made it over to the other side. One of them is already present on our side." The church's great hope is for that glorious day when heaven and earth are reunited once more, when God dwells among us in fullness, when we live in the presence of our Lord Jesus.

So the Gospel of Luke ends! It ends in the same location it began – in the Jerusalem temple (see 1:8-10). That is where an angel visited Zechariah and told him God's plan to redeem Israel was about to unfold. This is where Jesus's followers now wait for that unfolding plan to become their mission and their message. Readers of Luke already know the temple was once the center of God's interactions with God's people, but that Jesus already fulfilled the temple's functions and predicted the temple's demise. Now it remains for Jesus's disciples to become the new temple, Christ's body, the center of God's work in the world. As Jesus promised, the Spirit would soon fill this new temple so that it can move beyond its Jerusalem center to the goal of all this: the ends of the earth!

Implications of the Text for Today

Hearing Individual Resurrection Narratives

Many people believe that the main task with the four Gospels is to combine and harmonize them, recreating the "full story" that each writer only tells in part. When we do that to the resurrection narratives, we get quite a long list of resurrection announcements and appearances, but we get only one clear message: "Jesus really did rise from the dead!" As important as that message is, there is so much more to learn – if only we stop combining and harmonizing. A better approach is to listen to each Gospel individually. Only then can we recognize the deeper meaning and significance of these texts.

Matthew's account of the resurrection does seem aimed at persuading readers that Jesus did rise. But that is not the bottom line. Matthew's resurrection message is more like this: Jesus really did rise; therefore, when we disciple all the nations, Jesus's authority and presence really will go with us (see Matthew 28:16-20).

Mark's Gospel emphasizes something different: because Jesus died and rose again, disciples who have failed can be forgiven and begin the life of discipleship all over again (see Mark 14:27-28; 16:7).

John's Gospel presents the resurrection life of Jesus as the beginning of eternal life (see John 5:21-26; 11:25).

What then is the unique resurrection message of Luke's Gospel? I think one emphasis stands out more clearly than any other: because Jesus is alive again, he is present to minister to the community of faith. He does it by opening up the Scriptures to them (24:32). He does it by being present in their Christian fellowship, in their "breaking bread together" (24:30). He does it by rekindling hope in those who are dismayed (24:17), by offering peace and reassurance to those who are confused and frightened (24:36-39). He does it by revealing truth (24:45). He does it by restoring joy (24:52).

And how do we then respond appropriately to Luke's resurrection message? By studying the Scriptures, by breaking bread together, by watching for glimpses of the resurrected Jesus among us, by worshiping and waiting, and then, when Jesus sends the Spirit, by living in the power of that Spirit and carrying out Christ's mission on earth.

Scripture, Experience, Understanding, Community

Luke 24 suggests that many factors contribute to understanding God's Word and God's ways. A very strong emphasis in this chapter is on correctly understanding the Scriptures. On the road to Emmaus, Jesus explains the Scriptures to those who are confused and downcast (24:27). When the resurrected Jesus appears to the believing community in Jerusalem, he explains how "the Law of Moses, the Prophets and the Psalms" (24:44) all bear witness to Jesus. That is how first century Jews named their entire Bible (our Old Testament).

This chapter makes clear that Scripture is not self-interpreting. There are many ways to understand and misunderstand the Old Testament. Jesus provided the appropriate key – himself! When we read the Old Testament with an eye toward its fulfillment in Jesus, we read it appropriately. That does not mean we find detailed predictions of Jesus on every page. It means we allow the climax of the story (Jesus's life, death and resurrection) to shape our reading of the whole narrative.

There's more: Jesus is not only the central message of the Bible (24:44); Jesus is also the prime interpreter of it. Therefore, we read and apply the Old Testament the way Jesus did, emphasizing what Jesus emphasized, relativizing what Jesus relativized. And the same Jesus who teaches us is the one who shows up in our Christian fellowships. Our best opportunities to understand God's Word and

God's ways are not when we study the texts in privacy and solitude (something virtually no Christian did for the first 1,500 years of church history), but when we gather in Jesus's presence and learn God's ways as we fellowship and worship in Christian community.

The Resurrection Body

Christian theology has often made claims about life after death and about our future resurrection that actually resemble Greek philosophy more than the Bible. Greek philosophers spoke of "the immortality of the soul." The Bible speaks of the resurrection of the body. These are not the same thing!

Actually, the Bible speaks of two separate stages after death. First there is an intermediate state, which we could call "life after death." At the end of the age, when Jesus comes again, there is the resurrection of the body, something we might call "life after life after death" (an expression from N.T. Wright, whose book, *Surprised by Hope*, I highly recommend).

We know very little about what happens immediately after death. My comments on 20:27-40 suggest caution in claiming too much knowledge about that.

The truth is we also only have hints and glimpses and images and metaphors about our final state, after we are given resurrection bodies designed to live forever in God's presence. But the images we have do not suggest something "purely spiritual." They suggest a new kind of transformed resurrection body. Jesus's resurrection body provides perhaps the best set of clues we will get, until that great day when the dead are raised, those alive are transformed and heaven and earth become one.

Personal Reflection Questions

- How has the material in this chapter provided glimpses into what is involved in learning God's ways? What is the role of Scripture in learning God's ways? What are effective means of interpreting it? How is Jesus the center of Scripture? Do you also experience situations where the presence of Jesus, the power of the Spirit or the influence of believing community help to "open your eyes" or "open your mind" to what God is saying and doing?
- In many ways Jesus was unique: he was the incarnation of God, God living as a sinless human person. Yet Jesus's life on earth was intended not only to show us what God is like, but to help us understand what humans living according to the will of God are like. And Jesus's resurrection provides clues as to what awaits us at the end of the age, when we too receive new resurrection bodies. How do you respond to these claims? Do you agree that we can learn about our own "humanity" by looking at Jesus, both in his earthly life and in his post-resurrection state?
- In what ways has this study of Luke's Gospel encouraged and inspired you? In what ways has it challenged you? What are some of the unanswered questions that you would like to explore more fully as a result of spending time with this Gospel?

Bibliography of Works Cited and Resources for Interpreting Luke:

Bailey, Kenneth. *The Cross and the Prodigal: Luke 15 through the Eyes of Middle Eastern Peasants.* Downers Grove, Ill: InterVarsity, 2005.

______. *Poet and Peasant: A Literary Cultural Approach to the Parables in Luke.* Grand Rapids, Mich: Eerdmans, 1976.

______. *Through Peasant Eyes: More Lucan Parables, Their Culture and Style.* Grand Rapids, Mich: Eerdmans, 1980.

Bartholomew, Craig, Joel B. Green, and Anthony C. Thiselton. *Reading Luke: Interpretation, Reflection, Formation.* Grand Rapids, Mich: Zondervan, 2005.

Bock, Darrell L. *Luke 1:1–9:50; Luke 9:51–24:53* (Baker Exegetical Commentary on the New Testament). Grand Rapids, Mich: Baker, 1994, 1996.

Bovon, François. *Luke: A Commentary on the Gospel of Luke.* 3 Vols. (Hermeneia). Minneapolis, Minn: Fortress, 2002.

Byrne, Brendan. *The Hospitality of God: A Reading of Luke's Gospel.* Collegeville, Minn: Liturgical, 2000.

Caird, George. B. *The Gospel of St. Luke* (Pelican Gospel Commentaries). Baltimore, Md: Penguin, 1963.

______. *New Testament Theology.* Oxford: Oxford University Press, 1994.

Carroll, John T. *Luke: A Commentary* (New Testament Library). Louisville, Ky: Westminster John Knox, 2012.

Craddock, Fred B. *Luke* (Interpretation). Louisville, Ky: Westminster John Knox, 1990.

Danker, Frederick. *Jesus and the New Age According to St. Luke.* Rev. ed. Philadelphia, Pa: Fortress, 1988.

Edwards, James R. *The Gospel According to Luke* (Pillar New Testament Commentary). Grand Rapids, Mich: Eerdmans, 2015.

Ellis, E. Earle. *The Gospel of Luke.* 2nd Edition. Grand Rapids, Mich: Eerdmans, 1974.

Evans, Christopher F. *Saint Luke* (Trinity Press International New Testament Commentaries). Philadelphia, Pa: Trinity Press International, 1990.

Evans, Craig A. *Luke* (New International Bible Commentary 3). Peabody, Mass.: Hendrickson, 1990.

Fee, Gordon, and Douglas Stuart. *How to Read the Bible for all its Worth.* Grand Rapids, Mich: Zondervan, 2014.

Fitzmyer, Joseph A. *The Gospel According to Luke.* 2 Vols. (Anchor Bible 28). New York, NY: Doubleday, 1981.

France, R.T. *Luke* (Teach the Text Commentary Series). Grand Rapids, Mich: Baker, 2013.

García, César. *God Speaks Today: What does this mean in the midst of suffering and oppression? Revelation in contextual perspective.* Thesis: Fresno Pacific Biblical Seminary, 2011.

Geddert, Timothy J., *Commentary on Mark* (Believers Church Bible Commentary). Scottdale, Pa: Herald Press, 2001.

______. *Double Take: New Meanings from Old Stories*. Winnipeg, Man: Kindred Productions, 2007.

Geldenhuys, Norval, *Commentary on the Gospel of Luke*. Grand Rapids, Mich: Eerdmans, 1971.

Goulder, Michael D. *Luke: A New Paradigm* (JSNT Supplement 20). Sheffield: Sheffield Academic Press, 1989.

Green, Joel B. *The Gospel of Luke* (NICNT). Grand Rapids, Mich: Eerdmans, 1997.

______. *The Theology of the Gospel of Luke*. Cambridge: Cambridge University Press, 1995.

Jeffrey, David Lyle. *Luke* (Brazos Theological Commentary on the Bible). Ada, Mich: Brazos, 2012.

Johnson, Luke Timothy. *The Gospel of Luke* (Sacra Pagina 3). Collegeville, Pa: Liturgical Press, 1991.

Karris, Robert J. *Luke: Artist and Theologian* (Theological Inquiries). New York, NY: Paulist Press, 1985.

Keller, Timothy. *Prodigal God: Recovering the Heart of the Christian Faith*. New York, NY: Penguin, 2010.

Marshall, I. Howard. *The Gospel of Luke* (The New International Greek Testament Commentary). Grand Rapids, Mich: Eerdmans, 1978.

Morris, Leon. *Luke* (Tyndale). Downers Grove, Ill: InterVarsity, 1988.

Nickle, Keith F. *Preaching the Gospel of Luke: Proclaiming God's Royal Rule*. Louisville, Ky: Westminster John Knox Press, 2000.

Nolland, John. *Luke*. 3 Vols. (Word Biblical Commentary 35). Nashville, Tenn: Thomas Nelson, 1989-93.

Nouwen, Henri J.M. *The Return of the Prodigal Son: A Story of Homecoming*. New York, NY: Doubleday, 1994.

Ringe, Sharon H. *Luke* (Westminster Bible Companion). Louisville, Ky: Westminster John Knox, 1995.

Schweizer, Eduard. *The Good News according to Luke*. Translated by David E. Green. London: SPCK, 1984.

Shields, Bruce E. *From the Housetops: Preaching in the Early Church and Today*. St. Louis, Miss: Chalice Press, 2000.

Stein, Robert. *Luke* (New American Commentary). New York, NY: Holman Publishers, 1993.

Stott, John R.W. *Christ the Controversialist: A Study in Some Essentials of Evangelical Religion*. London: Tyndale Press, 1970.

Talbert, Charles. *Reading Luke: A Literary and Theological Commentary on the Third Gospel*. Macon, Ga: Smyth & Helwys Publishing, 2013.

Tannehill, Robert C. *Luke* (Abingdon New Testament Commentaries). Nashville, Tenn: Abingdon, 1996.

______. *The Narrative Unity of Luke-Acts: A Literary Interpretation. Vol. 1. The Gospel According to Luke*. Philadelphia, Pa: Fortress, 1986.

Tiede, David L. *Luke* (Augsburg Commentary on the New Testament). Minneapolis, Minn: Fortress, 1988.

Wright, N.T. *Luke for Everyone*. Louisville, Ky: Westminster John Knox, 2004.

______. *Simply Jesus*. New York, NY: HarperOne, 2011.

______. *Surprised by Hope: Rethinking Heaven, the Resurrection, and the Mission of the Church*. New York, NY: HarperOne, 2008.

Printed in the USA
CPSIA information can be obtained
at www.ICGtesting.com
CBHW070841250524
9097CB00010B/491